The Imaginative Prose of
Oliver Wendell Holmes

The Imaginative Prose of
Oliver Wendell Holmes

Michael A. Weinstein

University of Missouri Press
Columbia and London

Library of Congress Cataloging-in-Publication Data

Weinstein, Michael A.
   The imaginative prose of Oliver Wendell Holmes / Michael A. Weinstein.
       p.   cm.
   Summary: "Explication of Holmes's didactic works, including A Mortal
Antipathy and Over the Teacups, which substantiates Holmes as a serious
writer of the New England Renaissance whose ideology of self-
determination as an American value is as relevant to modern society as it
was to the agrarian and industrial societies he addressed"—Provided by
publisher.
   Includes bibliographical references and index.
   ISBN-13: 978-0-8262-1644-1 (alk. paper)
   ISBN-10: 0-8262-1644-7 (alk. paper)
   1. Holmes, Oliver Wendell, 1809–1894—Criticism and interpretation.
2. Didactic literature, American—History and Criticism. 3. Autonomy
(Psychology) in literature.   I. Title.
   PS1992.D52W45 2006
   818'.309—dc22

                                                                    2005036361

∞™This paper meets the requirements of the
American National Standard for Permanence of Paper
for Printed Library Materials, Z39.48, 1984.

Designer: Jennifer Cropp
Typesetter: Crane Composition, Inc.
Printer and binder: The Maple-Vail Book Manufacturer
Typefaces: Palatino and Bodoni

To my beloved colleague,

who distinguishes me from Holmes.

§

Contents

Acknowledgments   ix

Chapter 1.
Holmes's Imaginative Prose: Form and Contents   1

Chapter 2.
The *Autocrat* as an Account of Existential Doubt   24

Chapter 3.
The Power of Silence and the Limits of
Discourse at the Professor's Breakfast Table   47

Chapter 4.
The Denial of Freedom in *Elsie Venner:*
Holmes's *Romance of Destiny*   67

Chapter 5.
The Vindication of Freedom in *The Guardian Angel*   90

Chapter 6.
The Rise of the Specialist and the Eclipse of
the Humanist at the Poet's Breakfast Table   116

Chapter 7.

Morality in the New Society in *A Mortal Antipathy* 142

Chapter 8.

Over the Teacups as an Account of
Senescence and a Last Testament 168

Annotated Bibliography 195

Index 201

Acknowledgments

This book is a critical homage to Oliver Wendell Holmes, Sr., whose intellectual life is a model of genial, generous, and disciplined reflection on the human condition and American society. I have been impelled by gratitude to describe and interpret the complexity and insight of Holmes's thought, because he taught me how to affirm an American identity in a post-9/11 world, where aggressive nationalism and rigid cultural divisions threaten to push individual judgment aside.

Two people have been especially important in furthering my studies of and meditations on Holmes. For more than forty years, Deena Weinstein has been a continuous source of ideas and support, and so she continues to be. Bob Rinaldi is a present-day embodiment of Holmes's conversational Autocrat, presiding over the lunch counter at the White Hen Pantry that he owns in Chicago with intelligence, geniality, goodwill, and the courage of his libertarian convictions. As I wrote this book, I had before me a living example of Holmes's model of American democratic virtue.

The Imaginative Prose of
Oliver Wendell Holmes

Once fix a man's ideals, and for the most part the rest is easy.

—Oliver Wendell Holmes

Chapter 1

Holmes's Imaginative Prose

Form and Contents

One of the most prominent writers of mid-nineteenth-century America, Oliver Wendell Holmes, Sr., was a polymath spanning the two cultures of the sciences and humanities. He was one of the most important medical scientists of his era and also an admired poet, novelist, essayist, and memoirist with an intense interest in public affairs, gender relations, religion, and cultural politics. In his imaginative-prose works—three novels and four table-talk books—Holmes brought all of his resources to bear on a comprehensive reflection on personal and social life within his times, which were formative of our own. The purpose of the following readings of Holmes's seven works of imaginative prose is to disclose their richness and complexity of meaning.

With few exceptions, critics and commentators have failed to recognize the interconnected structures of meaning in Holmes's imaginative-prose works. They have dismissed him as a "dilettante" with flashes of insight and wit, but lacking system and seriousness. Holmes deserves better and so do contemporary readers, who have been deprived, through his critical slighting and neglect, of texts that offer enlightening examples of how to think about the scope of life experience intelligently, and that speak cogently to contemporary concerns.

Holmes's richness is obvious and undisputed. His range of topics—a variety of which appear in each work—includes epistemology, depth psychology, theology, the phenomenology of the life cycle, medicine, democracy, mass society, sex and gender, boxing, horse racing, literary criticism, houses, and trees, and that is only a beginning. Holmes's complexity is not so obvious because the interconnections among his topics and themes are made within hybrid genres and heterogeneous texts that initially seem to be far less organized than they appear after attention has been paid to their structures.

The term imaginative prose itself indicates Holmes's formal complexity. It is deployed here to bring under one heading the table-talk books and the novels, both of which are hybrids of essay and fiction. Holmes characterized his table-talk books as "connected essays" that are "gilded" by romance, and his novels as "physiological romances" that are "medicated" by intellectual discourse. In order to get at the meaning-structures of such texts, it is necessary to coordinate the plots and characters of the romances with the direct presentation of ideas in the mini-essays.

As hybrid forms that overlap one another, the connected essay and the medicated novel do not differ in kind but rather in the priority given to exposition in the former and the predominance of fiction in the latter. Holmes composed his imaginative-prose works from common "portfolios"—collections of raw and semi-finished writings that he would weave together into the final production. He opened two portfolios in the thirty years during which he wrote imaginative prose, one when he was nearing fifty in the late 1850s and the other when he was seventy, reflecting the change in attitudes and concerns that attended his transition from middle to old age and the simultaneous emergence of the new mass-democratic and industrial society.

Holmes's imaginative-prose works are always structured by levels of intellectual and dramatic-romantic narrative that refer to one another more or less intimately. In a table-talk book, which gathers rhetors and actors around a breakfast or tea table, mini-essays on major and related themes are informed by the romantic plot, particularly the strategic deeds of major characters. This creates what William Dean Howells called a "dramatized essay"—a form that he argued Holmes invented. Similarly, in a medicated novel, the romantic plot is informed by essays and expository passages. Failure to consider the relations that Holmes constructed between his intellectual and dramatic narratives has caused Holmes's critics and commentators to miss much of the coherence of his thought.

A second element of complexity in Holmes's imaginative prose is the heterogeneity of his individual texts. A Holmes portfolio contains poems, fictional documents of many kinds, bits of essays, and snatches of conversation, all of which find their way into his works. Both topics and literary forms replace one another abruptly, and the development of persistent themes occurs sporadically rather than continuously. Yet connections among the heterogeneous elements of the text abound, forged by analogy, contrast, reinforcement, and subversion. Again, critics and commentators have failed to attend carefully enough to how Holmes coordinated the variety of form and content in his texts into intelligible structures.

Most importantly, Holmes's texts are complex because he considered many sides of the same problem and balanced contending positions against each other through various characters and rhetors. Holmes projected different and conflicting aspects of himself into his rhetors and characters, proliferating personae such as the Autocrat (his conversationalist persona), the Professor (his medical-scientist persona), and the Poet (his poet persona). In each case the conversational dictator of a connected essay or the authority figure of a physiological romance is contested by other rhetors and characters with opposing viewpoints, and often the position of the text is undecidable.

Undecidability does not mean incoherence—Holmes's irresolution is most often deconstructive, revealing the supplements to and negations of a dominant thesis. His texts are not demonstrations of theses, but "tests" of them: considerations of structured problems that are focused by a dominant standpoint. Above all, Holmes's imaginative-prose works provide a model for how one might think through one's life sensitively, intelligently, and comprehensively. Such thinking is not narrowly systematic and ordered by formal logic on the whole, but resorts to the entire range of thought-forms, often proceeding in fits and starts, and leaving loose ends, but displaying—in Holmes's case—a tendency toward consilience.

Holmes's deployment of hybrid genres and heterogeneity of literary forms within them, and the tendency toward undecidability in his texts, resonate with contemporary "postmodern" literature, which often has similar characteristics. Holmes, however, did not—as many postmodernists do—fuse his genre experimentation to the premise that texts cannot evince closure of meaning and the imperative that meaning be perpetually deferred. While he tended not to let propositions go uncontested, Holmes clearly favored some of them over others and worked out a comprehensive humanist ethic that he consistently defended, although the balance between its Christian and scientific components shifted from work to work and sometimes within a single work. Rather than considering Holmes a forerunner of postmodernism, it is more accurate to say that he was an inventive modern experimentalist—an essayist in the freest and most generous sense of that term.

Describing the coherence of meaning in Holmes's imaginative-prose works demands attention to the relations among the variety of topics presented in them, the ways in which form and content refer to one another, and the relations among heterogeneous forms and diverse subject-positions. Such attention yields the result that each of his texts can be shown to evince the intelligible development of a theme or set of themes.

Two possibilities presented themselves for disclosing the structures of meaning in Holmes's texts. One was to pull out strands of meaning from all of the works and to compose studies of how Holmes treated the major themes that occupied him, such as the human life cycle, American national identity, freedom, determinism and individual responsibility, social differentiation and specialization, mass democracy and the invasion of privacy, and gender relations. The other possibility, which was chosen, was to consider the meaning-structure of each work separately, showing coherence within that text. That decision was based on the judgment that the individual texts had greater integrity than the canon as a whole, because of their complex constitution and the focus of each one on a particular theme or set of themes. The strategy of reading each text was determined uniquely, according to the ways in which Holmes structured its meanings. Sometimes the entire text evinced the intelligible development of a theme; in other cases meanings were organized according to the development of particular characters or separable topics, or the distinction between intellectual and romantic narratives.

Once the meaning-structure of each work was identified, its relevance to disputing or affirming claims in the critical literature on Holmes became clear. Each reading is focused on a claim or set of claims in the literature, giving it an element of argument in addition to the basic exegesis or immanent critique. All of the major critical claims are addressed in the readings and the ones that are contested have been found to neglect the complexity of meaning in Holmes's texts.

Holmes criticism is relatively sparse and scattered, considering that he was one of the most popular writers in mid-nineteenth-century America and that he was a key figure in the New England Renaissance who had close ties to such figures as Ralph Waldo Emerson, James Russell Lowell, and Nathaniel Hawthorne. Indeed, in the only major study to treat Holmes in depth as a theorist and philosopher, Peter Gibian writes: "Losing Holmes, we have lost a brilliant writer and a provocative thinker."[1] Relative inattention to Holmes by scholars and the general literary and intellectual community can be explained primarily by historical factors. His four books of table talk and his three novels have offended modernist critics because they are heterogeneous texts combining essays, aphorisms, romantic tales, and poetry. His political and social positions, particularly his strain of racism, his qualified anti-feminism, and his anti-abolitionism have offended left and liberal social and cultural critics. At the same time, he has not attracted conservative interpreters because he was also, in the main, a liberal and even a progressive, and not at all a traditionalist.

Gibian, whose thesis that Holmes anticipates postmodernist positions on discourse will be addressed in the third chapter of the present study, marshals impressive evidence for his interpretation, yet is far from comprehensive in his reading of Holmes's texts, failing to acknowledge how much Holmes's thought fits with the ideological patterns of his time, particularly the tendency to achieve closure through grand narratives of historical development—in Holmes's case, scientific and Christian humanism. More seriously, Gibian focuses so exclusively on Holmes's form of conversational discourse that he ignores Holmes's frequent insistence that nondiscursive elements are more fundamental to the course and character of human

1. Peter Gibian, *Oliver Wendell Holmes and the Culture of Conversation*, 1.

life than is verbal articulation. One aim of the readings to follow is to rectify the imbalance in Gibian's interpretation while preserving its positive contributions.

Other commentaries on Holmes over the past century—when they have dealt with general issues rather than specialized topics—have uniformly concentrated on Holmes's intellectual character, maintaining, even when sympathetic, that he was a "dilettante." David Hoyt titles one of the chapters of his biography of Holmes "The Perfect Dilettante Writer" and elsewhere calls him "Holmes, the dilettante." Walter Jerrold calls him "the dilettante speaker of the breakfast-table." Small remarks about the breakfast-table books that "The richness Holmes offered in his treatment was only rarely of philosophical depth or lyrical intensity." S. I. Hayakawa and Howard Mumford Jones comment that Holmes was "distinctly an amateur in letters. His literary writings, on the whole, are partly the leisure-born meditations of the physician, partly a means of spreading certain items of professional propaganda, partly a distil-lation of his social life." Holmes's major biographer Eleanor Tilton builds her entire interpretation of Holmes's life on his "habit of doing too many things too easily and quickly." Even Gibian calls Holmes the "philosopher-dilettante."[2]

In relation to Holmes criticism, the major purpose of the follow-ing readings is to dispute the claim that Holmes was a dilettante and to build a case that his thought evinces complex patterns of meaning, trenchant insight into the human condition, and sustained attention to persisting themes. If Gibian is correct that we have "lost" Holmes as a contributor to our cultural wisdom, much of that loss is due to the misrepresentation of his intellectual character by successive generations of critics from all camps. Recovering him demands attention to the meaning-structures that inform his wide-ranging and heterogeneous writings.

Holmes's integrity as a thinker does not proceed from any single doctrine that he propounded, but from his sustained attention to the vicissitudes of the human condition in his times. Therefore, no

---

2. David Hoyt, *The Improper Bostonian: Dr. Oliver Wendell Holmes*, 169; Walter Jerrold, *Oliver Wendell Holmes*, 66; Miriam Rossiter Small, *Oliver Wendell Holmes*, 90; S. I. Hayakawa and Howard Mumford Jones, "Introduction," in *Oliver Wendell Holmes: Representative Selections, With Introduction, Bibliography and Notes*, xli; Eleanor Tilton, *Amiable Autocrat: A Biography of Dr. Oliver Wendell Holmes*, 22; Gibian, *Oliver Wendell Holmes*, 118.

unitary interpretation of Holmes emerges from the readings to follow. Each text has its integrity and its ruptures, its resolutions and
irresolution. The readings are meant to show how Holmes thought
through the problems that he addressed, in successive clusters,
making reference to continuity and discontinuity along the way, but
avoiding detailed comparative analysis. Their emphasis is intratex-
tual, on the subject-positions within each text and not on the man
Holmes or the strands of meaning that one text shares with others.
Although they are sensitive to Holmes's intellectual and social environment, the readings are not studies in cultural history, but immanent analyses of meaning. Rather than reading the interpreter's
own philosophical, ideological, and critical positions into Holmes's
texts, the studies attempt to bring the structures with which Holmes
invested his texts forward, with sparing and strategic critical commentary.

Had the decision been made to follow strands of meaning through
the texts, the most important of them would have been Holmes as
primarily a moralist in his imaginative prose. The following section
traces the strand of Holmes's moral thought as it bears on one of his
major concerns—American national identity. It is meant to intro-
duce the readings by providing a general orientation to the texts
that they address, but should not be understood as a comprehensive understanding; it is just a central strand. Many others are apparent throughout the readings, supplementing and subverting
Holmes the moralist of American identity.

Moralist of American Identity

In his imaginative-prose works, Holmes is more than anything
else a moralist, in the broad sense of modern Western letters: a critic
of human life, deploying scales of value and knowledge of human
nature and wisdom to urge people to their betterment. The tradition
of modern Western moralism to which Holmes belongs reaches
back to the sixteenth century and is epitomized by Montaigne's essays. At the same time that Montaigne was inventing the modern
essay, a parallel initiation was occurring in England, with Francis
Bacon and, in the seventeenth century, the diarist Samuel Pepys and
the polymath thinker Thomas Browne. Holmes explicitly credits the
English essayists as the forbears of his imaginative prose, singling

out the great "conversational dogmatists"—as he calls them—Pepys, Samuel Johnson, and Thomas Carlyle, and giving special favor to Browne in *The Autocrat of the Breakfast-Table*. Although Holmes defended what he considered to be a distinctively American morality with universal import, his literary models are English.

If any previous thinker approximates Holmes, it is Browne, who was a physician, a partisan and practitioner of early modern empirical science, and a Christian humanist advocating an ethic of tolerance. Like Holmes, Browne was a devotee of classical and modern learning with broad interests and the creativity to articulate those interests in a variety of genres. His *Religio Medici*—an account of the physician's view of the world—connects directly with Holmes's own humane reflections on medicine, and Browne's free and experimental approach to writing helped form the free approach of the English essay that Holmes received and elaborated in new ways.

Pepys, Johnson, and Carlyle—the "conversational dogmatists"— are not models, as Browne is, for the form and content of Holmes's thought, but exemplars of a spirit of determined individuality backed up by erudition, reflection, engagement with the public world, and the courage to form one's own opinions and state them forthrightly. They are generalists and humanists in the early modern sense that combined religion and classical and modern learning in a free criticism of life. That combination was imagined by Holmes in the figure of the Master of Arts in *The Poet at the Breakfast-Table*— the last of the conversationalist dogmatists as the generalist was swept aside by the rising tide of specialization.

Johnson, in particular, is Holmes's connection to the past, although his skepticism is antithetical to the metaphysical and moral attitude that marks many of Johnson's writings. Through his adult life, Holmes measured himself year by year against Johnson, who was born one hundred years before him. For Holmes, imaginative prose is a way to consider and vent his opinions and speculations on the human condition, and to give copious moral advice.

Metaphysical Skepticism

Since Holmes's moral discourse is embedded in and contextualized by the epistemological reflection and philosophical psychology associated with German idealism and romanticism, it is more similar to Carlyle's than to Johnson's discourse. An attempt to mine Holmes's imaginative prose for insight into a nonimperialist conception of American identity must acknowledge that it grows out of a coherent philosophy and does not float free of explicit presuppositions.

Although Holmes makes scant mention of technical philosophy in his imaginative prose, one name and theory—Kant and his critique of metaphysics—dominates his references and reflections. In his first work, *The Autocrat of the Breakfast-Table*, the narrator-character of the title approves of Kant's thesis that time and space "are nothing in themselves, only our way of looking at things." Holmes puts that thesis to the test in his fifth work, *The Poet at the Breakfast-Table*, through the character of the Master of Arts—the fictional last-in-the-line of conversational dogmatists—who has devoted his life to understanding the entire universe in its fundamental interconnections. The Master, however, is not content with his project because it has been confined to understanding phenomena within the perspective of space and time; he wants to "'subject the formal conditions of space and time to a new analysis, and project a possible universe outside of the Order of Things.'"[3] Holmes shows the vanity of that project by having the Master withdraw his offer to tell the narrator-character (Holmes's poet-persona) "'*The one central fact in the Order of Things which solves all questions*'" (339). The Poet reflects that the Master probably doubts his own conclusion.

In his late work, the novel *A Mortal Antipathy*, Holmes comes down decisively on the side of Kant: "When you see a metaphysician trying to wash his hands [of space and time] and get rid of these accidents, so as to lay his dry, clean palm on the absolute, does it not remind you of the hopeless task of changing the color of a blackamoor by a similar proceeding? For space is the fluid in which he is washing, and time is the soap which he is using up in the process, and he cannot get free from them until he can wash himself in a mental vacuum."[4]

Holmes's metaphysical skepticism, which he maintained throughout his imaginative prose, is the epistemic ground of his moral vision. He is not concerned with critiques of any kind of reason, but

---

3. Oliver Wendell Holmes, *The Autocrat of the Breakfast-Table*, 266; Oliver Wendell Holmes, *The Poet at the Breakfast-Table*, 27.
4. Oliver Wendell Holmes, *A Mortal Antipathy*, 26–27.

uses the Kantian thesis as the most abstract context for advancing a philosophical anthropology. He expands the epistemic principle that each individual has "an imperfectly-defined circle which is drawn about his intellect" into a metaphorical account of self-conscious personal experience as the core of a series of wrappers. Variations of that image recur throughout his works. In *The Autocrat*, Holmes suggests that "the soul of man has a series of concentric envelopes around it," including body, clothing, domicile, and the entire visible world, all of which "Time buttons . . . up in a loose wrapper" (241).

The image recurs in *A Mortal Antipathy*, where Holmes's physician-hero and stand-in, Dr. Butts, comments that people are so deeply concerned about their bodies because they are the most intimate of a series of wrappers that enclose personal consciousness and include "'the house we dwell in, the living people round us, the landscape we look over, all, up to the sky that covers us like a bell glass,—all these are but loose outside garments which we have worn until they seem part of us'" (37).

For Holmes, human consciousness is enveloped in space and time and the "accidents" that occur within them, and is incapable of knowing what if anything is outside them. Sometimes that self-enclosure is not felt as a loose wrapper or even imprisonment under a bell glass, but is existentially agonizing. In *The Autocrat*, the narrator-character equates the brain to a seventy-year clock with "wheels of thought" that tick inexorably and cannot be stopped by will, sleep, or even madness, but only by death, which breaks the body's case, "seizing upon the ever-swinging pendulum, which we call the heart" and silencing "the clicking of the terrible escapement" (27).

In his last imaginative-prose work, *Over the Teacups*, the horror of time recurs in a short story inserted into the narrative. "The Terrible Clock" is the tale of a man who is driven mad by his fascination with a clock's ticking and striking of the hour. Each tick seems to say "Quick" and each striking of the hour to say "Gone." Reduced to its primal experienced form, the loose wrapper becomes a hideous straitjacket, goading to action and then imposing the despair of irretrievable loss. The story's protagonist is broken by his obsession.

It is important to keep in mind the pessimistic strain in Holmes's metaphysical skepticism. He was not a philosophical pessimist, but a struggler who strove to overcome agonizing despair by engaging in the world and attempting to hold to a faith in the triumph of humanist morality. Yet he sounded the existential bottom many times, and those experiences provided him with a temperamental pity and tolerance that form the background of his moral discourse. He responded to the adversity and failures of embodied life with a Buddha-like compassion that is at the antipodes from arrogance and triumphalism. Metaphysical skepticism played out in an existential key brings the pangs of the foreclosure of transcendence to not only the intellect but also the soul (psyche) that desires a better form of existence than the one it has been allotted.

Most representative of Holmes's response to envelopment in the phenomenal world is his philosophical poem that appears in *The Autocrat,* "The Chambered Nautilus," which describes how the sea creature builds new chambers for itself over its life cycle, but never leaves the confines of its shell. Moralizing metaphysical skepticism, Holmes compares his soul to the nautilus and exhorts it to continue to put the past behind and to build new temples that will shut it from heaven, each time with "a dome more vast" (98). For a metaphysical skeptic, the only cure for pessimism about time's grim reaping is the vital time of action in the world that widens the scope of life and thought, despite uncertainty about final meaning.

A more direct moral consequence of metaphysical skepticism is the relativity of beliefs about ultimate reality to the concrete make-up and circumstances of the individuals who hold them, leading to a disposition to tolerate diversity of religious and existential commitments. If it is impossible to know the "central fact" that "solves all questions about the 'Order of Things,'" then the choice of one's horizon is a personal matter and should be respected as such. Holmes makes this plain in his second work, *The Professor at the Breakfast-Table,* where the narrator-character (Holmes's medical scientist persona) says that each individual "has a religious belief peculiar to himself."[5] None of them can claim the whole truth, because, although "[t]ruth is invariable," each person gets only a partial allotment of it mixed with their specific psychic constitution:

5. Oliver Wendell Holmes, *The Professor at the Breakfast-Table,* 296–97.

"Smith is always a Smithite" and "Brown a Brownite" . . . "the *Smithate* of truth must always differ from the *Brownate* of truth" (297). For Holmes, it is futile and brutally evil for people to try to convert others and even more to excommunicate or execute them for what they see as heresies.

Wrapped within and sometimes overwhelmed by phenomenal experience, human beings nonetheless have at their core a "self-determining principle," which the Autocrat compares to a "drop of water imprisoned in a crystal . . . one little fluid particle in the crystalline prism of the solid universe" that is "very strictly limited" by physical constitution, education, and economic circumstances (86). Self-determination is, for Holmes, "the highest function of being" at the same time that it is the most fragile and problematic element of being. Nurturing the possibility of self-determination is the prime motivator for Holmes's moral discourse and the issue that he struggles with most in his imaginative prose. It is the energy that opposes the mechanical entropy of pitiless time and redeems, if that is possible, the insults of death, disease, decay, and injustice that life inevitably visits on the self.

It is too much to say that Holmes has a tragic sense of life, because he holds himself open to a generous belief in the possibility of an afterlife. Much more, his metaphysical skepticism leads to a complex dance within phenomenal experience between self-determination and the determinism of all the circumstances symbolized by the wrappers. Determinism often threatens to overwhelm freedom, more than anywhere else in the psyche itself. Within the context of space and time, and all the accidents that fill them, the battle for morality is fought within the embodied self.

Self (-) Determination

In Holmes's imaginative-prose works, psychological discourse serves a moral function, indicating the conditions in which self-determination is encouraged or thwarted. The highest function of life, self-determination does not stand outside and above the immanent flow of temporal experience, but emerges and operates within it, appearing sporadically rather than being a constant structure of it. As the core of a human being that is enveloped in wrappers of accident, self-determination is deeply personal, working on radically individualized contents. The world external to the body is only available to the conscious self through its most intimate wrapper, which conditions thought. Human beings cannot transcend the proclivities and perspectives that crystallized their particularized responses to accident, which impacts conscious experience most proximately through a psyche constituted by strata of unconscious experience, some of which emerges into awareness.

Holmes's metaphysical skepticism is accompanied by a skepticism toward the possibility of self-knowledge that is grounded in depth psychology. By the time people get to the point where they can try to decide who they should be, the resources that they deploy to make their decisions have already been prepared by processes, most of which they are incapable of entertaining in reflective thought. Holmes puts the point directly in his conclusion to his final testament, *Over the Teacups:* the individual "is unconscious of the agencies which made him what he is. Self-determining he may be, if you will, but who determines the self which is the proximate source of the determination?"[6]

The thesis that conscious thought is determined by unconscious experience is a constant in Holmes's imaginative prose. As a dedicated medical scientist, Holmes approached psychology through a naturalistic paradigm, rejecting any notion that the form and content of mentality could come from anywhere else but the flow of forces and phenomena within space and time. In *The Autocrat,* he introduces the idea that there are six selves present in any conversation between two interlocutors: the self-image of each one, each one's image of the other, and whom each one actually is, which is known only to God (54). Science can map the vicissitudes of experience—and it is to be treasured for its endeavors—but it can never bring any self to full definition.

In *The Professor at the Breakfast-Table,* Holmes presents his most complete discussion of the dependence of conscious experience on unconscious processes. Remarking that human beings know "something of the filmy threads of this web of life in which we insects buzz awhile, waiting for the old gray spider to come along," the narrator-character adds that he is "twirling on his finger the key to

6. Oliver Wendell Holmes, *Over the Teacups,* 312.

a private Bedlam of ideals" (23). The psyche's madhouse is brimming with hidden and unbidden thoughts, the entirety of which do not form a coherent and meaningful pattern. The individual who has risen to a moment of self-determination cannot halt the heterogeneous flows of thought or even determine definitively what their contents will be, but is like "a circus-rider whirling round with a great troop of horses," able to exert some guidance by taking "his foot from the saddle of one thought" and putting it on another (38). Choices never take place in a state of suspension from the phenomenal world, but always occur "on the run." Human beings are enmeshed in a moving experience that they cannot fully master: self-determination is relative to the reception of the given—Holmes's early formulation of human being as being-in-the-world, here existing in a web presided over by death that can never be fully comprehended.

The saddles of thought on which the circus-rider ego successively leaps are words. Consistent with his emphasis on the unconscious ground of thought, Holmes does not believe that language can be used logocentrically to define metaphysical reality. In *The Professor*, the narrator-character takes the two extreme positions that language is "a solemn thing"—"a temple, in which the soul of those who speak it is enshrined"—that is built out of life's "agonies and ecstasies, its wants and its weariness"; and that it is a "shallow trick," a "set of clickings, hissings, lispings" that represent the residual ashes of a wider and richer experience (43, 181). At either pole and in between them, language remains a derivative element of phenomenal experience, carrying with it perspectives that cannot be controlled by will.

The bedlam of ideals that people carry within their personal experience means that the self never has perfect integrity. A consequence of the fecundity and heterogeneity of thought is the multiplicity of the individual personality. In *Over the Teacups*, Holmes calls himself a "partnership of I-My-Self & Co." (166). He is most interested in the "second member" of the partnership—the individual's emotional and intellectual character, including self-image—that itself is pluralized and is at best only partially under the control of the executive ego. The root problem of the self, for Holmes, is "disordered volition," caused by conflict among its multiple personae and the tendency of some of them to rebel against the adversities and limitations of phenomenal experience, with consequences destructive to self and others.[7]

Holmes's three novels are studies in disordered volition and how it is or fails to be overcome. The moral implications of his psychology are expressed most completely in his second novel, *The Guardian Angel,* which he wrote explicitly to advance and test the doctrine of "limited responsibility."[8] Its heroine, Myrtle Hazard, is a beautiful, vital, and intelligent orphaned adolescent girl who has been raised in her aunt's repressive Calvinist household and who contains within herself the conflicting personalities of four of her female ancestors—a man-taming woman of the world, a Puritan martyr, a wild half–Native American, and a seeress accused of witchery.

The novel tells the story of how Myrtle comes to the peak of self-determination by integrating her complex tendencies into a personality principled by the ethic of benevolent and sympathetic service, with the help of a support network of "guardian angels" and against her own temptations to excess and the invasions of a series of male predators who want to capture her. Myrtle's successful development comes from good initial personal inheritance, nurturing from others, and concentrated work on herself. The moral personality is, for Holmes, a hard-won achievement, dependent on favorable circumstances: "The World, the Flesh, and the Devil held mortgages on [Myrtle's] life before its deed was put into her hands; but sweet and gracious influences were also born with her,—and the battle of life was to be fought between them, God helping her in her need, and her own free choice siding with one or the other" (27).

The most formidable predator against whom Myrtle must defend herself is the young lawyer Murray Bradshaw, a fortune-hunting possessive individualist who calculates his every action according to his perceived selfish interest. He is a master of impression management, able to separate his external demeanor from his inward thoughts and motives. When Bradshaw faces defeat in his efforts to woo Myrtle, his personality structure breaks down and he gives way to destructive and nihilistic impulses that he was not aware he harbored.

Holmes insists in *The Guardian Angel* that multiplicity in the self

7. Oliver Wendell Holmes, *Elsie Venner,* ix-x.
8. Oliver Wendell Holmes, *The Guardian Angel,* viii-ix.

does not exclude "a special personality of our own" (94). That personality only reaches its fulfillment in an ordered integrity if it is moralized. The self sometimes has the freedom—to different degrees in different individuals—to choose between good and evil, but only determination to the good is healthy and productive of self-determination, which is thereby limited. Holmes records declarations and moments of pure existential freedom, but his proclivity is to moralize freedom—one is free by choosing to be sympathetically benevolent.

The moralized and integrated self is not, for Holmes, sacrificial, although Myrtle is capable of voluntary sacrifice when she reaches maturity and has ordered the sides of herself into a coherent hierarchy, in which her Puritan martyr ancestor presides as the dominant element. The individual's own development of their moral potentialities and nondestructive personal tastes and talents is what makes for the good life. In *The Autocrat*, the narrator-character quotes Thomas Browne approvingly: "'EVERY MAN TRULY LIVES, SO LONG AS HE ACTS HIS NATURE, OR SOME WAY MAKES GOOD THE FACULTIES OF *HIMSELF*'" (93). The fact that human beings cannot fully know what their natures are does not contradict Holmes's formulation of a humanistic psychological ethic of self-actualization. All growth—and "grow we must"—occurs in the web, within the wrappers, under the bell glass and in the shell of the nautilus, building new chambers until it expires.

Rather than installing it as an ontological foundation, Holmes tends to interpret self-determination phenomenalistically as, in his first novel *Elsie Venner*, a "sense of freedom," which, "whatever it is, is never affected by argument. *Conscience won't be reasoned with. We feel that we can practically do this or that, and if we choose the wrong, we know we are responsible; but observation teaches us that another race or individual has not the same practical freedom of choice*" (317). The "little fluid particle in the crystalline prism of the solid universe" is fragile and easily occluded—it is not a foundation, but a fragile fruition, yet it remains, despite its immanence and relativity to unconscious experience, the highest function of life. Skepticism about the possibility of complete self-knowledge and tenacious awareness of the limits and conditions of self-determination and moral integrity lead Holmes to cherish the fruitions all the more and to be keenly aware that they do not come into being effortlessly.

The Etiquette of Liberty

Holmes identifies his affirmation of self-determination with the core of American identity, which is grounded not in a political arrangement, a social system, or an ethnic, racial, or specific cultural tradition but in the fulfillment of the self in its natural and essential human form. For Holmes, America is the universal nation, representing the possibility of complete spiritual freedom, which is the most that a human being can ask for from the phenomenal world. In *The Professor*, Holmes's work most concerned with national identity, the narrator-character says that "our free institutions . . . are nothing but a coarse outside machinery to secure the freedom of individual thought" (115).

Freedom of opinion gains its importance not primarily in its civic or economic dimensions, but as the social recognition of self-determination of the individual's orientation to existence. The American, asserts the Professor, inherits "as his national birthright" the freedom "to form and express his opinions" and is "assured that he will soon acquire the last franchise which men withhold from men,—that of stating the laws of his own spiritual being and the beliefs that he accepts without hindrance except from clearer visions of truth" (284).

American identity, for Holmes, is a moral ideal—respect for, indeed, affirmation of each individual's right to make decisions about what the world is and how to dispose oneself toward it: who one is and should be, and what one's metaphysical horizon is. In terms of today's public situation and discourses, Holmes's interpretation of American identity is at the polar opposite of cultural imperialism and culture wars—of any claims to religious superiority or to the superiority of secularism. He is not simply saying that freedom of expression of ultimate commitments should be tolerated, but that it should be deeply respected.

Holmes's valorization of respect for the freedom to state the laws of one's spiritual being follows directly from his philosophical psychology. Such a complex and dynamic entity as the personality should not be straitjacketed by outside imposition. Only the individual is competent to determine what position to take toward life as a whole, because that determination is based on what goes on within the wrappers enveloping consciousness, to which only the individual has (imperfect) access. To be coerced or even pressured to deny one's spiritual nature by inquisitions and invasions of privacy is, for Holmes, to impair, distort, indeed to corrupt life's highest function. Smith should be allowed to discover and then to express his Smithate of truth, and the same applies to Brown and his Brownate.

It is not a matter simply of legal and political protection of civil liberties, which Holmes affirms, along with political democracy as its correlative, but of a social ethos that honors self-determination through its recognition that there is nothing more personal and important in life than coming to terms with it in one's own way. Holmes's most forthright affirmations of liberty are backgrounded by the silent virtues of appreciation, forbearance, humility, and metaphysical modesty. The ideal American would vigorously express a worldview and also appreciate its relativity and problematicity, simultaneously sympathizing with the efforts of others to define and determine themselves—the formal/social conditions of freedom of conscience.

Holmes attempts to provide cultural support for the virtue of respect for self-determination through a humanist ideology that is not meant to substitute for traditional faiths, but to limit their pretensions. In *The Professor*, he advances the concept of the Broad Church, which is a "communion of well-doers" that has "its creed in its heart, and not in the head,— . . . we shall know its members by their fruits and not by their words" (xx). Holmes's moralization of religion does not lead him openly to advance the case for a humanist movement, but to propose, in *Over the Teacups*, an "etiquette regulating the relation of different religions," based on the "true human spirit" of mutual comprehension, respect, and appreciation (195–96). Endorsing a sympathetic ecumenism, he suggests that "[i]f the creeds of mankind try to understand each other, they will be sure to find a meaning in beliefs which are different from their own" (196). Addressing the relation of Judaism and Christianity specifically, Holmes chastises Christians for failing to acknowledge that Jews might have had their own good reasons for rejecting Jesus and opines that the two faiths will only establish "intimate relations" when they have been sufficiently "rationalized and humanized" to render their differences "comparatively unimportant" (199). He sees promise for the Broad Church in "the extreme left of liberal Christianity" and "modern Judaism" (199).

Although Holmes generally keeps his religious humanism free from direct reference to his metaphysical skepticism, in *The Poet* he drives skepticism about religious claims to transcendental truth to its extremity in remarks by the Master of Arts, one of the major rhetors at the table who represents the dying social type of cultural generalist. Taking up Holmes's critique of the limits of language, the Master argues that all religions "come to us through the medium of a preexisting language; and if you remember that this language embodies nothing but human capacities and human passions, you will see at once that every religion presupposes its own elements as already existing in those to whom it is addressed" (183). The Master contrasts the arrogance of traditional theology to "the utter humility of science." He urges the cultivation of "comparative theology": "You cannot know too much of your race and its beliefs, if you want to know anything about your Maker" (149). Later in the text, the Poet echoes the Master, asserting that "we must study man as we have studied stars and rocks" (272).

Holmes is confident in the moral consequences of his scientific humanism, because he holds the romantic idea that there is a "natural conscience" which, if uncorrupted by dogmas of human depravity, points "to the poles of right and wrong only as the great current of will [flows through] the soul" (268). Natural conscience can only be operative if, as the Master puts it, people understand the obvious historical fact that "humanity is of immeasurably greater importance than their own or any other particular belief" (327).

Holmes's most extreme defenses of humanism make his position partisan and partial, undermining his etiquette of ecumenical generosity. Does respect for self-determination of the laws of one's spiritual life imply a common faith in scientific humanism as John Dewey would later argue? Here Holmes is subject to the problem that plagues every attempt to articulate a permissive form for diversity of ultimate commitments as a cultural paradigm. His humanism is a variant of American civil religion, with its own beliefs, rather than an enabling concept. Rather than respecting individual self-determination, it enforces its own dogma, standing as an option between traditional faith and secular humanism, with a bias toward the latter—Holmes's personal and moral interpretation of Unitarianism and Universalism.

The tension between Holmes's ethic of sympathetic and humble respect for self-determination of ultimate commitments and his ideology of ultra-liberal Protestantism indicates the difficulties of overcoming the mentality of rigid cultural politics. It is unlikely that someone who believes in the transcendental truth of a faith commitment would practice Holmes's etiquette in spirit, which leads to the attempt to prove to such a person that they must value a certain conception of what it means to be human above the directives that, for example, they believe that God has given them. Rather than revealing some essence of American identity, Holmes has provided—as should be expected—one interpretation among others, which is conditioned epistemologically by skepticism about claims to metaphysical truth and complete self-knowledge, and ideologically by religio-scientific humanism.

Holmes does not present his appeal for the Broad Church as simply the Holmesate of truth—his personal commitment—but as a paradigm for American culture, marking a disconnect or rupture in his thinking about American identity. Freedom of conscience is grounded for him in the concept of self-enclosure in wrappers, which tends toward solipsism, although he only embraced that extremity in his most mordant reflections. If self-enclosure is taken too far, it means that orientations toward existence are purely private concerns—centered in Holmes's thinking on the afterlife—that do not have import for public affairs, which are left to the play of material interests. Unwilling to accept that implication, Holmes introduced his humanist ideology to enforce respect. In *Over the Teacups*, he was optimistic that American religious culture would move toward the Broad Church. As the contemporary public situation clearly shows, his hope has not been realized.

Yet if Holmes has something significant to offer contemporary discussions of American identity, it is his emphasis on freedom of conscience and existential self-determination as core values, and his acknowledgment that they cannot become operative without respect for the right of each individual to determine their own basic response to life. The idea that each person's experience is particular and unfathomable, and that they are the only one who should legitimately decide their ultimate commitments is alien to contemporary invasive culture in which incessant advertising, erosion of privacy, and myriad forms of evangelism are taken for granted. It is one thing to proclaim liberty and another to enable it with an ethic of respect. Holmes's defense of self-determination is riddled with problems, but the ideal of self-determination is arguably the only nonmaterial value that is distinctive in American culture. Holmes's contribution is to have placed the Puritan quest for freedom of conscience in a form that can be generally received and that shows that a social ethos—a non-Puritan etiquette—is necessary to sustain it.

Effective freedom of conscience is not a dominant feature of contemporary life and it is the province of minorities to defend it, vigorously yet with humility. It is a matter of tact and discretion—one would prefer not to say tactics—how far to take the defense to the ideological extremities toward which it tends, whether Holmesian-style humanism or some variant of radical individualism—left or right—that would be more consistent with the thick interpretation of individuality embedded in Holmes's philosophical psychology. Thinking of American identity in terms of freedom of conscience is, at least, an antidote to arrogance, triumphalism, and cultural imperialism that are rooted in American culture. Holmes brought that idea front and center.

A Structure for Holmes's Thought

It does both justice and injustice to Holmes's thought to conclude this introduction with a rough systematization of his major ideas. The injustice is clear, in that Holmes eschewed philosophical systems and was deeply skeptical about the possibility of rationalizing the nature of things and the self. Yet although Holmes's thought neither strives for nor achieves closure, it evinces consilience among its major themes, which are only intelligible in their relations with one another. Showing a pattern in Holmes's philosophical reflections that he did not articulate consciously also saves him from the charge levied by many of his commentators that he was a dilettante.

The structure proposed here for Holmes's major ideas is a loose dialectic that does not take the form of deductive logic, but presents a set of meaningful relations. Following a broadly Hegelian pattern, the dialectic begins with determination, moves to freedom (self-determination), and concludes with forbearance (self-limitation). The order of terms represents an intelligible development toward a moral life that preserves radical individuality.

In the grand opposition between determinism and freedom in modern Western philosophy, Holmes accords privilege to the former. Human beings are first and foremost constituted by their bio-psychological organization, their socialization (education), and the immediate circumstances in which they are emplaced, which are always constraining. Holmes's emphasis on determination, which he never carries to a strict and dogmatic determinism, reflects the centrality of the scientific attitude in his thinking; as a medical scientist, professor, and practitioner, he had ample occasion to observe how the freedom of individuals is limited by their total life situations. Holmes deployed his understanding of concrete, experiential determination as a polemical weapon against the unforgiving Calvinism of his time and as the impetus for compassion that reached fruition in his ethic of active sympathetic benevolence, which he linked to his Christian humanism through such scriptural imperatives as "Forgive them for they know not what they do."

Although human beings find themselves caught in webs of determinations, at least some of them develop the potentiality to exercise a measure of freedom to determine themselves. Self-determination is, for Holmes, a hard-won, tenuous, and restricted victory that encounters its primary scope within individual consciousness as the power to explore for oneself and then to state one's judgments about the meaning of life. Freedom is less a practical matter for Holmes than a reflective process of coming to terms with personal existence and figuring out for oneself what his student William James called a conception of the frame of things. Since there is no positive knowledge of the nature of things and the self, Holmes, like James, leaves metaphysics up to the real assents of the individual. He does not, however, as James did, appeal to a "will to believe," but advances a more reflective process of self-understanding aimed at achieving clarity of judgment. Holmes identified self-determination of one's existential horizon with American national identity; America's gift to the world would be to create a society in which individuals would have the freedom to state the laws of their own being.

The matter could be left at the possible emergence of self-determination, as a direct experience from a healthy physical and psychological constitution, a nurturing education, and favorable circumstances (all of them determinations) were it not for the fact

that one's conception of the frame of things has practical social consequences. Individuals' ultimate commitments lead them to act on
their beliefs about how social relations should be ordered within
their frames, leading almost certainly to some degree of conflict,
given the great variety of human motivations and temperaments.
No less an individualist than his New England contemporaries
Ralph Waldo Emerson and Henry David Thoreau, Holmes resisted
religious and moral imposition through the political state, although
he affirmed the necessity of the state as an arbiter of conflicts of material interest.

Rather than advocating political settlements of cultural conflicts,
Holmes found that the only solution consistent with his individualism was a final step of self-limitation involving not only tolerance of
but also respect for the freedom of others to determine their existential
horizons. That respect most importantly involved noninterference in
the reflective process of reaching real assents and was fulfilled in a
disposition of generous forbearance. The loose dialectic linking determination, self-determination, and self-limitation is Holmes's bil-
dung—the moments in the formation of a mature character.

Chapter 2

The *Autocrat* as an Account of Existential Doubt

Addressing Oliver Wendell Holmes's *The Poet at the Breakfast-Table,* his biographer Eleanor Tilton writes that as Holmes "knew and said in the book, his writing was a means to liberate his soul."[1] Although the variety of genres in which Holmes wrote (poetry, table talk, periodical essay, novel, memoir, scientific essay, and travelogue) and the diverse purposes that they bespeak make Tilton's claim ambitious, it applies to Holmes's most famous work, *The Autocrat of the Breakfast-Table.* Here, in Holmes's first work of imaginative prose, to be followed by three more table-talk books and three novels, he produced, as he neared the age of fifty, a text that partakes of ironic autobiographical writing and middle-age reflection on life and death.

In the process of working out his response to middle age, Holmes set the pattern for his succeeding works of imaginative prose and articulated a philosophy of life and a romantic (erotic) imaginary that would continue to recur throughout his writings. *The Autocrat* is read in the following reconstruction as an account of Holmes's existential doubt when confronted with his full assent to the fact that he would inevitably die.

1. Tilton, *Amiable Autocrat,* 311.

Tilton's claim that Holmes's literary project was an essay in self-discovery echoes a long and dominant line of Holmes interpretation. Samuel McChord Crothers, writing a century ago, argues that the subtitle of *The Autocrat, Every Man His Own Boswell*, justifies "the reader's assumption that the author and his hero are one." For Crothers, Holmes was engaged in "the business of self-revelation" in his table-talk books, and he "found it convenient to create an artificial person" who lacked "self-consciousness" and could "say 'I' as often as he pleases, without giving offense."[2]

In light of contemporary understandings of literature, it is problematic to identify authors, as living human beings, with their writings, rendering the work as the expression of the life. Narrators, characters, and narrator-characters (like the Autocrat) are subject positions functioning in the text. Acknowledging the distance and difference between the person who writes a text and the subject positions that are written into it does not imply, however, that a text cannot be an author's account of what they understand to be their life experience, articulated indirectly through analogical fictions and substitutions, and/or more directly through what they believe to be facts about themselves and others. The purpose in the present writing is to show that *The Autocrat* gains intelligibility as a whole by reading it as Holmes's account of (his) engagement with aging and mortality, not that it is a key for understanding Holmes as a historical individual; the focus is on the meaning-structure of *The Autocrat* as a text, not on its relation to Holmes, the man.

Literary works are (self-) conscious constructions, and that is very much the case for Holmes's writings, as is made clear by his deployment of "artificial persons" (personae) to (re)present himself. *The Autocrat* is particularly refined in this respect; Holmes articulates not only through the Autocrat but also through documentary and conversational reports about the Professor and the Poet, two figures who will be the narrator-characters, respectively, of his next two table-talk books. The Professor is Holmes's medical-scientist persona and the Poet is his imaginative persona. The Autocrat mediates between these two figures as Holmes's conversationalist persona, which does not mean that the Autocrat is more Holmes than the other two. Each figure plays an essential role in the text's

2. Samuel McChord Crothers, *Oliver Wendell Holmes: The Autocrat and his Fellow Boarders*, 9, 10.

economy—the Professor as existential doubter, the Poet as provider of problematic imaginary redemption, and the Autocrat as final judge and dramatic hero.

As Walter Jerrold puts it, Holmes's table-talk books are structured by the narrator-character functioning as a "conversational leader" for a group of characters who meet at a breakfast or tea table. Jerrold notes that "the boarders around the table are scarcely ever allowed a word and if they are it is only as in the Platonic dialogues, as a leading up to some utterance of the principal speaker."[3] Although Jerrold's observation is an exaggeration when applied to Plato and to Holmes's later table-talk books, it holds for *The Autocrat*. In that text, the Autocrat does almost all of the talking and the other characters function as objects of identification or of positive and negative cathexis for the leader: the disruptive and playful yet ultimately supportive young clerk John is the Autocrat's adolescent alter-ego; the old gentleman is the benign presence of good-willed senescence; the schoolmistress is the Autocrat's romantic object; the stiff lady in Bombazine is her negative; and the divinity student represents the orthodox evangelical Calvinism that Holmes rejected.

All of the characters will be understood here as the dramatis personae in a "dramatized essay" with a tight narrative structure.[4] This approach to Holmes's table-talk books gives them far more coherence than they are traditionally accorded. Crothers, for example, says that in *The Autocrat* Holmes "follows his mind about, taking notes of all its haps and mishaps." Jerrold speaks of Holmes's "Protean performances" in his "gossip-volumes." I intend to show that *The Autocrat* is far more than a vehicle for Holmes "to dogmatize all matters."[5] Although it is an extremely heterogeneous text, containing conversation, philosophy, "talking in a cheap way" meant simply to amuse and divert (286), poetry, student translations, scientific papers, stories within the story, "private journals," and some of

3. Jerrold, *Oliver Wendell Holmes*, 97, 98.

4. William Dean Howells is the only one of Holmes's commentators who understands that the basis of the meaning-structure of Holmes's table-talk books is narration. He asserts that Holmes "invented" "the form of the dramatized essay" in *The Autocrat* ("Oliver Wendell Holmes," http://www.blackmask.com/books26c/whowh.htm [downloaded 3/28/03]).

5. Crothers, *Oliver Wendell Holmes*, 10; Jerrold, *Oliver Wendell Holmes*, 101, 98.

Holmes's most famous poems, *The Autocrat* has a strict dramatic development around the theme of middle age.

As the first of Holmes's dramatized essays, *The Autocrat* is unique in that the romantic hero of the work is the conversational leader, rather than a younger man who is assisted by the narrator-character; the Autocrat gets the girl after suffering his middle-age pangs. The peculiarity of *The Autocrat* makes it the Holmes text that most fully accords with Tilton's and Crothers's thesis that Holmes was writing to reveal himself and to "liberate his soul." The following reconstruction of the dramatic structure of *The Autocrat* will progress in stages according to the development of the text, from a meditation on truth conducted by the Autocrat, to a reflection on old age and death presented through the Professor's papers, to a halting assertion of life through imagination provided by the Poet, ending with the Autocrat's affirmation of love through his report of his romance with the schoolmistress.

Truth

The Autocrat's first six chapters are a philosophical prolegomenon or prelude to the existential drama that unfolds in the last six chapters. *The Autocrat's* first half most fully approximates the dominant judgment, made about all of Holmes's table-talk books, that they are discursive essays in which the narrator-character jumps from one theme and level of discourse to another without any logical rhyme or reason, and controls the discussion summarily and peremptorily; the other characters serve here at best as foils and usually simply as willing or bored listeners. Yet the first six chapters are also filled with observations on discourse centered around the proper relation of the individual to truth, and culminate in a coherent reflection on the truth about the structure of human life that leads to the encounter with mortality in the seventh chapter.

The first half of *The Autocrat* is also the most philosophical of Holmes's writings, in the sense that it addresses in general terms, albeit metaphorically, issues such as the nature of the self, language, life, and truth that are traditionally associated with Western philosophy. That is not to say that Holmes is a philosopher in the conventional sense; he makes no effort to systematize his reflections or even to respond to possible objections to his assertions. He presents, instead, a series of suggestive mini-essays that can be drawn together into an intelligible vision. There is no evidence that Holmes planned the first six chapters as a discourse on truth; they read as if he was feeling his way toward the drama, unaware of the sharp break that comes in the seventh chapter. Once he discovers his guiding theme, the text takes off along an explicit trajectory.

In the first chapter, the Autocrat remarks: "I value a man mainly for his primary relations with truth, as I understand truth,—not for any secondary artifice in handling his ideas" (14). This statement implies that Holmes has some idea of what truth is, but he does not articulate a theory of truth here or in any of his other writings. "Truth" stands as an undefined idea in Holmes's discourse, yet it functions as a lodestar in the first half of *The Autocrat*, as when the narrator-character announces: "I love truth as chiefest among the virtues; I trust it runs in my blood" (115).

It would be easy to discuss Holmes as an incoherent philosopher, but it is fruitful to take another approach and think of him as a critical philosopher in the line of Plato's Socrates and Kant. Following Socrates, Holmes is concerned with a person's "primary relations with truth," whether or not they love knowledge. From the Kantian viewpoint, Holmes uses "Truth" as a regulative ideal that guides his intent, rather than an achieved accomplishment that can be known without the bias imposed by each individual's "understanding" of it. For Holmes, the love of truth is a matter of personal candor, disciplined by receptivity to opposing perspectives, decent respect for fact, attention to logic, and commitment to the provisionality of conclusions.

Holmes's first approach to philosophical themes in *The Autocrat* comes at the outset of the first chapter in the context of the norms of good conversation among a select company of interlocutors, what he calls a "Society of Mutual Admiration." His initial discourse in the text is a defense of "algebraical intellects" who think in terms of general ideas against "arithmetical intellects" who calculate about particular eventualities (1). The good conversationalist is large-minded; even though the capacious intellect has "the third vowel at its center, it does not soon betray it. The highest thought, that is, the most seemingly impersonal; it does not obviously imply any individual centre" (10). A little further comes the observation that "the great minds are those with a wide span, which couple truths related to, but far removed from, each other" (14).

Holmes's ideal conversationalist is foremost a constructor of fresh perspectives who stimulates the minds of the select society. The enlivening function of spoken discourse is inhibited by a number of conversational moves that lower its algebraical level and stop its free flow. The first of these is the intrusion of "fact" to deflect a suggestive general reflection: "Who does not know fellows that always have an ill-conditioned fact or two which they lead after them into decent company like so many bull-dogs, ready to let them slip at every ingenious suggestion, or convenient generalization, or pleasant fancy?" (5). The second subversion of good conversation is the rigid use of logic to drive home an ill-considered premise; the "most frequent work" of the "logical mind" is "to build a *pons asinorum* over chasms which shrewd people can bestride without such a structure" (14). "Some of the sharpest men in argument are notoriously unsound in judgment" (8). The third conversation stopper is the conclusive phrase, such as "'That tells the whole story,'" which "is intended to stop all debate, like the previous question in the General Court. Only it doesn't; simply because 'that' does not usually tell the whole, nor one half of the whole story" (28).

The Autocrat's polemics against the misuse of fact and logic in conversation do not mean that Holmes was a partisan of undisciplined fancy at the expense of such common understandings of truth as accuracy and consistency. "Spoken language," for Holmes, does not get directly at truth, but is a primary means for opening oneself up to it, a preparation for other forms of thinking. Conversation has its own social end in the sheer pleasure of intellectual stimulation characteristic of a Society of Mutual Admiration, but it also has a more important personal end of roughing out thoughts "as an artist models in clay": "Spoken language is so plastic,—you can pat and coax, and spread and shave, and rub out, and fill up, and stick on so easily when you work that soft material, that there is nothing like it for modelling. Out of it come the shapes which you turn into marble or bronze in your immortal books, if you happen to write such" (19–20).

Despite the impetus for openness in good conversation, there are limits on expression. The most serious hindrance to good conversation is "long arguments on special points between people who differ

on the fundamental principles on which these points depend"
(10–11). (Think of almost all contemporary American political discourse.) For Holmes, "a code of finalities is a necessary condition of
profitable talk between two persons" (11). Participants in conversational society need to agree on "certain *ultimata* of belief not to be
disturbed in ordinary conversation," unless they are able to "trace
the secondary questions depending upon these ultimate beliefs to
their source" (11). There should be no expectation that conversation
will lead to conversion of ultimate beliefs or to their reconciliation;
truth about the larger questions remains relative to the individuals'
own meditations: "I show my thought, another his; if they agree,
well; if they differ, we find the largest common factor, if we can, but
at any rate avoid disputing about remainders and fractions, which
is to real talk what tuning an instrument is to playing it" (15).

Holmes's conversational persona ends his reflection on conversation as a specific language game at the beginning of the third
chapter, where he defines his conversational ideal. Remarking that
conversation is "the noblest, the most important" of the fine arts
and that it is "spoiled by the intrusion of a single harsh note," the
Autocrat advocates "conversation which is suggestive rather than
argumentative, which lets out the most of each thinker's results of
thought" (52). The first two chapters of *The Autocrat* can be understood as laying a suggestive context for what follows in the next
four chapters, where Holmes exposes his philosophy of life experience. The text's first half falls somewhere between the roughing out
of spoken language and an accomplished literary sculpture. In the
third through sixth chapters, Holmes is no longer concerned with
the rules of conversational discourse, through which he has revealed the relativity of truth about *"ultimata"* to the individual's
judgment, but with working out his understanding of the truth
about individual life experience, his *ultimata.*

In the third chapter, Holmes clears the path for his plunge into
philosophy. Much of the chapter is a running attack on wit (Holmes's
major claim to popular fame) and an account of how it degrades its
practitioner's social dignity: "The wit knows that his place is at the
tail of the procession" (50). Epistemologically, the "essence" of wit
"consists in a partial and incomplete view of whatever it touches. It
throws a single ray, separated from the rest,—red, yellow, blue, or
any intermediate shade; never white light; that is the province of

wisdom" (50). It is the white light that the Autocrat wants to shine at this point in the text. That light will be diffracted, as it almost always is in Holmes's writings, through metaphors, images, and analogies, but they function to illustrate algebraic ideas.

Building on his general premise that truth about *ultimata* is relative to the individual, Holmes makes his first foray into philosophy in his famous discussion of the six selves that are present in conversation between two people; each interlocutor is a "real" individual whose nature is known "only to his Maker," a self-image, and the image that the other person has of him (53). For Holmes, human beings constitutionally misrecognize themselves, breeding illusions about themselves. They live in self-generated imaginaries and are enclosed in their own conversations with themselves. Indeed, the "least important, philosophically speaking," of the selves "is the one that we have called the real person" (54). Human beings, after all, act on the definitions that they have of themselves and others, not on knowledge of who they actually are. Given this account of the self, truth about life experience must be personal, if not solipsistic; the self-image is an enclosure that cocoons the real individual. At best, a capacious mind will have a rich, generous, and wide-ranging imaginary.

In the fourth chapter, the theme of self-enclosure is deepened and brought to fruition conceptually, as the motif of death is introduced. Addressing the problem of free will, Holmes calls upon science and asserts that "the more we observe and study, the wider we find the range of the automatic and instinctive principles in body, mind, and morals, and the narrower the limits of the self-determining conscious movement" (85). He makes this remark in the context of his longstanding polemic against extreme claims for moral responsibility grounded in Calvinist theology, but it also flows into a more existential discourse. Carrying his reflection to its conclusion, Holmes imagines "the self-determining principle" in relation to "its prearranged and impossible restrictions" as a "drop of water, imprisoned in a crystal . . . One little fluid particle in the crystalline prism of the solid universe!" (86). Unpacking his image, Holmes states that "the fluent, self-determining power of human beings is a very strictly limited agency in the universe," hedged by physical constitution ("organization"), education, and economic condition (89). Human beings not only are incapable of knowing themselves by

virtue of their enclosure in their imaginaries but also are volition-
ally imprisoned in their circumstances.

As the fourth chapter draws to a close, Holmes gathers his resources and brings his philosophical reflection to a synthesis.
Recurring to his attack on wit, the Autocrat tells the boarders that
he is not averse to entertaining them, but that he will also give them
his "serious thoughts" and perhaps his "sadder fantasies." Then
Holmes immediately quotes Thomas Browne, one of his favorite
authors: "'EVERY MAN TRULY LIVES, SO LONG AS HE ACTS
HIS NATURE, OR SOME WAY MAKES GOOD THE FACUL-
TIES OF HIMSELF'" (93). Browne's definition of true life as self-
actualization seems to contradict Holmes's assertion that the self
misrecognizes itself, since one can never know if one is acting one's
nature. Yet Holmes's intent becomes clear in the passages that follow. Emphasizing the norm of making good on one's faculties, he
launches into a defense of life as growth ("grow we must . . .")
against nostalgia for past attachments (". . . if we outgrow all that
we love") (93).

The reflection on growth leads into a discourse on the "race of
life," first imagined as a sailing regatta and then as a horse race, at
which point old age and death intrude decisively. The sailing race
ends for the participants when "the black steam-tug with the skele-
ton arms" takes them in tow (94). In the horse race, the contenders
drop out over the decades, until those who remain at three score
and ten stumble to the finish line: "Who is ahead? Ahead? What!
and the winning-post a slab of white or gray stone standing out
from that turn where there is no more jockeying or straining for victory! Well, the world marks their places in its betting-book; but be
sure that these matter very little, if they have run as well as they
knew how" (96). Under the mordant reflection on life's finality, acting one's nature has become doing one's best with the expectation
of release. This is the culmination of Holmes's meditation on life,
which anticipates notions of the "absurd" that would mark mid–
twentieth century existential philosophies.

The fourth chapter ends with Holmes's most philosophical poem,
"The Chambered Nautilus," which summarizes the preceding discussions and brings them to fruition. The nautilus is a sea creature
that builds its shell in a "series of enlarging compartments" that
take the form of a "widening spiral," as the animal abandons each

chamber for the next. The poet contemplates the creature's empty shell on the beach, remarking on its "dim dreamy life" as it "left the past year's dwelling for the new" and "stretched in his last-found home, and knew the old no more" (98).

At the end of the penultimate stanza, the poet hears a voice singing "through the deep coves of thought" that consummates, in the final stanza, the wisdom that Holmes has achieved through his meditation on self-enclosure: "Build thee more stately mansions, O my soul, / As the swift seasons roll! / Leave thy low-vaulted past! / Let each new temple, nobler than the last, / Shut thee from heaven with a dome more vast, / Till thou at length are free, / Leaving thine outgrown shell by life's unresisting sea!" (98).

The telling lines are "Let each new temple, nobler than the last, / Shut thee from heaven with a dome more vast." Although we live in our own imaginaries and are determined by nature, nurture, and social condition—that is, we are shut from heaven—we can build a life that is noble and capacious. Yet, as we do so, we reaffirm our self-enclosure. If it does not aspire to tragedy, Holmes's wisdom is wistful, a consolation prize won from metaphysical skepticism, the noble possibility of the absurd life.

Holmes's philosophy of life as articulated in the fourth chapter is usefully contrasted with Ralph Waldo Emerson's transcendentalism. In his study of Emerson, Holmes explicitly rejects "mysticism" in the sense of a claim to have contact with absolute reality: "The knowledge, if knowledge it be, of the mystic is not transmissible. It is not cumulative, it begins and ends with the solitary dreamer, and the next who follows him has to build his own cloud-castle as if it were the first aerial edifice that a human soul had ever constructed."[6] Ultimately life is a dream, and Holmes chooses to take it seriously. That is his answer to the dominant philosophical discourse of his historical time and place, which thrived on metaphysical optimism.

In the fifth and sixth chapters, Holmes winds down his meditation on life experience with a defense of the expediency and dignity of the virtue of truthfulness, along with acknowledgment of the powerful inducements to stray from it, such as timidity, good nature, and polite behavior (116). Existential concerns are held in

6. Emerson, *Works*, vol. 2, 307.

abeyance until the seventh chapter, where there is a rupture in the text and radical personal doubt emerges in the person of the Professor who is unwilling to accept the Autocrat's vision of the nobility of the absurd life. Critical philosophy and metaphysical skepticism give way to personal and very particular discontents about aging and the inexorability of finitude. The philosophical context of self-enclosure takes on at times a more bitter tone, a passage from "serious thoughts" to "sadder fantasies."

Death

The seventh chapter marks a sharp formal break in the text. The feeble gestures toward conversation around the table that were in the first six chapters are now absent, and the Autocrat no longer vents his own opinions; instead, after his brief report of a conversation with his friend the Professor (Holmes's physician persona), he reads a paper by the Professor reporting how the latter worked through his discontent at his growing recognition that he was getting old and would inevitably die. The seventh chapter is one of Holmes's most thematically coherent and structured writings. It is a wildly heterogeneous text containing an edifying personal report; a dialogue between the Professor and Old Age; a newspaper review, in the contemporary style of Holmes's Boston, of a lyceum lecture delivered by Cicero; and several poems. Yet all of the different literary forms are deployed to tell the story of the Professor's successive attempts to reconcile himself to old age and death.

Holmes presents in the seventh chapter the Professor's self-analysis of his anxiety about mortality. That analysis is not based on depth psychology and probing the unconscious, but instead follows the pattern that became familiar in American psychology in the twentieth century of working through resistances to inevitable transitions in the life cycle and moving toward acceptance of loss and affirmation of the positive elements of each of its successive stages. A healthy adjustment to life is the aim of Holmes's philosophical psychology, and it is achieved first by overcoming denial and then by finding reasons to affirm engagement in life, thereby avoiding despair and cold resignation. Existential moments occur in the process of working through, but they never reach the points of angst and agony, nor is the confrontation with nothingness ever broached; in their place is a deep sense of the world's insult to the self and a mood of reluctant resignation. The chapter records mood swings and shifting perspectives, bouncing from humor to mordancy—a literary construction to be sure, but also an account of how thoughtful people actually come to terms with a disturbing change in life.

It is significant that Holmes chooses the Professor to express his report of existential doubt. That persona, representing Holmes the scientist and physician, is the figure of himself that is most committed to accepting the inconvenient facts of life and the least likely to entertain transcendental or imaginary escapes from them. The Professor will not accept imaginary palliatives for the human condition, so he is left with the options of trying to deny the inevitable, resigning himself to decline, or—and this last alternative is the desired one—making the best of a bad situation. Ironically and appropriately, just because the Professor is a this-worldly character, he suffers the most of Holmes's personae from existential limitations and is most likely to cling to the mechanism of denial when he has to face facts about himself that he has seen and acknowledged daily in the lives of others. By choosing the Professor as his expositor, Holmes also chose not to evade the pangs of confronting recognition of old age and death.

The chapter begins with a conversation in which the Professor comes to the Autocrat in a "dreary" mood and complains about having been called an "old man," a designation that he is unwilling to accept and against which he protests. The Autocrat makes him submit to a physical examination that shows incontrovertibly that he has all the signs of impending old age. The Professor resists and challenges the Autocrat to a boxing match, showing the latter his bicep, to which the Autocrat replies: "Pluck survives stamina." The Professor departs, "a little out of humor" (150).

A few weeks later, the Professor again converses with the Autocrat, and this time he is "good-natured," having written his "paper." Taking a strictly materialist approach, the Professor has reduced life and death to energy and entropy, likening the body to a furnace that works up to "full blast" until age forty-five and then declines in its production of energy until it gives out: "We are old fellows from the moment the fire begins to go out. Let us always behave like gentlemen when we are introduced to a new acquaintance"; there is no use in "fighting against . . . this ebb in the wave of life that flows through us" (151).

Then follows the Professor's dialogue with Old Age, which reprises the earlier conversation with the Autocrat. Confronted again with evidence of his old age, the Professor still defies the facts, goes out for a walk, suffers a fall, catches cold, and is laid up with lumbago, which gives him the opportunity to reconsider his rebellion. He has persisted in fighting the inevitable and has not behaved like a gentleman. The Professor's reconsideration of his rebellious stance leads him initially to his most bitter and existential reflection. Thomas Browne comes in for another decisive citation, this time not affirming self-actualization, but making the severe judgment that death is "the very disgrace and ignominy of our natures" (158). With bitterness, the Professor comments: "Collectively, the changes of old age appear as a series of personal insults and indignities, terminating at last in death" (153).

As his meditation deepens, the Professor penetrates to the existential dimension of his perplexity. In terms of human life experience, entropy means habit. Old age that submits to decline means that the individual "shrinks into himself," adopting repetitive patterns of behavior that are "as positive and as much beyond the reach of outside influences as if they were governed by clock work" (155). Making the basic conceptual distinction that governs his discourse, the Professor contrasts the Animal and the Organic functions; the former engage the vicissitudes of the world, whereas the latter work according to strict periodicity: "Habit is the approximation of the animal system to the organic. It is a confession of failure in the highest function of being, which involves a perpetual self-determination, in full view of all existing circumstances" (155). Here, in the guise of the "highest function of being," is the description of the human condition that characterized twentieth-century existentialism—Heidegger's being-in-the-world, Sartre's being-in-situation, and Ortega's "I am myself and my circumstances," all of which incorporate the idea of perpetual self-determination. Habit is the opposite of existential freedom, "an action in present circumstances from past motives. It is substituting a *vis a tergo* [force from behind] for the evolution of living force," the latter being the standard advanced by the Autocrat in the fourth chapter (155). Old age, at its core, threatens the surrender of self-determination.

Having scraped existential bottom, the Professor provides comic relief with a parodic newspaper review of Cicero's *De Senectute* presented as a lyceum lecture. The first of Holmes's many attacks on critics, the review comments unfavorably on Cicero's dress and appearance, and offhandedly ticks off some of the points he made, registering agreement and disagreement, and concludes that "the lecture was on the whole acceptable, and a credit to our culture and civilization" (159).

Returning to his meditation, the Professor makes another attempt at reconciliation, saying that "science and history agree in telling me that I can claim the immunities and must own the humiliations of the early stage of senility" (160). Yet he immediately reflects upon the insults of old age and finds himself groaning. The best he can summon is a mordant comment: "I have no doubt we should die of shame and grief at the indignities offered us by age, if it were not that we see so many others as badly or worse off than ourselves" (160–61). At this juncture, the Autocrat reports that his reading of the Professor's paper to the boarders was broken off. He returns to the next breakfast with a poem of uncertain authorship, "The Last Blossom," which records the ultimate insult and indignity of an old man who realizes that the hopes and enthusiasms nourished in him by a young woman's smile were vain and foolhardy, because it was meant for a young man "walking close behind" him (162). Self-mockery and self-irony are the final results of the Professor's inconclusive and unsuccessful meditation on death and old age.

When the Autocrat takes up the Professor's paper again, its tone has changed. The Professor has decided that he has "no intention" of *"giving up"* on life; he has found out how he can treat the "epidemic, endemic, and sporadic . . . malady" of old age, and he will share his wisdom (162–63). The Professor's prescription will be familiar to contemporary Americans; one does well to take up new hobbies and studies, and one will be surprised at how many benefits healthy and even vigorous exercise will bring (he renounces boxing, cautions against horseback riding, and strongly recommends walking and rowing). Justified in terms of scientific principle, exercise provides pleasurable sensations and "a sense of power in action," the psychological correlate of energy (167).

All the good exercise in the world, of course, will only improve the quality of old age; the furnace will eventually grow too cold for exertion. When the flames of vitality have been replaced by "the

sombre stain of regret," the Professor can only advise that one should
not let one's "heart grow cold." It is always possible to retain "cheer-
fulness and love" (173–74). Gone is the groaning over insult and injury, relieved by a disinterested sentiment that knows better than to
hope, for example, for a warm smile from a young woman be-
tokening erotic passion.

The Professor cannot sustain his final judgment unaided. His scientific reason can only go so far, so he calls upon the third of
Holmes's personae, the Poet, the master of imagination, quoting
some of the latter's "old-fashioned heroics." The Poet suggests that
if a "maiden's smile, or heavenly dream of art / Stir the few life-
drops creeping round his heart," all the old man's gray hairs "cannot make him old" (174). Emotional responsiveness is the last stand
that the self can take before it "shrinks into" itself and walls off the
world, the extremity of self-enclosure, the retraction from capa-
ciousness, and the extinction of energetic commerce with the world.
The Professor's paper ends with the Poet's verses. There is no rational, empirical, and scientific resolution of existential doubt for him,
only imaginary compensation.

The Poet's verses are not the last word in the seventh chapter; the
Autocrat concludes it by inserting a poem by the Professor that the
latter reads to his medical friends and that he titles "The Anatomist's Hymn." Retitled by the Autocrat as "The Living Temple,"
the poem is a celebration of the beauty of the human body's mechanism which ends with a prayer that "When wasting age and
wearying strife / Have sapped the leaning walls of life," God would
"Take the poor dust thy mercy warms / And mould it into heavenly forms!" (176). This move to the transcendental does not square
with the Professor's preceding efforts at science-based discourse
and is not part of his "paper." In Holmes's account of (the Professor's) encounter with mortality, there are many suggested recon-
ciliations but no definitive resolutions. In the eighth chapter, the
Poet takes over and the text moves on haltingly and doubtfully to
romantic drama and compensatory fantasy.

Imagination

The eighth chapter opens affirmatively enough, with the narrator-character proclaiming in a parenthetical statement to the reader

that "Spring has come." Yet he immediately counsels the "impatient reader" to skip over the chapter and read the poem at the end of it, minus two verses marked off by parentheses (176–77). There is good reason for his caution: seasonal spring may be upon him, but Holmes remains in the winter of his discontent. Indeed, the Autocrat's initial discourse concerns the boarder called the old man, who had taken to the streets in a white hat and had returned disheartened by an incident in which a young man had called him an "old daddy" and had asked him where he had his hat whitewashed (177). The Autocrat's reflection on the insult leads him to the conclusion that the hat is the last of one's "artificial integuments" to die (178).

The eighth chapter is one of Holmes's most tortured texts; he needs to move on from the inconclusive resolution of the Professor's meditation on old age and death, but is unwilling to take the plunge into imagination. The Poet is the only saving figure in his personality to whom he can have recourse. Yet the Poet's way is not altogether trustworthy. The eighth chapter is shot through with doubt.

After his discourse on the hat, the Autocrat introduces the Professor and the Poet, putting all of his personae into play. The Autocrat considers the Professor "a useful and worthy kind of drudge," who probably has reservations about science's labored and halting pace "while the trumpets are blowing and the big drums beating" (179). Springtime brings the Autocrat closer to the Poet; the latter is "more alive to life" than anyone else (180). Yet as the Professor has noted, the Poet has to do heavy lifting to soar; he has to carry his materials to the "upper chambers" of his brain, whereas the Professor works on the ground floor (179). The Poet also suffers from "a fit of despondency" (180). He is irritated that "when he feels most he can sing least," "ashamed" about the uneven quality of his creations, disconcerted about the meager number of standard songs that he can evoke, and insistent on the harsh labors of poetic creation (180–81).

Leaving the Poet's complaints aside, the Autocrat opines that "the true sunshine that opens the poet's corolla" is women, at which the schoolmistress blushes, but looks "pleased" (182–83). The Autocrat's romance with the schoolmistress has begun, but before it can blossom, he must go through psychological tribulation.

Doubts about poetry begin to deepen as the Autocrat distinguishes between the constitutionally weak poets who use the art as a compensation for their diminished life and "the great sun-kindled, constructive imaginations," which are very rare (184). Reflecting on the pale "albino-poets," the Autocrat says: "And so singing, their eyes grow brighter and brighter, and their features thinner and thinner, until at last the veil of flesh is threadbare, and, still singing [about how they have been unloved and misunderstood], they drop it and pass onward" (185).

Having trenched upon death once again, the text suddenly lurches into Holmes's grimmest meditation, bringing back the theme of self-enclosure with its fullest force. The Autocrat suggests that "Our brains are seventy-year clocks" that are wound up by the Angel of Life, locked up in the skull and left to run out; only the Angel of Resurrection has the key (185). Nothing can stop the inexorable ticking of the "wheels of thought," not the will, nor sleep, nor madness; "death alone can break into the case, and, seizing upon the ever-swinging pendulum, which we call the heart, silence at last the clicking of the terrible escapement we have carried so long beneath our wrinkled foreheads" (185–86). The irresistible mechanism of thought is here something "dreadful" that drives some people to madness and even suicide. The Autocrat articulates what he takes to be a universal wish that our thought, which unwinds "the endless tapestry of time, embroidered with spectral figures of life and death, could have but one brief holiday!" (186).

His meditation having reached the extremity of not being able to live with his own experience, the most agonizing of alienations, the Autocrat has no exit. There is no hint of animal functions; in this vision, the mind is thoroughly organic. The Autocrat's alter-ego, John, comes to the rescue by suggesting alcohol as an escape from the escapement, which allows the Autocrat to reflect on the effects of mind-altering drugs. He asserts that the will can "maintain a certain control" over the movements of the brain, but that when it fails, "men are apt to try to get at the machine by some indirect system of leverage or other" (182). Poets and artists, "who follow their imagination in their creative moments," are especially prey to the (ab)use of mind-altering drugs, which eventually ruin the machine, but also have real, albeit temporary benefits, such as expansiveness and generosity: ". . . the alcoholic virtues don't wash; but until the water takes their colors out, the tints are very much like those of the true celestial stuff" (189).

Now the Autocrat is at the core of his reservations about poetry. "Spasmodic cerebral action" is not only a consequence of intoxication but also takes the true celestial forms of music, poetry, religion, and love (189). Creativity is not voluntary; one can "put the mind into a proper attitude," but then one must wait for the winds of inspiration. The "true state of creative genius is allied to reverie," yet "the dreaming faculties are always the dangerous ones, because their mode of action can be imitated by artificial excitement; the reasoning ones are safe, because they imply continued voluntary effort" (192). It is clear why Holmes would have doubts about poetry and the saving power of the imagination; if recourse to the imagination implies the abandonment of self-control, it not only opens up the possibility of madness and the temptation to addiction but also subverts the life experience that the Autocrat has treasured most in the first half of the book: "the fluent, self-determining power of human beings."

Holmes does not resolve his disquiet with poetry in the eighth chapter. The imagination can so easily be delusive; it is not disciplined by standards of truth. Life in the higher stories of the brain can always fall to the basement. Yet the man of scientific reason, the Professor, has not provided a satisfactory resolution to his existential doubts. In the eighth chapter, Holmes is consumed by doubt; he cannot go back to the Professor's existential quandaries, but he cannot go forward into a life of imagination, because of his psychological doubts, his fear of losing his grip on himself. There seems to be no just middle to serve the Autocrat to mediate the crisis.

After his meditation on imagination and addiction, the Autocrat comments on what he calls "the *terrible smile*" that some people put on when they believe that they have been caught by others in a state of self-preoccupation: ". . . they begin to smile, with an uncertain movement of the mouth, which conveys the idea that they are thinking about themselves, and thinking, too, that you are thinking they are thinking about themselves,—and so look at you with a wretched mixture of self-consciousness, awkwardness, and attempts to carry off both" (193). Is this the way that Holmes is looking at the reader?

The chapter draws to a hopeful close with remarks on the "ovarian eggs of thought" that eventually hatch into cultural change and concludes with the poem "Spring Has Come." The first five stanzas celebrate the beauties of fresh life, but the next two parenthetical verses look back on springtime from the perspective of summer, which contemplates the "withering" tulip and urges roses to bloom from the time of their ripened future. The celebratory tone is renewed in the succeeding five stanzas, but the concluding verses strike a supplicant note in the image of "some poor bird with prisoned wing / That sits and sings, but longs to fly;" and in the anonymous poet's prayer: "Oh for one spot of living green, — / One little spot where leaves can grow, — / To love unblamed, to walk unseen, / To dream above, to sleep below!" (198). Perhaps there is no such place on earth, but Holmes will find a substitute in fantasy and indulgence in his imaginary. Abandoning his doubts, he will arrange a liaison between the middle-age Autocrat and the young and adoring schoolmistress, inverting in the process the norms of good conversation that he had defined at such length in the first six chapters of the text.

Romance

Spring at last arrives in force at the Autocrat's table in the ninth chapter. He had warned young people not to read the Professor's paper in the seventh chapter and had advised all readers that they might want to skip the eighth chapter; now he tells people who are old in spirit not to read—he is addressing the young at heart from twelve to eighty (199). Launching into an apology for the writings that will follow, the Autocrat confesses that he has been confessing to the reader and has been spreading *"seed-capsules"* of his life: "These little colored patches are stains upon the windows of a human soul" (199–200). Seen from the outside, they are "meaningless spots of color," but, from within, "they are glorified shapes with empurpled wings and sunbright aureoles" (200). "My hand trembles when I offer you this," the Autocrat tells the reader.

His reflection on confession leads the Autocrat to invert the talk-form that he advocated in the first six chapters. The insightful abstraction knitting together disparate regions of experience gives way to a defense of concrete particularity: "It is by little things that we know ourselves; a soul would very probably mistake itself for another, when once disembodied, were it not for individual experiences which differ from those of others only in details seemingly trifling" (200). The Autocrat appeals to a "genius" to read his reflections: "But if you can read into the heart of these things in the light of other memories as slight, yet as dear to your soul, then you are neither more nor less than a POET" (201). The Autocrat wants sympathy and understanding for what he is about to undertake, his romance with the schoolmistress.

The last four chapters of the text are taken up with that romance, which forms the paradigm for the dramas that structure Holmes's six other works of imaginative prose. The only difference is that, in *The Autocrat*, the middle-age narrator-character is the romantic hero and gets the girl; in the other works, the narrator-character or stand-in middle-age intellectual is a benign presence or benevolent helper, presiding over or assisting a liaison between a suitable well-bred rescuer and object of rescue.

There is every reason for the Autocrat's (or Holmes's) hand to tremble. The Professor's paper seemed to have decisively established that the one thing that a middle-age man could not hope for, even if it was what he wanted most, was a young woman's erotic love. In addition, up to this point in the text, one could establish some congruence between the Autocrat's persona and Holmes the living man; nothing that the Autocrat had said was inconsistent with how Holmes expressed himself socially. A romance with a younger woman leading to marriage is not something Holmes ever experienced; it is a pure fantasy. Spring means submission to the imaginary, a season for the young.

The romance begins when the Autocrat decides to "make a few intimate revelations" at the table about his past experiences. He sees the schoolmistress and is suddenly pierced with a vision of marital bliss that does not explicitly feature her. Recovering, he finds that the schoolmistress is particularly interested in hearing his "confessions." Most of the others leave the table, and the Autocrat is free to fall into a Proustian discourse of remembrance with only the schoolmistress and the old man as listeners. Then the old man departs and the two presumptive lovers are left alone.

The contents of the Autocrat's confession in this first conversation and subsequent chats with the schoolmistress are consistent with what is known about Holmes's life and are not particularly revealing. They constitute first encounters with sin, death, and love that do not lead to further insight; accounts of his affinities; paeans to beauty; what he calls cheap talk in the twelfth chapter; and some philosophy. The lack of depth is explained when the Autocrat several times states that he has not reported what he actually said to the schoolmistress, but has been dissimulating to the reader.

The need to use filler while his romance is ripening behind the print allows the Autocrat to reprise some of his philosophical concerns. Overcoming the doubts about poetry expressed in the eighth chapter, the Autocrat contrasts scientific to poetic discourse, giving the clear advantage to the latter. When he speaks of his "passionate fondness for trees," he will not use Linnaean classifications, but will "speak of trees as we see them, love them, adore them in the fields, where they are alive, holding their green sun-shades over our heads, talking to us with their hundred thousand whispering tongues. . . ," and so forth (231). He is after "the meaning, the character, the expression of a tree, as a kind and as an individual," its personification, which will always evoke a sense of beauty (232). After he has completed his account of his "romantic attachments" to trees, the Autocrat is ready to take the schoolmistress on the first of their series of walks.

Covering over what is said on the first walk is a new reflection on self-enclosure, which persists as a constant theme. The Autocrat reports that the Professor has remarked that "the soul of a man has a series of concentric envelopes around it," including his body, his clothing, his domicile, and the whole visible world, "in which Time buttons him up as a loose wrapper" (241). Self-enclosure is depicted much more benignly than in its previous appearances (rather than the locked watch of the eighth chapter, time here is a "loose wrapper"). Concentrating on the domicile, the Professor reprises the chambered nautilus, building its series of shells, but now to a more humble and homely purpose: "A house is never a home until we have crusted it with the spoils of a hundred lives besides those of our own past. See what these are and you can tell what the occupant is" (242). Yet humans are still encased in their brains. The Autocrat later allies himself explicitly with Kant, insisting that Time and Space "are nothing in themselves, only our way of looking at things," and that each individual has "an imperfectly-defined circle which is drawn about his intellect" (266). Self-enclosure is no longer terrible when the brain is filled with romance.

Before the Autocrat's courtship of the schoolmistress is consummated, he must accept it as such and face the doubts about middle-age romance articulated in the seventh chapter. The text ruptures abruptly after the Autocrat's first walk with the schoolmistress, when he introduces an "Extract from my Private Journal." He reports that he has been "low-spirited and listless" recently. He first attributes his state of mind to coffee, but it quickly becomes apparent that he has been fighting against "a *passion*" for the schoolmistress. He likens himself to an inmate of an insane asylum, a victim of delusion. To even think of the possibility of marrying the schoolmistress is horrifying: "Dying would be a much more gentlemanly way of meeting the difficulty" (248). The Autocrat fantasizes committing suicide and leaving his estate to the schoolmistress. Plunging into self-pity, he asserts: "I shall never be married" (248). Nonetheless, he decides that another walk with the schoolmistress will do him good and beseeches, in the poem that concludes the tenth chapter, the muse of Beauty to "fire" his brain "With thrills of wild sweet pain!" (250).

From then on, the text moves relentlessly toward its fantasy ending, with the eleventh chapter culminating in the Autocrat's proposal and the twelfth in the wedding. Before he moves to propose, the Autocrat reports that he has told the schoolmistress that he "would have a woman as true as Death" who would perish if she ever told a "real lie" (270). His ideal woman has "love-capacity" as a "congenital endowment" (270). He relates that he has bonded with the schoolmistress as a soul mate through their conversations about life, which have revealed that both of them "have fought all the devils and clasped all the angels of its delirium" (275). The Autocrat now has the confidence to propose and asks the schoolmistress if she will "walk the *long path*" with him; she consents. The old gentleman sees them walking arm in arm and blesses them. The reader never learns the schoolmistress's point of view; the story is told from the Autocrat's perspective and through the desires that condition his imaginary. The schoolmistress is an ideal object of cathexis who never shows a will independent of the place that she holds in the Autocrat's imaginary. She is too good to be true.

The twelfth and final chapter has a good deal of "talking in a cheap way" (for example, how church spires sway) until the Autocrat reveals the rest of his imaginary. He has not told the schoolmistress that he is a man of means who will save her not only from a life of quiet desperation in which her desires would go unful-filled, but from the drudgery of her work that would eventually kill her. He expresses his pity for women who are subject to "that larger Inquisition which we call Civilization!" (305). The Autocrat avers that "there is no depth of tenderness in my nature that Pity has not sounded" for "that great procession of the UNLOVED" (305). The schoolmistress will not have to join that multitude of the "voice-less," but she is distinctly unimpressed when she is told of her good fortune. "I never made a greater failure in an attempt to pro-duce a sensation," says the Autocrat (311). The schoolmistress is even better than the Autocrat's ideal woman; she is an angel of "charity," a "blessed little saint and seraph!" (310).

The old man gives the bride away, and the adoring couple go off to honeymoon in Europe. She is rich in spirit and tells the Autocrat that "'Heaven has given me more than I ever asked; for I had not thought love was ever meant for me'" (310).

If romance is a palliative for the existential doubts of middle age, it is a problematic one. As Holmes presents her, the schoolmistress is a woman who can only exist in the imagination—someone who serves as an object simultaneously of pity and adoration, who needs to be rescued, yet somehow is too strong to feel that need. She is Holmes's ideal woman, who gives unconditional love to her protector who saves her from the fate of being enslaved.

The figure of the schoolmistress—"the blessed little saint and ser-aph"—points to Holmes's insecurity about gender relations and a sense of unworthiness that colors the rescue romances that appear in all of his works of imaginative prose. Except for Euthymia Tower—another fantasy ideal in his late novel *A Mortal Antipathy*—Holmes's heroines are all needy, and when his female characters are not so, he treats them roughly. It is telling that the school-mistress should say that she had thought that love was not meant for her. Her humility indicates that in his insecurity Holmes de-manded more than any real woman could be or give. There is no logical contradiction between being needy and being capable of giving unconditional love, but it is a combination that at best is very rare in worldly experience.

Chapter 3

The Power of Silence and the Limits of
Discourse at the Professor's Breakfast Table

Peter Gibian—Holmes's most important and only philosophical
commentator—advances the thesis that Holmes articulated in his
table-talk books a "base model of conversation" that is particularly
adapted to civilizing the polyvocal public discussion of a democratic republic. Assimilating Holmes to Richard Rorty, Gibian argues
that Holmes sought "conversational 'civility'" through a talk form in
which "multivoiced interactions" never merge "incommunicable discourses into one": "For Holmes as for Rorty, such non-disciplinary,
non-directed dialogue does not put itself forward as a new authority but as a site for possible meetings between authoritative voices;
and it is seen to be not static but progressive in its effects."[1]

The most significant of Gibian's contributions is to save Holmes
from the clutches of modernist critics and to show that his writings are
intelligible in terms of contemporary understandings of discourse.
Gibian argues that Holmes has a "distinctive vision of dialogue as a
non-synthetic verbal form built out of explosive interruptions and al-
terations between the diverse views of multiple speakers."[2] That

1. Gibian, *Oliver Wendell Holmes*, 5, 129, 159.
2. Ibid., 8.

understanding is especially relevant to current discussions about diversity and culture wars in America, and it is also plausible when one simply follows the conversation in the table-talk books. In those works, a group of characters gathers around a breakfast or tea table presided over by a dominant narrator and rhetor—the Autocrat, the Professor, the Poet, and the Dictator, in chronological order. As Gibian shows, the titles Autocrat and Dictator are ironic; the other figures at the table do not usually submit to the leading rhetor, and deny and ignore him at their will.

Yet Gibian's contribution is also a limitation. There is no denying that the interlocutors at Holmes's tables never achieve a verbal synthesis and that Holmes was a partisan of free expression. Yet Holmes also had another side, the reconciler. Gibian leaps too quickly to the conclusion that Holmes embraced sheer continuation of polyvocal conversation as his formal absolute. Gibian's insistence on his thesis leads him to state that Holmes would agree with the proposition that "I do not make my talk, rather my talk makes me."[3] That proposition is foreign to Holmes's thought and forecloses consideration of his affirmation of nonverbal unity, which, obviously, cannot appear in the texts of imagined conversations. Such unity does become manifest, however, in the dramatic context in which the conversations occur. A consideration of the literary form in which Holmes organizes table talk provides a more complete view of the parameters of Holmes's thought on diversity and unity in a democratic republic. That consideration brings Holmes closer to a more traditional humanism than to ideals of interminable discourse.

Up to now, I have characterized Holmes's most distinctive literary works as table-talk books, which is the way that Gibian understands them. That was not, however, the way in which Holmes's turn-of-the-twentieth-century commentators understood them. For those critics, the works were "discursive essays" or, in the precise terms of William Dean Howells, "dramatized essays." In the dramatized essay, conversation takes place within a frame provided by a developing narrative that involves the interlocutors in a plot in which their characters are evinced in action as well as talk. In order to grasp the full range and content of Holmes's thought, it is neces-

3. Ibid., 107.

sary to examine his essays as proto-novels, in which meaning is communicated as much or more by deeds as by words.

In order to show how plot supplements conversation in Holmes's dramatized essays, I will focus on *The Professor at the Breakfast Table*, which is the text that addresses most directly and extensively the issues of unity and diversity in American society, culture, and politics that Gibian takes to be the core of Holmes's concerns. By coordinating Holmes's narrative with the flow of conversation, his move to reconciliation will emerge side by side with his defense of open discourse. *The Professor* lends itself particularly well to an approach to Holmes through the dramatized essay. Tilton notes that its full characterization of major figures, action scenes, and mysteries of plot make it a vehicle for practicing novel writing (Holmes would soon after publish his first novel, *Elsie Venner*, which was initially titled *The Professor's Story*).[4] The plot of the work is centered on the nearly platonic love relationship between a physically crippled figure named successively the Sculpin, Little Boston, and the Little Gentleman, and Iris, an adolescent art student, with the Professor (Holmes in his persona as medical scientist) performing the function of discursive mediation for the reader.

Little Boston, which is the name by which commentators ordinarily refer to him, is one of Holmes's most complex and problematic inventions. He has two inverted club feet, a curved spine, a withered right arm, and a perfectly formed left arm, and his heart is displaced from his left to his right side. Yet he is also an indomitable and forceful advocate of freedom of conscience and expression. As the Sculpin, he is compared to a grotesque aquatic creature with a large head and a rudimentary body; as Little Boston, he is a chauvinistic provincial declaring his native city the hub of the universe and the brains of America; and as the Little Gentleman, he is a man of honor who has made the best of his sorry inheritance. Iris is nearly inarticulate, but expresses herself passionately and precisely in her sketch book. She is endowed with the ability and will to love and serve, and is subject to spiritual/hysterical trances and sleepwalking. If the Little Gentleman is the head, then she is the heart.

In sketch, the plot develops as Iris and the Little Gentleman form an unspoken bond of affection with one another, and culminates

4. Holmes, *Elsie Venner*.

with Iris's performing acts of devotion and sacrifice that redeem the Little Gentleman from having to die with the sense that he was incapable of being loved by any woman but his mother, who had died long ago. The Professor is fascinated by both of these figures and even more by their relation, and becomes a detective, attempting to solve the mysteries of the characters and reporting on the results of his investigations.

Within the frame provided by the plot are conversations, discourses, and poems on the nature of thought and language; freedom of conscience and expression, American national identity, Calvinism, medical quackery, and liberal reformism; the nature of the female personality; and spiritual humanism. Some of the discourses are delivered by the Little Gentleman and most by the Professor. Their appearance is not random, but follows an intelligible pattern coordinate with the plot: the reflections on thought provide a psychological ground for the defense of freedom of conscience and expression, which is tempered by the female principle of the heart; the strands are finally tied together by the proclamation of a common faith. Andrew Lang called Holmes the "unassuming philosopher."[5] The following reading of *The Professor* aims at giving Holmes's thought a systematic configuration that is present within it, but that Holmes did not explicitly provide.

Life, Thought, Language, and Opinion

Early in *The Professor*, after some initial skirmishing that establishes Little Boston as a coequal rhetor to the Professor and before Iris enters the scene, Holmes introduces the dramatis personae around the breakfast table and immediately launches into a mini-essay on the nature of thought in the Professor's voice. The occasion of the discourse is a warning to the Professor from his predecessor, the Autocrat, that the former should be careful to expend his insights wisely, lest he run out of original thoughts. The Professor dismisses the warning because he is convinced that thought is indefinitely fecund. Dipping into metaphysics through a

5. Andrew Lang, "Oliver Wendell Holmes," http://www.mastertexts.com /adventures;among;books/chapter00004.htm (downloaded 3/28/03).

grim image, the Professor opines that human beings know "something of the filmy threads of this web of life in which we insects buzz awhile, waiting for the old gray spider to come along" (*The Professor,* 23). Yet the Professor claims that he is "twirling on his finger the key of a private Bedlam of ideals," (23), which, along with his catholic interests, will provide him with sufficient new material even after his "lively friend," the Autocrat, "has had his straw in the bung-hole of the Universe!" (24).

Far from asserting the primacy of discourse, the Professor traces the fecundity of thought to the life process, of which thought is merely "the residuum," "the gaseous ashes of burned-out *thinking,*—the excretion of mental respiration" (24). The Professor admits that if and when a man has exhausted his "elective affinities" with the world around him, "there is an end of his genius as a real solvent" (25). That has not happened to him yet, and the Professor is confident that the critics will inform him if and when it does.

Holmes next takes up the nature of thought in the second chapter, where the Professor adds to the fecundity of thought its appearance in simultaneous strata; he often thinks of several things at once. Acknowledgment of polyphasic thinking leads to the assertion that thought is not only fecund but also, along with the rest of life and the world itself, a plenitude: "The inner world of thought and the outer world of events are alike in this, that they are both brimful. There is no space between consecutive thoughts, or between the never-ending series of actions" (38). Having embedded thought in what his student William James would later call "the blooming and buzzing confusion" of life experience, Holmes is ready to move on to the relation between thought and language. He makes the transition through one of his most striking and famous images, the mind as "a circus-rider whirling round with a great troop of horses" (38). Just as the rider cannot stop the horses, but can only guide them by stepping from one saddle to the other, the mind must mount the events that it would master "on the run"; an individual "can only take his foot from the saddle of one thought and put it on that of another" (38). The saddle of a thought is a word.

The Professor then remarks that the will cannot "act in the interspaces of thought," because there are none, but is exercised only by switching from one "moving thought" to another. This conclusion awakens a response from the Divinity-Student, an important supporting character representing Calvinist orthodoxy, who asks "how you can admit space, if all things are in contact, and how you can admit time, if it is always *now* to something?" (39). The Professor as unassuming philosopher chooses not to hear the question, and his reflection on thought and language is abruptly broken off, but only momentarily.

The topic is taken up again when the Professor calls for a copy of *Webster's Unabridged,* which brings forth an expletive from the Little Gentleman who will only countenance a British dictionary until Boston produces an American dictionary. The Little Gentleman's complaint runs deeper than his claim that Webster did not know how to spell correctly; if words are saddles, then he wants their definitions to be as good as possible: "'Language!—the blood of the soul, Sir! into which our thoughts run and out of which they grow!'" (49). As the figure in the conversation who is most decided in his advocacy of an American national identity based on freedom of thought and expression, the Little Gentleman is concerned with the political uses of language. He relates how Samuel Adams taught people how to spell the world "resistance" and concludes: "'We know what language means too well here in Boston to play tricks with it. We never make a new word till we have made a new thing or a new thought, Sir!'" (41).

As he spoke, the Professor reports, the Little Gentleman rose "until his stature seemed to swell into the fair human proportions" (41). This is the prelude to his being taken down by jests, derision, and trivial recollections, which open the way for the Professor's rejoinder to linguistic purism and provincialism. Expanding on and deepening the Little Gentleman's train of thought, the Professor observes that "language is a solemn thing," which "grows out of life—out of its agonies and ecstasies, its wants and its weariness. Every language is a temple, in which the soul of those who speak it is enshrined" (43). Yet, having affirmed the Little Gentleman's line, the Professor glides into a more latitudinarian position: "it is likely that the language will shape itself by larger forces than phonography and dictionary making. You may spade up the ocean as much as you like, and harrow it afterwards, if you can,—but the moon will still lead the tides and the winds will form their surface" (44). Even if language is a temple enshrining the speaker's soul, it is subservient to the flow of life, and even the Little Gentleman shares that understanding. Later in the book, after Iris has taken her place at the table, the Professor devalorizes language even further. "Articulation is a shallow trick. . . . Words, which are a set of clickings, hissings, lispings, and so on, mean very little compared to tones and expressions of the features" (181).

In his response to the Little Gentleman, the Professor performs a mediating role between the position that language is the very "blood of the soul" and the position that it is a "shallow trick." Taken as a whole, the discourses on life and language in *The Professor* do not support Gibian's claim that, for Holmes, "I do not make my talk, rather my talk makes me." Holmes's reflection is far more complex than that, being constructed on a pattern of depth levels that inform one another mutually. Within the web spun by the life process and absent metaphysical speculation about the whys and wherefores of things, life in human beings generates thought, which is articulated imperfectly in language; and then there is feedback down the line. From the viewpoint of understanding, language is a tiny and dependent element of an embracing and preponderantly inarticulate process; from the perspective of action, it is our primary resource for a very limited control over events. We do learn who we are by talking, as Gibian affirms, but we also come to ourselves through nonverbal experience. For Holmes, the masculine principle of precision, advanced by the Little Gentleman, must be balanced by a feminine principle of ease, permissiveness, and trust in forces beyond the control of will. The Professor performs the balancing act between the two poles of life experience, and he has the last word.

The major theme that runs through *The Professor* is freedom of expression, which is justified by Holmes not so much for its public function as for its appropriateness to the individuality that he finds essential to the life process. Embedded in a discussion of American institutions is a telling remark by the Professor that links Holmes's philosophy of experience and language to his political ideas: "A man's opinions, look you, are generally of much more value than his arguments. These last are made by his brain, and perhaps he does not believe the proposition they tend to prove,—as is often the case with paid lawyers; but opinions are formed by our whole nature,—brain, heart, instinct, brute life, everything all our experience has shaped for us by contact with the whole circle of our being" (114). The root political freedom for Holmes is freedom of opinion, which acknowledges each one's "private Bedlam of ideals" and each one's efforts to ride and guide the dense, racing pack of thoughts.

Freedom, Provincialism, and American National Identity

The Professor's reflection on the centrality of opinion to personality appears in the fifth chapter in an extended set of conversations with the Divinity-Student, who criticizes the Professor for bringing up religious ideas at the table that might disturb the Calvinist faith of the boarders. In defending his forthright expression, the Professor enunciates the core of Holmes's political theory: "We talk about our free institutions;—they are nothing but a coarse outside machinery to secure the freedom of individual thought" (115). For Holmes, the freedom of individual thought is not instrumental to the realization of other values, but is an end in itself. Toward the conclusion of the book, the Professor describes "the one great thought" that the American "inherits as his national birthright; free to form and express his opinions on almost every subject, and assured that he will soon acquire the last franchise which men withhold from men,—that of stating the laws of his spiritual being and the beliefs he accepts without hindrance except from clearer views of truth" (284).

Political liberty, then, is the condition for the essential freedom to work out one's own relation to life for oneself. Given Holmes's philosophy of experience and philosophical psychology, only individuals can disentangle their real assents from the web of life, and nothing is more important for individuals than to have opinions that are genuinely their own; for Holmes, free institutions serve the free personality, which is formed through free thought: politics most deeply has a psychological purpose.

Holmes's advocacy of free thinking runs through *The Professor* as its dominant theme, taken up at every turn in a variety of contexts. Although Holmes has been slighted by his commentators as a political theorist, *The Professor* is a political work. Tilton notes that when he wrote the book in 1859, as a series of papers for the *Atlantic Monthly,* Holmes was smarting from attacks on his public statements on three fronts: orthodox Calvinists were inflamed by his polemic against original sin, the abolitionist and temperance movements were angered by his failure to support their causes, and much of the medical profession was hostile to his argument that childbed fever was spread by doctors and to his criticism of over-medication. Holmes's Unitarianism, support of slavery as the price of union, and insistence on a positivistic approach to medicine placed him outside any definable camp. Tilton suggests that *The Professor* was Holmes's attempt to get back at his critics, often through the voice of Little Boston.[6] Holmes gives support to her suggestion in his 1882 preface to the book, where he admits that it was "more aggressive" than *The Autocrat* (vi).

All of Holmes's specific concerns and conflicts are addressed abundantly in *The Professor*, but they are always referred back to and intertwined with his defense of free thinking and his identification of it with American national identity. That defense and identification were complicated respectively by the failure of Holmes's psychological interpretation of freedom to provide grounds for political unity and by the fact of provincialism, which would soon tear the country apart in civil war. Holmes responds to those problems by tempering excesses of expression with nonverbal gestures of healing and by contrasting the Little Gentleman's provincial defense of freedom with the Professor's more generous interpretation.

Holmes's thought on freedom and national identity proceeds in fits and starts, developing momentum and direction as his dramatized essay unfolds. His first effort to address the tangle of questions comes at the beginning of the second chapter, right before his discussion of polyphasic thinking. Imagining a conversation with an "intelligent Englishman," the Professor decides that he "would let out the fact of the real American feeling about Old-World folks," which is that "they are children to us in certain points of view. They are playing with toys we have done with for whole generations" (35–36). Mocking "the Old-World puppet-shows" of pomp and circumstance, and social rank and deference, he admits to "the Englishman's concentrated loyalty and specialized reverence," quickly

6. Tilton devotes extensive attention to Holmes's political opinions and his multifaceted conflicts and controversies. She suggests that "In the first person singular, Holmes maintained some kind of poise in the face of the violent attacks of the evangelical press; in the disguise of Little Boston, he could, conveniently, lose his temper and at the same time laugh at himself for doing so" (*Amiable Autocrat*, 250).

adding that Americans "think more of a man as such (barring some little difficulties about race and complexion which the Englishman will touch us on presently), than any people that ever lived did think of him" (36). The reflection ends inconclusively with the Professor's affirmation of a "thorough interpenetration of ideas" among contrasting civilizations, with no implication that either one would benefit or change from contact and conversation with the other.

When Holmes addresses the issue again, in the fourth chapter, Iris has taken her place at the table and the Little Gentleman has become a major rhetor. The stage is set for a dramatic confrontation of views that is also a decisive moment in the plot and one of the few conversations that fulfills Gibian's model of polyvocal interchange. The conversational baton has passed to the hands of "the deformed little gentleman" who espouses provincialism, identifying freedom of thought with American nationality, which in turn is defined and propagated exclusively by Boston. Shifting and sharpening the contrast of civilizations to one between Boston and Rome ("the three hilled city against the seven-hilled city"), the Little Gentleman asserts: "The *battle* goes on everywhere throughout civilization; but here, here, here is the broad white flag flying, which proclaims, first of all, peace and good-will to men, and, next to that, the absolute, unconditional spiritual liberty of each individual immortal soul!" (75). The clash of civilizations is presented starkly: either Boston will melt "the accidents and hindrances of humanity" or Rome will consume "man himself" (78).

The Little Gentleman's harangue is met with jest, mild sarcasm, and derision, and a fight nearly breaks out over an unrelated side issue, at which point the Professor intervenes to defend cosmopolitanism, suggesting that the English have as much "practical freedom" as Americans. The Little Gentleman responds that the Englishman holds freedom *"antagonistically,"* against a society that does not really believe in it, whereas "the American baby sucks in freedom with the milk of the breast at which he hangs" (81). After some more jesting about Irish wet nurses, the Little Gentleman slogs on, proclaiming that America is "making man over again" and that the horizon is opening up now that "the provisional races" (the Native Americans) are "dying out." Brushing aside the Divinity-Student's reservations about his racism, the Little Gentleman announces: "A new race and a whole new world for the new-born human soul to work in! and Boston is the brain of it. . . . That's all I claim for Boston,—that it is the thinking center of the continent, and therefore of the planet" (83).

The Little Gentleman's chauvinism awakens vigorous opposition at the table, leading to amusing slams as he is called upon to justify Boston against Baltimore ("the gastronomic metropolis of the Union"), Philadelphia ("What do we know about Philadelphia except that the engine-companies are always shooting each other?"), and New York ("The order of its development is just this:—Wealth; architecture; upholstery; painting; sculpture") (84–85). Finally, the young man from Maryland, who will at the end of the book become Holmes's model American unionist and be married off to Iris, has enough of the Little Gentleman's excesses and repeats one of the Professor's earlier comments that "every American owns all America," adding: "I am an American,—and wherever I look up and see the stars and stripes overhead, that is home to me!" (87). Whereupon everyone looks up, gazing upon "the sight of the dingy ceiling and the gas-fixture depending therefrom" (87).

Then it is once again time for the Professor to intervene, and he does so disastrously, saying that it "dwarfs the mind . . . to feed it on any localism. The full stature of manhood is shrivelled" (87). This personal attack on the Little Gentleman, supposedly inadvertent, is an instant conversation stopper, and its victim gets up to leave the table. The battle for a more generous, unionist definition of American identity has not been won by discourse; indeed, it has not been won at all. The Professor is deeply ashamed of himself; he has spoken in a most uncivil way, has violated the norms of democratic discussion and has no words to heal the wound. In the starkest fashion, the episode that most fully approximates the talk form that Gibian associates with Holmes breaks down entirely.

But that is not the end of the story. In a "kind voice," Iris begs the Little Gentleman to stay and puts her "soft white hand" on his arm.[7] They "look straight into each other's eyes" and bond with each other, initiating their spiritual romance. "A lady's wish . . . makes slaves of us all," says the Little Gentleman, and he resumes his seat at the table, falling into a reverie of "wordless passion" (88). In the wake of insult and injury, inclusion is restored not by the

7. Iris's use of speech here is performative.

determination to keep talking, but by a sympathetic and benevolent deed. From then on, the Professor changes his role from conversational dogmatist to investigator and detective: "Chance has
thrown together at the table with me a number of persons who are
worth studying, and I mean not only to look on them, but, if I can,
through them" (89–90).

In succeeding discourses on American identity, the Little Gentleman is left free to express himself without jest, derision, or opposition, always under the protection of Iris's beneficent smile and
gaze. He expands upon his vision in later chapters, concentrating
on the need to "Americanize" religion on the pattern that politics has
been Americanized, going so far as to say that if a person "chooses
to vote for the Devil, that is his lookout;—perhaps he thinks the
Devil is better than the other candidates; and I don't doubt he's
often right, Sir!" (207). Similarly, "a man's soul has a vote in the
spiritual community," and nobody should be called a schismatic or
a heretic (207). The Little Gentleman is even permitted to get away
with extreme Boston patriotism, as when he claims that Boston
might launch the ark of a pure Christianity ("I love to hear the
workmen knocking at the old blocks of tradition and making the
ways smooth with the oil of the Good Samaritan" [219]). The other
boarders meet his proclamations with no more than smiles, and
Iris's is "the radiant smile of pleasure" (219).

As the book nears its conclusion, the Professor introduces an appreciation for the richness of history in the Old World, which nur-
tures poetry in a way that the New World cannot (244–46). And in
the peroration in which he describes "the one great thought" of "freedom to state the laws" of one's own spiritual being, he adds that
the "chief danger" that Americans face is that they will think that
the whole planet is made for them "and forget that there are some
possibilities left in the *debris* of the old-world civilization which deserve a certain respectful consideration" (284).

The tensions, strains, inconclusiveness, and air of impracticality
in Holmes's political thought can be traced to his radically psychological interpretation of freedom. The Little Gentleman cannot be
made to submit to argument, because he is stating his real assents,
and that is the aim of discursive life. Holmes finds no political resolution to the problem of unity and diversity, not even in a commitment to continue conversation; talk, for him, is not directed at

reaching even provisional consensus, but is the vehicle of personal expression. The interlocutors at his table do not change their opinions; one would not expect them to do so, since opinion is at the core of personality. Holmes was well aware of the compromises and deal-making of ordinary politics, but he had no use for them.[8] Instead, he sought for reconciliation in what he called "social quality," which he identified with feminine virtue.

Social Quality, Virtue, and the Feminine Touch

However democratic one might find Holmes's political ideas and his table-talk form, he is no champion of social democracy. If political democracy left to itself provides no guarantee of national unity and no harmonization of diversity, then politics must be limited by some other principle. Holmes finds that principle in a social aristocracy that moderates and uplifts the political hurly-burly by surrounding it with a civilized atmosphere, which is created in great part by well-bred women. His discussion of social aristocracy takes up most of the sixth chapter and is pursued as a dialogue between the Professor and the Model of All Virtues, a middle-age woman in comfortable circumstances who adopted Iris after her father died and who has cared for her education. The Model brings Iris to the table and stays there until this decisive interchange, withdrawing after her defeat. All of the boarders agree that the Model is a perfectly good person, but they dislike her intensely because she is joyless and faultless, the essence of pure duty. She has raised Iris according to her pattern, suppressing but not stifling her charge's passionate, loving, and sympathetic spirit. The Model is also somewhat of a feminist.

The Professor initiates the conversation with some remarks on "the manners of well-bred and ill-bred people," asserting that "good-breeding is *surface-Christianity*. Every look, movement, tone, expression, subject of discourse, that may give pain to another is habitually excluded from conversational intercourse. This is the reason why

8. That Holmes understood the workings of ordinary politics and despised their pettiness and narrow self-interest is evidenced abundantly in his memoir of his friend John Lothrop Motley (John Lothrop Motley, *Works*, vol. 11, 325–526).

rich people are apt to be so much more agreeable than others"
(133). The Model interrupts: "I thought you were a great champion
of equality." In response, the Professor enunciates Holmes's basic
social belief: "I go politically for equality,—I said,—and socially for
the quality" (133).

The Model presses on, asking the Professor to identify "the quality." He admits that it is difficult to define "the distinction of social
ranks," adding that he only believes in distinctions that "follow the
natural lines of cleavage in a society which has crystallized according to its own true laws" (134). He is adamant, however, that "the
core of all the great social orders the world has seen has been, and
is still, for the most part, a privileged class of gentlemen and ladies
arranged in a regular scale of precedence among themselves, but
superior as a body to all else" (134). America cannot avoid such
stratification; its division of classes is simply "more completely
elective," rather than hereditary (134). The Model wants to know
how the "election" is conducted, and the Professor replies that
there is never a formal vote, but that "the women settle it mostly";
they know all the signs, mainly nonverbal, that betray "a coarse
fibre and cheap training" (135). Money also has a role in subduing
human nature "into suavity," but "quality ladies" are the key to a
beneficent social atmosphere: "there is less self-assertion in diamonds than in dogmas" (136).

Moving to the attack, the Professor launches into a comparison
between dowdy intellectual women and quality ladies who enact
"flattery" rather than speak it, to which the Model replies: "A woman
of sense ought to be above flattering any man" (136). The Professor
is now ready to plunge the dagger into his opponent: "But a
woman who does not carry about with her wherever she goes a
halo of good feeling and desire to make everybody contented,—an
atmosphere of grace, mercy, and peace, of at least six feet radius,
which wraps every human being upon whom she voluntarily be-
stows her presence, and so flatters him with the comfortable thought
that she is rather glad he is alive than otherwise, isn't worth the
trouble of talking to *as a woman;* she may do well enough to hold
discussions with" (137). The Model is displeased and remarks that
a "sensible man" would get sick of too much praise. The Professor
deflects her with an analogy: "Oh, yes, . . . just as men get sick of
tobacco. It is notorious how apt they are to get tired of that veg-
etable" (137).

Here is an opportunity for the young man John, the table's jester and the Professor's raucous ally, to rout the Model. He announces that he has gotten tired of his cigars and has burned them all. The Model is taken in and approvingly suggests that John convince his friends to consummate the same "noble sacrifice." When he reveals that he has burned his cigars by smoking them, Iris suddenly bursts out in a "clear, loud laugh," which gets everyone around the table to join her, except the Model; she "wanted that one little addition of grace, which seems so small, and is as important as the linchpin in trundling over the rough ways of life"—she "had not the tact to join" (138).

The laugh is Iris's declaration of independence and genuine womanhood: "It was plain that some dam or other had broken in the soul of this young girl, and she was squaring up old scores of laughter, out of which she had been cheated" (138). The laugh is also a conversation stopper, and this time nobody acts with the grace and sympathy to bring the victim back into the conversational fold. The Model will soon leave the table, defeated in her plans for Iris, her position thoroughly discredited. From then on the Professor will be able to pontificate about women undisturbed by criticism. And so he does, repeating in several variations his invidious comparison between "brain-women" and "heart-women," for example: "Intellect is to a woman's nature what her watch-spring skirt is to her dress; it ought to underlie her silks and embroideries, but not to show itself too staringly on the outside" (147). The point is always that the woman's role is to ingratiate and by so doing to reconcile and become a "sister of conversational charity," along with her "high-bred" brothers.

The Professor's espousal of the feminine mystique reaches its farcical conclusion in his fanciful example of how women might function in politics. Free now to speculate unhindered, he imagines the case in which the president of the United states is "an unpresentable boor sucked into office by one of those eddies in the flow of popular sentiment which carry straws and chips into the public harbor, while the prostrate trunks of the monarchs of the forest hurry down on the senseless stream to the gulf of political oblivion" (141). No reason to worry: "there will be angels of good-breeding then as now, to shield the victim of free institutions from himself and from his torturers" in high-bred society (141–42). Social quality rescues political equality from its blunders and fiascoes.

The genuine Model of All Virtues is, of course, Iris, who is not merely a heart-woman, but a genius of the soul. She talks very little and is never a disputant, but her beneficent presence and especially her decisive deeds tell the book's story, move the plot along, and illuminate Holmes's viewpoint (*The Professor* is subtitled *With the Story of Iris*). The key to Iris's character is her private, locked sketch book, to which the Professor gains access late in the narrative. The book contains a poem, in which Iris pleads for the scope to love, and her telling drawings. The most important of those drawings come on a page in which Iris has created "an Eden of all the humped and crooked creatures," and not one of them is "a mean figure to look at" (236–37). The Professor speculates that "she is trying to idealize what we vulgarly call deformity, which she strives to look at in the light of one of Nature's eccentric curves, belonging to her system of beauty, as the hyperbola and parabola belong to the conic sections, though we cannot see them as symmetrical and entire figures, like the circle and the ellipse" (237). The reference to the Little Gentleman is obvious and noted, but the point goes deeper; Iris's character actualizes the benevolent sympathy of the heart-woman at its perfection—not only does she have the surface Christianity of the well-bred; her goodwill comes from her depths. Her book, says the Professor, is "full of the heart's silent longing" (230).

Before Iris is saved from the clutches of the Model of All Virtues, who returns to take her home after her year of art study, by the young man from Maryland, she has one more crucial deed to perform. After one of the Little Gentleman's harangues, Iris notices that he looks very ill. From then on, his decline is swift and culminates in a deathbed scene. With passionate devotion, Iris has attended to the Little Gentleman through his suffering, caused by a heart problem. At the end, the Little Gentleman reflects that although he has "known what it is to dream of the great passions," he has not felt a woman's lips since his mother kissed him before she died, and he never will. Moved without forethought and "with a warm human instinct that rushed up into her face with her heart's blood," Iris kisses the Little Gentleman, performing a sacrament that "washed out the memory of long years of bitterness" (302).

As he slips into death, staring at a crucifix, the Little Gentleman holds Iris's hand, and at the moment he succumbs, he involuntarily grips her in a "terrible dying grasp" (305). Iris remains silent as her hand is crushed: "It was one of the tortures of the Inquisition she was suffering, and she could not stir from her place" (305). Focusing on the crucifix, Iris feels that, as Jesus did, she must "suffer uncomplaining," and, indeed, go further and wipe the Little Gentleman's brow. Where conversation fails, sacrificial love fills the breach, and who but a woman is more fit to serve? Free expression and free service, the masculine and feminine principles, make the human whole.

The Broad Church

At the beginning of the final chapter, before the deathbed scene and in preparation for Iris's marriage to the young Marylander, the Professor describes the ideal American, the "finest sight" on the planet. He is a member of the natural aristocracy, well bred, "born of good stock, in one of the more thoroughly civilized portions of these United States of America, bred in good principles, inheriting a social position which makes him at his ease everywhere, means sufficient to educate him thoroughly without taking away the stimulus to vigorous exertion, and with a good opening in some honorable path of labor" (283), the democratic aristocrat. The young Marylander, who is studying to be an engineer, fits this portrait admirably. He is ready to take advantage of technological advances that make the entire continent open to his talents and to be one of the founders of a new civilization based on "the one great thought" of "stating the laws of his spiritual being and the beliefs he accepts without hindrance except from clearer views of truth." The new American "belongs where he is wanted; and that young Marylander of ours spoke for all our young men when he said that his home was wherever the stars and stripes blew over his head" (285).

Shortly after describing the new American, the Professor delivers a peroration, encapsulating the themes that have been developed in the dramatic essay. He begins with a radical defense of freedom of expression against those who would restrict it: "If to question everything be unlawful and dangerous, we had better undeclare our independence at once; for what the Declaration means is the right to question everything, even the truth of its own fundamental proposition" (295). And the last, of course, is just what Holmes has done, presenting a case through much of the essay that people are not "created equal"; indeed, they both form natural social hierarchies and are radically individualized through their specific response to particular circumstances, including most importantly their inheritance and nurture.

The "right to question everything" by itself is an opening to proliferate diversity and provides no way of reconciling differences. Practical and material conflicts have to be settled, and the political mechanism is not sufficient to perform that function unless there is some principle of social solidarity that motivates conciliation. Gibian's principle of interminable discussion does not do the job, because, for Holmes, conversation serves individual development of personality, not consensus-building, even the consensus on conducting a civil discussion and the commitment to continue it; the crucial discussions in *The Professor* are stopped dead or saved by deeds. Discourse does not heal, and the healing function is not slighted by an essayist who was also a famed physician and medical scientist.

The Professor's peroration is interrupted by the Divinity-Student, who takes the young Marylander to task for attending a Unitarian church with Iris. The latter answers that he is "a Churchman . . . by habit and education," but adds that his old church has educated him "out of its own forms and into the spirit of its highest teachings": "I think I belong to the 'Broad Church,' if any of you can tell what that means" (296). The Professor is more than willing to oblige. He distinguishes between the idea that the Broad Church "means the collective mass of good people of all denominations" and the notion that it must be based on a consensus on doctrine, arguing vigorously against the latter, because it is impossible to make even "a village or a parish or a family think alike," much less an entire nation; each individual "has a religious belief peculiar to himself" (296–97). "Smith is always a Smithite," and Brown is always a Brownite. Their efforts to convert, excommunicate, or burn each other are futile and destructive. "Truth is invariable," but Smith only gets a Smith's-worth of it, mixed with his psychic constitution, and the same holds for Brown: ". . . the *Smithate* of truth must always differ from the *Brownate* of truth" (297).

The radical relativity of truth about the meaning and destiny of human life leads the Professor to the conclusion that the Broad Church "will never be based on anything that requires the use of

language" (298). It has "its creed in the heart, and not in the head,—
... we shall know its members by their fruits, and not by their
words" (298). The Broad Church is a "communion of well-doers."
Concluding with an image, the Professor revives the Little Gentleman's ark of pure Christianity. The Narrow Church is composed of
people in little boats surrounding the great ship, "thanking god that
they are safe, and reckoning how soon the hulk containing the mass
of their fellow-creatures will go down" (298). The Broad Church is
aboard the "poor old vessel," "working hard at the pumps and very
slow to believe that the ship will be swallowed up with so many
poor people in it, fastened down under the hatches ever since it
floated" (298–99). We can recognize Iris as a saint of the Broad
Church. We can also recognize the Broad Church in later attempts
to articulate an American civil religion, most notably, John Dewey's
"common faith."[9]

Whatever one thinks of the desirability or practicability of
Holmes's vision of American identity, and of its foundation in a
gendered binary of head and heart, it is clear that his political and
social thought does not valorize conversation over sentiment, will,
and nonverbalized thought. One might claim that the vision appears within the context of an unresolved series of conversations,
but that would ignore the fact that the Professor does reach a synthesis, such as it is, in his peroration. Even more importantly, that
claim has to discount the dramatic structure of the essay, in which
passions and deeds that are lauded in the peroration are enacted in
the preceding text, and are synchronized with the presentation of

---

9. Dewey, in fact, uses the same image as Holmes did in articulating his
"common faith," stating that the "fact" that we are "all in the same boat tra-
versing the same turbulent ocean" has potentially "infinite religious significance," and that faith in humanity's improvement "has always been implicitly
the common faith of mankind" (*A Common Faith* [New Haven: Yale University
Press, 1934], 87). Dewey's move was to carry the notion of the Broad Church
from Christianity to humanity as a whole, the last moment of a process of gen-
eralizing and secularizing New England Protestantism. See *George Santayana's
Character and Opinion in the United States, vol. 8 of The Works of George Santayana*
(New York: Charles Scribner's Sons, 1936) for an extended statement and attempted demonstration of the thesis that turn-of-the-twentieth-century New
England philosophers secularized their Protestant heritage and generalized its
categories. Recent contributors to the pragmatic tradition, such as Rorty, have
dispensed with a humanist faith in favor of interminable conversation, abandoning substance for process.

the thesis. Far from being a "discursive" thinker, Holmes emerges from this reading of *The Professor* as surprisingly coherent and systematic, both at the level of political ideas and the level of literary construction. *The Professor* is less a book of table talk defending and evincing a form of democratic discussion than a dramatic critique of the limits of conversation with a message of Christian humanism and a foundation in wordless thought.

Chapter 4

The Denial of Freedom in *Elsie Venner*

Holmes's *Romance of Destiny*

Following shortly upon the publication of his second table-talk book, *The Professor at the Breakfast-Table*, Holmes published his first novel, *Elsie Venner*. That work did not mark a substantial break in the form of Holmes's imaginative prose, but only a shift in emphasis; now the rescue fantasy is front and center, whereas the descriptive, analytical, and polemical mini-essays function as explanations of the fictional characters and events. Indeed, Holmes explicitly acknowledged that he intended *Elsie Venner* to be more than an entertainment, approving of the characterization of it by "a dear old lady, my very good friend," as a "medicated novel" (*Elsie Venner*, xi).

Although Holmes was comfortable with the term "medicated novel," it does not suggest his strategy precisely. In the second preface to *Elsie*, he states that the "real aim" of the work was "to test the doctrine of 'original sin' and human responsibility for the disordered volition coming under that technical denomination" (ix-x). The strategy of using fiction as a test of a doctrine resonates much more with Holmes the professor of medicine, demonstrating a general principle through observation and experiment, than it does with Holmes the physician's healing practice. Later on in the second preface, Holmes offers a more accurate term, "physiological romance," to describe the work; he is employing the form of romantic narrative to make a point about moral theology from a scientific perspective (x).

Holmes encapsulates the thesis of *Elsie Venner* succinctly in his third preface to the work: "Believing, as I do, that our prevailing theologies are founded upon an utterly false view of the relation of man to his Creator, I attempted to illustrate the doctrine of inherited responsibility for other people's misbehavior" (xii). In order to "test" the doctrine of original sin, Holmes created the character of Elsie Venner, who had been poisoned prenatally by rattlesnake venom as the result of a snake bite suffered by her mother. As a consequence of the poisoning, Elsie comes into the world as a creature divided between an ophidian and a human nature, spending the eighteen years of her life in a silent struggle that ends in her sacrificial death. Her ophidian nature impels her to sociopathic behavior, for which, according to Holmes, it is an abomination to blame her.

Holmes did not intend his conceit of "moral poisoning" by physiological means to be taken as a scientific hypothesis; it is an extreme and imaginary case that serves to underscore the more general point that it is wrong, even criminal, to hold people responsible for impulses and deeds that they cannot control. The "dogma of inherited guilt," from whatever source, is the target of Holmes's polemic, as the author makes clear in the third preface: "But what difference does it make in the child's responsibility whether his inherited tendencies come from a snake-bite or some other source which he knew nothing about and could not have prevented from acting?" (xii). Indeed, many of the characters who populate the novel are presented as cases in which blame, disapprobation, and punishment are inappropriate because their inherited character and their circumstances effectively determine their dispositions and deeds. Far from being the anomaly or freak of nature that she would appear to be among the normal inhabitants of the town of Rockland in western Massachusetts, Elsie is emblematic of all of them.

Elsie Venner is a complex work in which the title character's agony serves as the focus for the story of the failure to rescue her from her predicament, several successful romantic rescues, an adventure of male rivalry, the criss-crossing of spiritual journeys of the town's leading clergymen, and the ideological interplay between the country doctor and the Calvinist minister, among other subplots and ramifications of the major plot. The critical strategy employed here is to examine Holmes's "test" of doctrine first by specifying and analyzing the author's explicit position, which appears in a conversation that is set off from the rest of the text between Dr. Kittredge, who represents Holmes's perspective, and the Calvinist Rev. Honeywood. Then the criticism moves on to test Holmes's test—to test his own doctrine—against the narrative development of the text at some of its significant moments.

Freedom

From the standpoint of general ideas and a philosophical problematic, Holmes's first three works of imaginative prose are dominated by the issue of freedom and determinism. For Holmes, the tension between those polar ideas is not so much an intellectual concern as a practical and even an existential quandary. In both *The Autocrat* and *The Professor*, Holmes advanced and defended the thesis that freedom to determine one's response to being-in-the-world is the highest peak of the human condition, and the notion that existential self-determination is (drastically) limited by genetic inheritance, natural environment, early childhood experience, social class, race, ethnicity, gender, and (local) culture—in a word, circumstance.

Holmes never reconciled the tension between freedom and circumstance in an explicit philosophical discourse. His comments and mini-essays scattered through the first two table-talk books range from empyrean laudation of freedom to bitter acknowledgment of determinism, with attempts to achieve some balance between the extremes. In *The Autocrat*, Holmes claims that the "highest function of being" is bound up with "perpetual self-determination, in full view of all existing circumstances" (*The Autocrat*, 155). Then, a little later, he reaches the mordant conclusion that the human brain is a "seventy-year clock" that is "wound up by the Angel of Life, locked up in the skull and left to run out" (185). Earlier he had suggested that the "self-determining principle" is like "a drop of water imprisoned in a crystal . . . One little fluid particle in the crystalline prism of the solid universe" (86).

Holmes's vacillation and indecision about the roles of freedom and circumstance in human existence was built into his personal history. The son of a Calvinist minister, he became a professor of medicine and a physician, absorbing the naturalistic perspective of his profession and breaking with the theology of his childhood. Yet he did not go over to scientific naturalism unequivocally and affiliated himself religiously to Unitarianism, maintaining an affirmation of a spiritual dimension in human existence, a belief in monotheism, and a commitment to Jesus-centered humanism. He also embraced the credo of freedom of expression that was, for him, the lasting contribution of the American Revolution to world civilization. Each of these sources of his views took him in different directions and came into conflict with one another. Calvinism bequeathed to him a preoccupation with the doctrine of original sin, medical materialism gave him the means to criticize that doctrine, Unitarianism provided an ethic of Christian humanism, and American civil libertarianism was a starting point for his full-blown declaration of existential independence. When he came to face his nest of issues most directly in *Elsie Venner,* Holmes put all of his cards on the table.

The conversation between Dr. Kittredge and Rev. Honeywood is placed two thirds of the way through the book, taking up all of chapter 22, entitled "Why Doctors Differ." It follows upon a tea party at Widow Rowens, at which all of the major characters are present and during which their relations are determined for the rest of the narrative. Having gathered his stories together and crystallized his plot, Holmes is ready to reflect upon the general ideas that it exemplifies.

As the other guests pair off and Elsie studies a stereoscopic image of the Laocoon—the ancient Roman sculpture of the Trojan priest of that name being crushed to death by serpents—Kittredge and Honeywood sit down in two armchairs, "squared off against each other" as "two representatives of two great professions brought face to face to talk over the subjects they had been looking at all their lives from such different points of view" (*Elsie Venner,* 313). The conversation is framed by a challenge to and provocation of Kittredge, placing him on Honeywood's ground. The minister brings up the old shibboleth that where you find three physicians, two of them will be atheists, forcing the doctor to defend the theory and practice of medicine against materialism. The interlocutors spar for a while over the various issues surrounding the problem of freedom and circumstance, until Kittredge asks Honeywood to let him express his "real thoughts," at which point the Professor as narrator-character intervenes to shape the physician's discourse into a more systematic exposition than conversation allows.[1]

The conversation-confession can be usefully understood as a restaging of Holmes's break with his Calvinist father, an *apologia pro vita sua*. Like Holmes's father, Honeywood is a Calvinist with a difference who mixes affirmation of traditional dogma with a generous spirit, a combination that often leads to performative contradictions. He provokes Kittredge more as a devil's advocate than as an ideologue, seducing the latter into making his confession. Holmes gives himself the opportunity here to explain himself to his father in the context of a friendly inquisition.

After some initial and inconclusive exchanges on the question of whether or not physicians believe in Nature rather than God, Kittredge attacks ministers for believing that "the same kind of truth" suits everyone. Physicians understand that "food and physic act differently with different people"; the same principle of relativity should also apply to religious beliefs. Honeywood replies by raising the crucial question: "Do you mean to say that every man is not absolutely free to choose his beliefs?" (316). Faced with the challenge to resolve or reconcile the tension between the freedom that Holmes most prized and the determining power of circumstance, Kittredge begins his response with the thesis that "constitution has more to do with belief than people think," illustrating that principle with the claim that Native Americans are unfit for civilization and that adherence to Catholicism and Protestantism is "a good deal a matter of race" (317).

Honeywood cuts to the core of the controversy by objecting that

1. The Professor, one of Holmes's table-talk leaders, narrates *Elsie Venner* and plays a minor part in the plot. When the novel was first published in the *Atlantic Monthly*, it was subtitled "The Professor's Story," establishing a link between Elsie and the table-talk book that preceded it, *The Professor at the Breakfast-Table*. As Holmes's professor-of-medicine persona, the Professor emphasizes Holmes's scientific and deterministic side, in contrast to his two other table-talk personae, the Autocrat and the Poet. The novel was later subtitled "A Romance of Destiny."

if people believe that their wills are determined by circumstance, they will lose hold of their "moral and religious nature." In response, Kittredge attempts to rescue freedom by qualifying his thesis of the relativity of belief; although inferior races are not spiritually free, "our own sense of freedom, whatever it is, is never affected by argument. *Conscience won't be reasoned with.* We feel that we can practically do this or that, and if we choose the wrong, we know we are responsible; but observation teaches us that this or that other race or individual has not the same practical freedom of choice" (317). Under Honeywood's pressure, Kittredge has abandoned the heights of existential self-determination and retreated to a lower ground where freedom is a subjective state—a sense of practical efficacy, an experience of choice, and an acknowledgment of responsibility that characterizes individuals with an advanced and superior constitution. Kittredge's defense of freedom breaks off here and the exchange moves on to a vindication of scientific knowledge against Honeywood's suggestion of the sufficiency of faith. Here Kittredge strengthens the case for determinism, listing the discoveries of modern science, such as the heliocentric theory and historical geology, that have undermined received religious dogma.

Once he has entered into his confession, Kittredge returns to the problem of freedom, reprising his first defense with greater precision and a touch of bitterness. Transferring existential freedom to the province of the clergy, he says: "Ministers talk about the human will as if it stood on a high look-out with plenty of light, and elbow-room reaching to the horizon" (323). In contrast, doctors learn through harsh experience that "Hottentots and Indians—and a good many of their own race" appear to be "self-conscious blood-clocks with very limited power of self-determination" (323). It is inappropriate and morally obtuse for people who "belong to the thinking class of the highest races" and who are "conscious of a great deal of liberty of will" to project their own mentality on the rest of humanity. In sum, physicians are "constantly seeing weakness" where ministers see "depravity" (323).

That is Kittredge's last word on freedom, and it moves him very close to the extreme image of determinism in *The Autocrat*, where Holmes compared the brain to an inexorable clock. The only room left for freedom is subjective, and it is not clear what the sense of freedom and the consciousness of liberty signify. If Holmes were to be consistent with the premises that he puts in Kittredge's mouth, people will feel free and acknowledge responsibility when their constitutions permit. If they do not act morally or do not hold themselves accountable for their misdeeds, they will be suffering from some weakness and should not be held accountable by others. Holmes does not explicitly draw this conclusion in the Honeywood-Kittredge encounter, but he comes to the brink of doing so. The substitution of weakness for depravity medicalizes the problem of sin, which is the ideological purpose of *Elsie Venner*. Holmes can claim victory over his father, but it comes at a price.

In addressing the problem of freedom in the context of moral theology, Holmes not only disposed of the Calvinist will to censure and punish that he despised so deeply but also scuttled the freedom to determine one's response to existence that was his supreme value in *The Autocrat* and *The Professor*. Unable to liberate existential freedom from its enslavement to a moral point of view, he subsided into a reluctant and halfhearted embrace of determinism. In *The Professor*, Little Boston, the character who most staunchly defends freedom of expression and existential self-determination, suggests that, in a polity based on liberty, people should be free to vote for the devil if that is their preference, going so far as to say that maybe the devil is the best candidate (*The Professor*, 207). Holmes allows no such fancy into *Elsie Venner*; he is out to finish off Calvinism, once and for all, let the sacrifices fall where they may. As will become clear in the "test" of Holmes's doctrine to follow, even the glimmers of freedom that might remain subjectively for superior and advanced human beings are excluded from the text.

Character

The most important subplot in *Elsie Venner* concerns the fates of the two main Protestant ministers in Rockland, the Calvinist Rev. Honeywood and the Unitarian Rev. Fairweather. Both of these figures are divided souls whose doctrines are at war with their temperaments. Honeywood is committed to the harsh doctrine of inherited guilt on an ideological level, yet his personality and deeds evince a practical affirmation of open-hearted and generous Christian humanism rooted in the example of Jesus in the Gospels. Fair-weather is ideologically committed to Unitarianism's rationalism and focus on universal moral duty, but his entire character drives him to surrender freedom and reason, and to seek the comfort of submission to the authority of the Roman Catholic Church. Both of these characters are members of an elevated social class and an "advanced" race. If anyone might be expected to exercise existential freedom, these intellectuals who specialize in ultimate concerns would be prime candidates. Yet Holmes never allows either one of them a moment of choice as they work their ways, respectively, toward healing their alienated souls through processes of conversion.

Honeywood's case is both comic and triumphal. For years, he has been progressively moving away from concern with human depravity toward engagement with benevolent causes and emphasis in his sermons on love and charity. This development has not gone unnoticed by his congregation, especially his senior deacon, who pressures him to remind the members of "the great fundamental doctrine of the worthlessness of all human efforts and motives" (233). One of Holmes's most sympathetic characters, Honeywood is treated with lighthearted irony. He has managed the tension between doctrine and disposition by holding on to the former and indulging the latter as much as feasible, while apparently failing to notice his performative contradiction enough to bring it to critical reflection and conscious resolution. His conversion does not come as the result of an agonizing self-appraisal, but from an awakening that lifts to awareness a process that was already essentially complete and was not a matter of choice.

Honeywood's conversion occurs halfway through the book when he is drawn into the plot that swirls around Elsie's predicament. Having given way to his deacon's desire for an old-fashioned doctrinal sermon, Honeywood riffles through some of his past efforts and finds one on human nature that fills the bill. He then enters "that curious state which is so common in good ministers," in which they "switch their logical faculties on the narrow side-track of their technical dogmas, while the great freight-train of their substantial human qualities keeps in the main highway of common-sense" (233–34). Enveloped in his theological zone, Honeywood embraces his premises and follows "the chain of reasoning without fairly perceiving where it would lead him, if he carried it into real life" (234). This has been his habitual strategy of avoidance and denial through compartmentalization and splitting—his evasion of existential self-determination, which will soon melt away.

Just as he is about to put the finishing touches on his sermon, Honeywood is interrupted by his beautiful, charming, and selfless granddaughter from Boston, Letty Forrester, who announces a visit from Sophy, the black servant of the Venner family, who is the only person who has bonded with Elsie emotionally. Sophy has come to seek Honeywood's counsel and help, because she feels that Elsie is in danger of giving way to the destructive tendencies of her ophidian nature. Under the impact of Letty's obvious goodness and vitality, and Sophy's revelation of Elsie's predicament, Honeywood is forced to question the doctrine of inherited guilt. Letty's example makes him wonder if it is not possible that many people simply have a good nature and are not masking a deeper depravity. The story of Elsie makes him question whether people should be blamed for dispositions and deeds over which they have no control.

When Honeywood returns to his sermon, it looks "very differently from the way it had looked at the moment he left it." He cannot believe that Letty or Sophy are naturally selfish, and that Elsie is anything but a "blameless child of misfortune" (246). "[B]ewildered with doubts and tossed to and fro on that stormy deep of thought heaving forever beneath the conflict of windy dogmas," he sets aside his sermon and opens up the book of Genesis at the eighteenth chapter to the story of Abraham's "remarkable argument" with God (246–47). Taking the passage "Shall not the Judge of all the earth do right?" he composes a new sermon, "On the Obligations of an Infinite Creator to a Finite Creature," maintaining that human beings have a right to demand that God be reasonable. Following the same method of abandoning himself to first premises that he had always employed, Honeywood relentlessly pushes on to Christian humanist conclusions, "which not only astonished people, as was said, but surprised himself" (247).

Far from being an act of self-determination, Honeywood's conversion is the last step of an unconscious process of self-actualization. As the Professor explains it, "the good man had got so humanized by mixing up with other people in various benevolent schemes, that, the very moment he could escape from his old scholastic abstractions, he took the side of humanity instinctively" (248). Holmes's lesson here is that the force of character wills out against beliefs that are incompatible with it. In Honeywood's case, the results are favorable: the healing of alienation removes his doubts about human goodness and allows him to affirm his best impulses self-consciously.

Rev. Fairweather presents a different and negative case that also demonstrates the force of character, in a much harsher way. He is introduced at the beginning of the book as a "down-hearted and timid kind of man" who preaches "as he had been taught to preach," but without full conviction. His doubts are not doctrinal, but psychological: "The intellectual isolation of his sect preyed upon him; for, of all terrible things to natures like his, the most terrible is to belong to a minority" (65). He experiences a fascinated attraction to the Roman Catholic church that he passes every Sunday on the way to his meeting house, fantasizing about losing himself in its congregation and indulging in the "luxury of devotional contact" (64). Fairweather's physiognomy reflects his disordered volition—"his thick and sallow cheeks, his tremulous lips, his contracted forehead" all emblematize an "inward conflict" (65). By the time that Sophy visits Honeywood, Fairweather is far along in his process of conversion to Catholicism. His "inward longing to be with the majority was growing into an engrossing passion," and he had established relations with the parish priest Father McShane, all the while continuing to go through the public motions of Unitarianism.

Fairweather's case is of particular significance to Holmes's problematic of freedom and circumstance, because he represents the rejection of spiritual freedom and self-determination. Holmes is here confronted with the question of whether the denial of freedom is a free choice, and he answers in the negative through a caustic commentary by the Professor on the escape from freedom. Anticipating Erich Fromm's famous thesis of a century later, the Professor remarks that "liberty is often a heavy burden on a man" because "it involves that necessity for perpetual choice which is the kind of labor men have always dreaded": "If a man has a genuine, sincere, hearty wish to get rid of his liberty, if he is really bent on becoming a slave, nothing can stop him" (252). Adopting the same position that Kittredge took in his conversation with Honeywood, the Professor advises generosity "in our judgment of those who leave the front ranks of thought for the company of the meek noncombatants who follow with the baggage and provisions" (254). Yet he is not willing to deny responsibility altogether and, breaking with the drift of the argument, he cautions "all who are disposed to waver that there is a cowardice which is criminal, and a longing for rest which it is baseness to indulge" (254).

The Professor's harsh conclusion to his reflections seems to deconstruct the medicalized discourse on good and evil that structures the book intellectually. He is not about to condemn Fairweather, although his contempt for him is obvious, even when veiled by pretensions to compassion. The judgment of cowardice and baseness is not levied against any character in the text, standing as evidence that Holmes was not fully reconciled to the logical conclusions of his own premises, yet was unwilling or unable to incorporate his reservations into his narrative. Perhaps there are human beings who willfully sin when they could do otherwise, but they are not to be found in Rockland, Massachusetts.

The Professor's comments on escape from freedom are the prelude to a visit by Honeywood to Fairweather. Sophy belongs to Honeywood's congregation, and the Venners attend the Unitarian meeting, so Honeywood cannot help Elsie directly, but must try to charge Fairweather with the task. He believes incorrectly that Fairweather knows about Elsie's history, which leads to misunderstanding and miscommunication that are compounded by the fact that neither minister is initially aware of the other's process of conversion. Their encounter is an amusing interchange in which each one adopts the theology with which the other is identified, causing both of them to be bewildered. As Fairweather approves the doctrine of original sin with the expectation of Honeywood's approbation, the latter compliments Unitarians on their acknowledgment of the possibilities of human goodness, anticipating corroboration from his interlocutor. This farce is a fitting end to the two stories of conversion, making Holmes's point that doctrine follows character.

When his conversation with Fairweather is over, Honeywood's case is successfully closed. In contrast, Fairweather still has some rough treatment to face. Preoccupied with his own spiritual perplexities, he has lost touch with his congregation and is focused only on himself. He is troubled by an anonymous letter asking for a public prayer at the next service and even more with doubts about his conversion. The letter is from Elsie who is making a desperate bid for love, and Fairweather will fail her through negligent forget-fulness that confirms the weakness of his character. He comes to Dr. Kittredge for counsel and reassurance, and receives a judgment that absolves him in advance for his malign neglect, but also hu-miliates him.

Although Fairweather is converting to Catholicism, Kittredge is his real father confessor, to whom he has recourse for his physical complaints (he is a hypochondriac) and his spiritual ills. He comes to Kittredge now for permission to consummate his conversion, which the physician provides: "You have got into the wrong pulpit, and I have known it from the first. The sooner you go where you belong, the better" (404–5). Fairweather is comforted by the words, but he also knows that Kittredge sees through him and that he has been "overmastered" and "humbled." Yet he does not sense con-tempt: ". . . it seemed as if the old Doctor did not despise him any more for what he considered weakness of mind than he used to de-spise him when he complained of his nerves or his digestion" (405–6). Indeed, Fairweather is "grateful" for Kittredge's paternal-istic manner. Understanding that Fairweather is "dreadfully sensi-tive to the opinion of the minority" that he is leaving behind, Kittredge refuses to let matters rest where they stand and insists on talking "honestly" with his patient. He tells Fairweather that he is not sure that the minister could have helped doing what he soon would do; he is one of those "spiritual patients" who "must have a great list of specifics for all the soul's complaints." He had simply gotten "accidentally shuffled in" with a stronger and more select group of believers "in wholesome ways of living" (407).

Fairweather departs from his consultation "with a hollow feeling at the bottom of his soul, as if a good piece of his manhood had been scooped out of him" (407). As the price of absolution, Kit-tredge had demanded that Fairweather understand that he was act-ing out of weakness; he had abjected his patient and treated him cruelly. He had imposed the deterministic thesis on Fairweather in such a way that the latter would see himself to be contemptible and be deprived of any illusion that he was free. Here the medicaliza-tion of sin becomes a weapon of punishment. Perhaps Fairweather cannot be blamed for his weakness—he is not one of those cowards who could have done otherwise—but Holmes allows no compas-sion for him. Rubbing in the truth of his weakness will do nothing for Fairweather but compound his suffering. There is a sadistic strain in the denial of freedom.

Holmes's Elsie Problem

The initial test of Holmes's doctrine of freedom and circumstance reveals the surrender of the first term of the polarity to determination by the force of character shaped by nature and nurture. Although the Professor holds out for a margin of responsibility when he introduces Fairweather's conversion in his discourse on the escape from freedom, his defense is no more than an ideological abstraction, because the narrative contains no instance of the exercise of free moral choice, even by the most likely candidates—the two reverends. Both the strong and vital Honeywood and the weak and devitalized Fairweather live out their respective characters, reaching a coincidence between personality and doctrine that, in Nietzsche's terms, confirms their ascending and declining trajectories.

When the focus shifts to Holmes's own test case, Elsie, there would seem to be no difficulty in showing the denial of freedom to the (anti-)heroine: she is the author's poster girl for a "disordered volition" beyond her control. Yet Elsie is more than simply a victim of prenatal poisoning; she is not a snake-lady pure and simple, but a divided soul who carries within her the germs of a select young woman from her genetic inheritance, in addition to her reactive, cold, and (self-)destructive ophidian nature. In terms of the way that Holmes has set up the problem of freedom and circumstance, Elsie might consistently either succumb to her ophidian nature—as she actually does—or be brought to the realization of her (female) human nature. At a limit, she might even be brought to a point of strength at which she would choose the direction of her character, vindicating freedom. Such an improbable solution would be an even more telling defense of humanism and rejection of original sin and depravity than Elsie's death. She could at least just as well be a Honeywood as a Fairweather. She could be rescued rather than sacrificed.

Every one of Holmes's works of imaginative prose is structured by a romance of rescue, in which, in its standard form, a worthy young person is saved from a life of quiet desperation by someone well bred who provides the love that the object of rescue most deeply needs and, in the case of the rescued woman, economic security that she does not seek, but that will make her life commodious. *Elsie Venner* is the most complex of Holmes's rescue romances; it contains successful rescues and a failed rescue—Elsie's. The novel is also the only one of Holmes's literary works to have inspired extensive criticism and commentary. Most importantly, four studies have addressed the work exclusively, all of them focusing on the question of why Elsie is sacrificed and providing different answers, each of which is plausible and enlightening, but none of which is entirely convincing.[2] The line of *Elsie Venner* criticism is inaugurated by Stanton Garner, who poses the problem directly and cogently. For Garner, "all of the elements of a redemptive comedy" are present in the situation that Holmes imagines, "the kind of comedy in which must inhere the optimism which is the point of Holmes's argument, for in Elsie resides the whole issue of the guilt or innocence of all mankind."[3]

In sketch, when Elsie is introduced into the text, she is seventeen and attending the Apollinean Institute, a girl's finishing school, at which the young medical student, Bernard Langdon, has taken up a teaching position for financial reasons. For all of her life, she has been protected by her widowed father, Dudley Venner, a Brahmin gentleman of leisure who has sacrificed his life to her, and the family servant Sophy. As a result of her poisoning, which has remained a family secret (except for its revelation to Dr. Kittredge), Elsie has exhibited a mix of inhuman coldness, reactive viciousness, bursts of self-absorbed passionate release, and faint traces of human-hearted emotion. From the outset, Bernard and Elsie are attracted to each other, but a romantic relation cannot be consummated because Elsie is as yet incapable of loving anyone except, perhaps, Sophy—

---

2. The major recent commentaries on Elsie Venner are Stanton Garner, "Elsie Venner: Holmes's Deadly `Book of Life,'"; Margaret Hallissy, "Poisonous Creature: Holmes's Elsie Venner,"; Anne Dalke, "Economics, or the Bosom Serpent: Oliver Wendell Holmes' *Elsie Venner: A Romance of Destiny*"; Bryce Traister, "Sentimental Medicine: Oliver Wendell Holmes and the Construction of Masculinity." Other comparative studies provide useful context: Abigail Hamblen, "The Bad Seed: A Modern Elsie Venner"; Kathleen Gallagher, "The Art of Snake Handling: Lamia, Elsie Venner, and `Rappaccini's Daughter'"; Alice H. Petry, "The Ophidian Image in Holmes and Dickinson."

3. Garner, "Elsie Venner," 291.

and their bond is inarticulate. Bernard is ambivalent, put off by her threatening strangeness and seduced by her beauty and individuality.

As the plot unfolds, Bernard must face the misconceived rivalry of Elsie's desperado cousin Richard, who wants her hand to gain control over the Venner's wealthy estate, but is rebuffed by her. The story reaches its climax when Richard fails to murder Bernard and is escorted out of Rockland by Kittredge, whereupon Elsie falls ill as her resurgent human nature struggles against her ophidian nature. It is then that she reaches out to Fairweather to say a public prayer and, after he fails her, overcomes the ophidian resistance and begs Bernard to love her. He also fails her, offering only brotherly love. From then on, Elsie is fated to die, her demise sealed by purple white-ash leaves—a snake repellent in folk wisdom—placed unwittingly by Bernard in a gift basket given to her by the community. The redemptive comedy that Garner poses as an alternative to Holmes's tragic/melodramatic narrative would have Bernard move on from his rescue of Elsie from Richard to save her by giving her the love that she needs and asks from him. Bernard would be "the Brahmin Galahad."[4]

Garner states his thesis with moral passion: "Having begun a novel which was to show that Elsie is without sin, Holmes ends it by showing how remorselessly she is sinned against, shunned by both the man of this world who should husband her body and by the man of God who should husband her soul." Initiating a line of criticism that will hold for all of the succeeding commentators, Garner throws the onus of failure on Bernard's character: "Elsie is punished, not because she deserves punishment, but because neither the settled order nor a presumptive benevolent agency can or will satisfy her need for a man whose blood is rich enough to accept her formidable offering." As a member of Holmes's cherished Brahmin caste—Holmes's famous description of which begins the novel—Bernard is incapable of fulfilling Elsie's "desperate need for affection and love." Comparing him to Jim Burden in Willa Cather's *My Antonia*, Garner argues that Bernard has lost part of his own "animal nature" in the process of his Brahmin breeding, which has given him in return an augmented intellect: "Had this one last chord not been bred out of Bernard, Elsie would have been saved. Is

4. Ibid.

the caste a step up or down the evolutionary ladder? No matter, it deserves neither praise nor blame."[5]

Echoing, extending, and intensifying Garner's criticism, Margaret Hallissy argues that "the serpent in Elsie is her sexuality." In order to be saved, Elsie "needs a man who is not only emotionally responsive but brave." Bernard is far from filling the bill. He is "ordinary," and Elsie is extraordinary in her "beauty and sensuality." He distances himself from her by adopting a clinical attitude toward her, projecting his own coldness of heart onto her. Elsie "loved someone not up to the challenge of loving her."[6]

The other two commentators, Anne Dalke and Bryce Traister, present independent and insightful interpretations of the work as a whole that support Garner's and Hallissy's core thesis. Dalke shows how *Elsie Venner* can be read as a critical comment on fortune hunting in mid-nineteenth-century capitalist America. Not only is Richard Venner money-mad, but Bernard finds his way into prosperity by marrying Honeywood's granddaughter Letty, who turns out to be from an exceedingly wealthy family and rescues him from any need to struggle in his medical career. For Dalke, Elsie is simply irrelevant to people who are in the clutches of the self-interested pursuit of economic success. Traister adds a complementary dimension by arguing that Bernard is not free to love Elsie because he is engaged in self-formation as a physician, which accounts for his clinical attitude toward her. Again, another interest gets in the way of the possibility for generous and saving love.

Whether it is his Brahmin breeding, his erotic inadequacy, or his financial or professional concerns, all of the commentators agree that the failure to rescue Elsie lies in Bernard's limitations. As the test of Holmes's doctrine moves to Elsie, it will proceed through a test of the regnant critical thesis about the work.

The Denial of Freedom to Elsie Venner

As plausible, careful, and insightful as the commentaries on *Elsie Venner* have been, their core thesis that Bernard's inadequacies are

5. Ibid., 292, 295.
6. Hallissy, "Poisonous Creature," 416–18.

responsible for Elsie's tragic/melodramatic death is not supported by the text. Dalke's and Traister's supplementary interpretations of the work do not establish that Elsie could not have been rescued. If Bernard is a kind of fortune hunter, as Dalke has it, he could just as well have married into the Venner family. If he is Traister's physician in training, he could have effected his first cure in Elsie's desperate case. Garner's and Hallissy's allied interpretations cannot be taken care of so easily. Their critiques are centered on the moment at which Bernard rejects Elsie's plea for complete romantic/sexual love, assuming that he is refusing a gift that he is too weak or deficient to receive. Neither of them considers how the narrative reached that point. A review of the relationship between Elsie and Bernard as it develops through the text shows that Bernard is hardly an overintellectualized member of the Brahmin case or an erotically and sexually challenged "ordinary" man. His rejection of Elsie is far more problematic than that and indicates less his own limitations than Holmes's own difficulties in managing his complex (anti-)heroine. Through their focus on Bernard, the critics have absolved Holmes of responsibility for Elsie, making it seem that the author is on her side; yet he is the one who imagined her.

Far from being devitalized, Bernard is an idealized figure, an instance of Holmes's exemplary American male—well bred, emotionally sensitive, virile, physically courageous, open-hearted, healthy-minded, and, yes, intellectual.[7] His character is established at the outset of the book when he takes a position in the hamlet of Pigwacket, prior to his move to Rockland. The boys in the local common school where he teaches have a penchant for harassing their masters, and their leader, the butcher's son Abner Briggs, had physically assaulted Bernard's predecessor, forcing him to depart in shame. Having received a generous dose of the permanent rebellion, during his first week in class, Bernard resolves to face the situation

---

7. Bernard Langdon is anticipated by the young man from Maryland in *The Professor at the Breakfast-Table*. He is "born of good stock, in one of the more thoroughly civilized portions of these United States of America, bred in good principles, inheriting a social position which makes him at ease everywhere, means sufficient to educate him thoroughly without taking away the stimulus to vigorous exertion, and with a good opening in some honorable path of labor" (283). The young Marylander, who is training to be an engineer, rescues the heroine Iris in the romance that structures *The Professor*.

head on, honing his impressive boxing and fencing skills in the evening. On the way to school on the day of his confrontation, he meets the buxom teenager Alminy Cutterr, who warns him that Briggs is planning to bring his vicious dog Tiger to class with mayhem in mind. Moved by Alminy's concern and her country charm, Bernard impulsively kisses her and then walks to school, where he dispatches Tiger with a swift kick and expertly manhandles Briggs and expels him permanently. Thereupon, the rest of the boys settle down: "What could be done with a master who was so pleasant as long as the boys behaved decently, and such a terrible fellow when he got 'riled,' as they called it?" (40). Having established his credibility as a "woman-tamer" and "one of the natural class of the sex-subduers," and as a virile, no-nonsense male, Bernard is ready for Rockland (37).

Bernard's relation with Elsie begins on his first day of teaching literature when he is fascinated by "that strange wild-looking girl" who sits apart from the other students (51). His attraction grows when he attends a party thrown by the local notable Colonel Sprowle. Taken up with erotic interest, he dances with his "over-womanized" student Rosa Milburn, who is delighted by his intimate attentions. The "flush of his new-born passion" is soon dimmed by the sense that a "counter-charm" is being exerted on him, and he sees that Elsie is "looking at him as if she saw nothing else but him" (105). The "glitter" of Elsie's "diamond eyes" seems, to Bernard, "to disenchant the air, so full a moment before of strong attractions" (105). Bernard becomes "silent and dreamy" (105). He excuses himself from Rosa's company and tries to seek out Elsie, but he is swept into a square dance and she is gone by the time he can extricate himself.

Elsie makes her next move when she puts a mountain flower that she picked on the ominous Rattlesnake Ledge—where no one but she dares to go—in Bernard's copy of Vergil. He sees that she is wearing the same flower that day, dismissing her gesture as "a young girl's graceful compliment," yet he is troubled and opens up his *Aeneid* at random, finding the story of Laocoon, which he reads "with a strange feeling of fascination," finally flinging "the book from him, as if its leaves had been steeped in the subtle poisons that princes die of" (126). Elsie's gift of the flower and Bernard's response to it establish the relation that will hold between them for the rest of the text. He will become progressively more distant from and resistant to her, and her passion for him will progressively intensify. Holmes has demonstrated that Bernard is both passionate and brave; he is not too weak to accept Elsie's gift—he is antipathetic to her ophidian nature at the same time that her wildness attracts him. If he were to rescue her, he would have to overcome his antipathy.

His bivalent fascination with Elsie drives Bernard to embark on an adventure up the mountain that dominates the Rockland landscape to seek out the flower that the wild girl had given him (185). Fitted out with heavy boots and a stick, Bernard comes upon Rattlesnake Ledge, where he finds Elsie's hair pin. Walking to the mouth of the cavern on the ledge, he is met "by the glitter of two diamond eyes" of a rattlesnake that paralyzes him. Unable to save himself, he awaits death until he sees the eyes growing dull and then finds that Elsie has rescued him by staring the snake down. She leads the way down the mountain in silence.

Elsie's rescue of Bernard brings forward the problem that Holmes has with his (anti-)heroine and his options for her. Although she has saved Bernard by recourse to her ophidian nature—the same gaze that so disturbed him at Colonel Sprowle's party—she could not have been motivated to undertake that deed of rescue by that nature. Here Holmes allows for the possibility that Elsie can use her dark powers for the good and that she can act from love or at least benevolence. The way is open for Bernard to acknowledge this immeasurable gift and to reciprocate, allowing Elsie to become a whole person who need not sacrifice the strength of her wildness. The alternative, which Holmes follows, is to increase the distance between them, heightening the cruel pathos that he has already built into the narrative.

The die is cast in the next chapter, which recounts a conversation between Elsie's father, Dudley, and the book's ideological authority, Kittredge. Since he learned about Elsie's condition after she had tried to poison a governess, Kittredge has become the Venner family's adviser. He has counseled Dudley to let Elsie have her way and to let her see young men when the opportunity presents itself. His prescription is that Elsie needs love: "She will not love anyone easily, perhaps not at all, yet love would be more likely to bring her right than anything else" (195). And then, "If any young person seems in danger of falling in love with her, send him to me for counsel" (195).

The meaning of the physician's advice becomes clear in the following chapter, when Bernard visits Kittredge, after deciding that his response to Elsie's rescue will be to "solve the mystery of Elsie Venner sooner or later" (204). For Kittredge, only love can save Elsie; yet neither Bernard nor, implicitly, anyone else should be the one to provide it: "'Her love is not to be desired, and'—he spoke in a lower tone—'her hate is to be dreaded'" (212). When Kittredge asks Bernard if he is in danger of falling in love with Elsie, he responds that she interests him "strangely," but that he pities her and does not love her: "I would risk my life for her, if it would do her any good, but it would be in cold blood" (214). Kittredge then warns Bernard: "Keep your eyes open and your heart shut" (214). Elsie's fate is sealed; she has become a terminal case, not (only) because Bernard must be interpellated into medical practice, but because Holmes, through Kittredge, will not allow her the possibility of freedom or at least of self-actualization that was posed by her rescue of Bernard. The physician has admitted that Elsie might be saved by love, but he will not permit his prescription to be filled.

Bernard's rejection of Elsie is made conclusive at the tea party thrown by the Widow Rowens, where he begins his romance with Honeywood's granddaughter Letty Forrester. Preoccupied with Letty as he was with Rosa Milburn at Colonel Sprowle's affair, Bernard notices that his companion has become discomfited and realizes that the cause is Elsie's jealous gaze. In yet another staring match, Bernard resolves "to look her down" and succeeds: "Presently she changed color slightly,—lifted her head, which was inclined a little to one side,—shut and opened her eyes two or three times, as if they had been pained and wearied,—and turned away baffled, and shamed, as it would seem, and shorn for the time of her singular and formidable or at least evil-natured power of swaying the impulses of those around her" (310). Bernard is able to subdue Elsie because of her sensitivity to him, a sensitivity that she shows to no one else but Sophy. He has taken advantage of her vulnerability to sacrifice her for Letty. His tawdry victory achieved, he is free to have "a snug *tête-à-tête*" with his new girlfriend "in the recess of a bay-window" (313). Elsie had saved Bernard with a stare on Rattlesnake Ledge; Bernard abjects Elsie with a stare, woman-tamer and sex-subduer that he is.

The plot moves on as Richard Venner realizes in an encounter with Elsie that she loves Bernard, when he vilifies the schoolmaster and she blushes with "shame or wrath" (359). He decides to murder Bernard and disguise it as a suicide, but his plans fail when Bernard has the presence of mind to defend himself. Elsie greets the humiliation of her cousin with "a look of contempt and of something like triumph," but immediately she notices that one of her beloved white pigeons that she fed with her own hands has died, and she falls into tearless weeping that releases "an unwanted tumult in her soul" (387–88). So begins Elsie's agonized struggle with herself that will soon lead to her death. She goes to school that day, her eyes now softened into "a strange, dreamy tenderness," as "the deep instincts of womanhood" strove "to grope their way to the surface of her being through all the alien influences which overlaid them" (393). She is unable to conceal her passion for Bernard, "the only person who had ever reached the spring of her hidden sympathies" (393). By this time, however, Bernard has become entirely insensible to her and has objectified her as a case. The Professor does not report that Bernard even notices Elsie's condition.

It is now time for Elsie to make her last desperate attempts to reach out for help—the request to Fairweather to say a public prayer for her and her plea to Bernard to love her. When she approaches Bernard after school, she has "none of the still wicked light in her eyes," but is "gentle" and "dreamy." When she is met with pity rather than love, it is "all over with poor Elsie" (423). She goes to her room and is found by Sophy suffering from an acute headache. From then on her decline is rapid, as she sheds her ophidian nature and takes on the image of her mother, a model of generous and self-sacrificial womanhood, void of any wildness. Bernard's gift of the white-ash leaves hastens her demise. She asks to see Bernard and gives him one of her bracelets: "I shall never see you again. Some time or other, perhaps, you will mention my name to one whom you love. Give her this from your scholar and friend Elsie" (447). Bernard takes the bracelet and moves to kiss Elsie's hand, but cannot accomplish the act: ". . . in that moment he was the weaker of the two" (447). He cannot even answer her good-bye. When Bernard leaves, Elsie briefly sobs and then composes herself.

Shortly thereafter, she expires, having shared a first and last kiss with her father.

Why must Elsie die? Why could she not have been rescued? Those questions become even more perplexing after reviewing her relation with Bernard. He was quite capable of saving her, a Brahmin with a difference. She showed abundant promise of humanization. Bernard's antipathy to Elsie is only sustained by his failure to move beyond the manifestations of her ophidian personality to see her possibilities of goodness—a failure that contradicts his character as Holmes sets it up. There is an answer in the text, provided by Kittredge: Elsie's ophidian nature had taken such hold of her that when it began to die out in her struggle for love, it proved to have "involved the centres of life in its own decay" (445). This brutal physiological explanation is consistent with Holmes's deterministic thesis, but it makes the entire story rest on a simple accident. Perhaps this is Holmes's point.

It is, however, neither emotionally nor intellectually satisfying to leave the matter there. If we cannot appeal to Bernard's weakness as the explanation of the failure to rescue Elsie, then we must look to the author. Elsie's double nature presents a problem for Holmes. There is a reptilian side of her that is genuinely inhuman, dangerously reactive and passionless, and there is a genteel side of her that emerges as her ophidian nature decays. Yet that bifurcation does not tell the whole story. Elsie also evinces a positive aspect of "wildness" in her love of nature, her courage, her communion with Sophy, her love of passionate dance, and her boldly beautiful taste in dress. Where does this positive side belong? It is neither reptilian nor genteel, and it is what gives Elsie individuality and makes her appealing; without it, Bernard could not have been attracted to her and there would have been no story. Elsie's positive wildness is simply anomalous in terms of Holmes's romantic imaginary, in which vital and capable heroes (like Bernard) save repressed and self-sacrificing victims of quiet desperation. Were Holmes to have rescued Elsie, he would have had to affirm a woman of great strength, which he was obviously incapable of doing when he wrote the novel. Instead, he lets the well-bred Letty rescue Bernard financially; she ends up wearing Elsie's bracelet. In his last novel, *A Mortal Antipathy*, written decades later, Holmes redeems himself by allowing a full-blooded heroine to save a male victim of traumatic neurosis.

Elsie is a cruel sacrifice to Holmes's deterministic thesis and to his imaginary. Of all of the characters in the book that bears her name, she is the one who most had to be deprived of freedom and self-actualization. Hallissy is correct that *Elsie Venner: A Romance of Destiny* inscribes the victory of the normal over the exceptional, but the injustice of that triumph must be borne by the author, not his characters.

Chapter 5

The Vindication of Freedom in *The Guardian Angel*

Holmes's first cluster of three imaginative prose works ended in 1861 with his first novel, *Elsie Venner,* conceived as a "test" of the Calvinist doctrine of individual responsibility for ancestral sin. Holmes succeeded effectively in disparaging that dogma. Yet he did not realize his purpose of grafting limited individual responsibility—and its presupposition of freedom as self-determination—to his naturalistic and mechanistic interpretation of moral character that reduced the latter to a summation and synthesis of hereditary and environmental influences. Voiding responsibility for the past's effects on the present, Holmes had also dissolved the self-determination required for any kind of responsibility. No character in *Elsie Venner* was given a moment of genuine choice.

Whether or not Holmes was aware of his failure, his Calvinist critics pounced on him for having opened the way to moral license and to the identification of evil with God.[1] The former line of attack had already been broached in *Elsie Venner,* through the Calvinist Rev. Honeywood. Holmes had met the problem with a warning by

1. See Tilton, *Amiable Autocrat,* 248–52, for an account of Holmes's "running warfare with the religious press."

the novel's narrator and minor character, the Professor (Holmes's medical professor persona), that "there is a cowardice which is criminal, and a longing for rest that it is baseness to indulge" (*Elsie Venner*, 254). The work showed no evidence of such states of being in its characters. The critics had a point.

Holmes's first postbellum work of imaginative prose was a novel, *The Guardian Angel*. Whereas the three earlier works had been set in their antebellum present, *The Guardian Angel* goes back to the same time, 1859–1861, when the first cluster was written. In his 1867 preface to *The Guardian Angel*, Holmes made the connection to *Elsie Venner* clear: "This tale forms a natural sequence to a former one . . . entitled 'Elsie Venner'" (*Guardian Angel*, vii). As the preface shows, the "natural sequence" is one of clarification and precision, and—although Holmes does not admit it—rectification; he is giving himself another chance to settle the problem of freedom and circumstance. The critics are on Holmes's mind, and he believes that he has been (perversely) misinterpreted. This time he will make sure that his position is well understood.

The Guardian Angel is a far more focused work than *Elsie Venner*. Rather than considering a range of issues surrounding Calvinist theology, the successor work concentrates relentlessly on one of them—moral responsibility. In the preface, Holmes vents his pique and defines his targets: "Should any professional alarmist choose to confound the doctrine of limited responsibility with that which denies the existence of a self-determining power, he may be presumed to belong to the class of intellectual half-breeds, of which we have many representatives in our new country, wearing the garb of civilization, and even the gown of scholarship" (viii-ix). He defends his project of following "the automatic machinery of nature into the mental and moral world, where it plays its part as much as in the bodily functions," and dismisses the accusation that he has laid "all that we are evil in to a divine thrusting on" by remarking that to admit that charge is to "reinstate the leader of the lower House in his time-honored prerogatives" (ix). Holmes is on the warpath.

Holmes's strategy for exemplifying, demonstrating, and vindicating his doctrine of limited responsibility is to write a morality play with complex characters who are faced with genuine choices and whose motives are often undecidable. Following in the line of *Elsie Venner*, *The Guardian Angel* is a "medicated novel" or "physiological romance" in which a "test" of doctrine is woven into a romance in which someone faced with a life of quiet desperation is rescued from their fate by a loving and generous savior. Unlike its predecessor, in which the characters were locked into their respective doctrines, even when they were not one-dimensional, *The Guardian Angel* is populated by multidimensional characters who are engaged simultaneously in "battles" within themselves and with others, which make their fates appear to be less than certain. As befits a morality play, the characters receive rewards and punishments in accordance with the moral quality of their deeds and their degree of responsibility for them. *The Guardian Angel* creates a moral universe, medicated by the doctrine of limited responsibility.

The Guardian Angel is the only one of Holmes's three novels to approximate the modern standards of its genre. In *Elsie Venner* and later in *A Mortal Antipathy*, Holmes wrote heterogeneous texts, replete with explanations and theoretical asides. In contrast, *The Guardian Angel* is tightly organized around its romantic narrative; the medication is introduced directly into the narrative, through the deliberations of its characters. The novel is also the most complex of Holmes's romances in its plot construction. There are exchanges of romantic partners, alliances in power struggles, subplots, personal growth and decline, mysteries, and a large cast of characters, all directly related to the test of doctrine. Whereas the spirit of logic had ruled *Elsie Venner*, the spirit of finesse takes command in *The Guardian Angel*. Finally, the work contains the only characters whom Holmes imagined who are willfully evil and deserving of punishment; that is, who are held responsible for their malign actions.

For the purpose of exposing how Holmes's doctrine of limited responsibility is exemplified in the text, it is necessary to provide a sketch of the plot, removing much of its richness. The multitude of relations and battles that constitute *The Guardian Angel* all make the same point that despite the presence of mechanism in moral experience, there is room for self-determination when individuals are strong enough to undertake it. The three major characters make that point most extensively, precisely, and convincingly: the novel's title figure, Byles Gridley, is a sixty-one-year-old retired professor and consummate generalist and humanist; Gridley's antagonist, William Murray Bradshaw, is a young lawyer who epitomizes unscrupulous fortune hunting and possessive individualism; and Myrtle Hazard is a young lady of fifteen whom Gridley helps to save from Bradshaw's clutches.

The most complex character whom Holmes ever imagined is Myrtle Hazard. She is the paradigm case of what Holmes had called "disordered volition" in *Elsie Venner* (*Elsie Venner*, ix), a compound of warring impulses that represent her ancestors. Among them are Judith Pride, a great beauty and woman of the world; Anne Holyoake, a martyr of Protestant faith; Ruth Bradford, a medium who was accused of being a witch; and Virginia Wild, who was part Native American. In addition, Myrtle has grown up as an orphan in the repressive Calvinist household of her aunt Silence Withers, where she suffered a traumatic incident of extreme psychological and physical abuse. She is further alienated from her New England environment by memories of India, where she spent her earliest years. Myrtle is beautiful and intelligent, but also wayward, over-sheltered, and rebellious.

The root story of *The Guardian Angel* is how Myrtle achieves self-determination by ordering and harmonizing the diverse elements of her moral makeup through her own acts of self-determination and the strategic help of Gridley and a support network of local notables (a minister, a physician, and a lawyer), a faithful Irish servant, and assorted other generous people.[2] In her process of coming to herself, Myrtle must fend off or be saved from the attempts of a series of male predators to captivate her. The assaults come after she has made a desperate break for freedom by taking a leaky stray boat down the river that runs through Oxbow Village, where the narrative is set, so that she can reach Boston and take a sailing ship to India, disguised as a boy. The adventure ends disastrously when she encounters rapids and is saved from near certain death by the young architecture student and sculptor Clement Lindsay, whom she will eventually marry.

Found recovering by Gridley in the Lindsay household, Myrtle returns to Oxbow Village in hysterical shock. During her convales-

2. In his perceptive commentary on *Elsie Venner*, Stanton Garner argues that Holmes's failure to allow his (anti-)heroine to be rescued followed from his failure to provide her with a social support network that could nurture her strength. In *The Guardian Angel*, Holmes supplies Myrtle Hazard with an abundant support network. See Garner, "Elsie Venner," 283–98.

cence, she falls in succession under the sway of the young Dr. Fordyce Hurlbut's "magnetic" hands, the handsome Calvinist minister Bellamy Stoker's spiritual intimacies, and Murray Bradshaw's courtier charms. Only Bradshaw knows that Myrtle stands to inherit a valuable piece of land; he has concealed the will that establishes her claim and plans to have it brought to light only after he has secured her hand in marriage. At every juncture of her adventure in self-formation, Myrtle is assisted by Gridley and the support network that he mobilizes, until she is brought, as her own person, safely into the arms of Clement.

Compounding all of the battles of the external narrative are internal struggles of all of the strong characters with themselves, as they come to turning points in the action. Their spiritual jihads are the focus of Holmes's test of his doctrine of limited responsibility, executed through descriptions of character-in-formation. The distinguishing characteristic of *The Guardian Angel,* which sets it apart from Holmes's earlier works of imaginative prose, is its concentration on the subjective side of the individual will, the dynamics of working through disordered volition, or failing to do so. His descriptions of moral experience are structured by a depth psychology that is explained in brief asides by the narrator and, more importantly, is evinced in accounts of the characters' deliberations.

Depth Psychology

That Holmes deployed a depth psychology that in some respects resembles twentieth-century psychoanalysis is widely acknowledged and undisputed. In the 1940s, Clarence Oberndorf published an abridgment of Holmes's three "psychiatric" novels with abundant annotations, attempting to show a connection between his insights into personality and Freudian concepts. Holmes, however, is not most adequately understood in terms of Freudian psychoanalytic theory. Although he employs the concept of the unconscious mind throughout his works, Holmes does not prefigure such standard Freudian notions as the Oedipal conflict and does not base his accounts of "disordered volition" on the primacy of sexual drives and their repression. A much more precise understanding of Holmes's psychology is provided by Charles Boewe, who explored the psychological theories grounding Holmes's novels in terms of the

emerging paradigms of his time, providing a persuasive understanding of how he conceived of unconscious mentality without recourse to psychoanalytic theory. Later, Karl Wentersdorf brought
forward the centrality of the unconscious—Holmes's "underground workshop"—to his psychology of creativity, recurring, as
Boewe did, to Holmes's own understandings rather than Freud's.[3]

As Boewe shows, Holmes was a forceful advocate of Marshall
Hull's experimentally verified theory of reflex action in animal behavior. Holmes extended it into the domain of human mentality
and expanded it to the point of including under it "any kind of force
beyond human control—. . . anything for which we cannot hold
ourselves responsible." Boewe uses his understanding of Holmes's
commitment to reflex psychology to argue that, in *The Guardian
Angel*, Holmes intended "to persuade his reader to believe that reflex functions operate in the higher spheres—that is, that his heroine [Myrtle Hazard] is not responsible for her actions; and the
method he chooses to relieve her of responsibility is to have her
subject to uncontrollable hereditary influences."[4]

The thesis guiding the present writing is at the polar opposite
from Boewe's—rather than being at the mercy of hereditary influences, Myrtle, as a strong character, has limited responsibility for
them. That disagreement, however, does not void Boewe's notion
that Holmes conceived of his psychology in terms of reflex action.
When he broadened the concept to include essentially any stimulus-
response process, including the vicissitudes of mentality, Holmes
opened up his scope to allow for the dynamics of conscious and unconscious experience, rather than reducing them to purely physiological process. Once implanted in the realm of experience rather
than simply behavior, Holmes left the rigid bounds of causality behind, acknowledging more complex states, such as conflict and ambivalence, and introducing the potential for self-determination. In
his study of Holmes's conceptions of unconscious mentality, Wentersdorf shows that Holmes's "advocacy of automatism was modi-
fied by his wavering but finally firm belief in free will."[5] Wentersdorf

---

3. Clarence Oberndorf, *The Psychiatric Novels of Oliver Wendell Holmes;* Charles
Boewe, "Reflex Action in the Novels of Oliver Wendell Holmes"; Karl Wentersdorf, "The Underground Workshop of Oliver Wendell Holmes."
4. Boewe, "Reflex Action," 312–13.
5. Wentersdorf, "Underground Workshop," 6.

does not, however, devote any attention to how Holmes attempted to make a place for free will, even in the restricted area of psychology of creativity.

As the final test of Holmes's doctrine of limited responsibility, *The Guardian Angel* both explains in sketch and evinces abundantly his depth psychology, which does not so much anticipate any movements in twentieth-century psychology as add the dimension of the unconscious mind to the norm—espoused by one of Holmes's favorite writers, the seventeenth-century humanist Thomas Browne—that individuals are fulfilled when they "make good" on their faculties. Holmes's unconscious is not merely a repository for repressed desires and fears (although it is that, too); it is also in part supportive of and essential to the actualization of the moral personality, and in part the resting place of unfulfilled possibilities that can be reawakened. Most importantly, the unconscious by itself is a field of unreconciled multiplicity, indeed, of disorder, containing myriad impulses and motives at cross purposes with one another. The art of life is to bring multiplicity into as generous a harmony as possible. For a personality in formation, that means working through one's conflicts with the aid of nurturance from others—one's guardian angels. The harmonization of the self requires acts of self-determination and makes self-determination possible—a virtuous circle.

In *The Guardian Angel*, Holmes introduces fewer explanatory and didactic mini-essays than he does in his other two novels, and, when his explanations appear, they are about psychology. Early in the text, before he describes Myrtle's complex makeup, the anonymous less-than-omniscient narrator sets out the psychological theory that will guide it, which is based on the principle that the self is a multiplicity. Remarking that "[i]t is by no means certain that our individual personality is the single inhabitant of these our corporeal frames," Holmes speculates that "some, at least, who have long been dead, may enjoy a kind of secondary and imperfect, yet self-conscious life, in these bodily tenements which we are in the habit of considering exclusively our own" (*Guardian Angel*, 22). Drawing upon reported cases of multiple personality and the common experience of surprising ourselves and of observing people who seem to be acting "in obedience to some other law than that of their own proper nature," he concludes by quoting his hero Byles

Gridley's neglected work of life-philosophy: "This body in which we journey across the isthmus between two oceans is not a private carriage, but an omnibus" (23).

Holmes's initial formulation of the multiplicity of the self is confused and imprecise. His medicated thesis in *The Guardian Angel*, derived from his expanded interpretation of reflex psychology, is that human beings inherit aspects of the personalities of their ancestors; individuals possess selves that they identify as their own along with "cotenants," all of which inhabit the same body and sometimes seize control of conscious expression. Although this case approximates what happens in multiple personality disorder, it is not adequate to understanding how multiplicity of the self can be generalized to include all human beings. It only allows for a plurality of separate and discrete selves, not for semi-detached sides of a single, complex self. If the human being was simply a tribe or family of fixed selves, one of which was the individual's "proper nature," there would be no room for growth, transformation, and self-determination, all of which are essential to Holmes's project of vindicating limited responsibility. The clinical case of multiple personality disorder would not be responsible for the acts of the body when the latter was under the control of an improper or alien nature. Indeed, there would be no play among multiple selves, only the replacement of one by another in an endless power struggle.

Holmes rectifies his static interpretation of multiple personality soon after the conclusion of his mini-essay. He summarizes Myrtle's predicament in a "formal statement" and sketches the course of her self-development, which is paradigmatic for successful reconciliation and resolution of psychological diversity. As the story begins, "[t]he instincts and qualities belonging to ancestral traits which predominated in the conflict of mingled lives lay in the child in embryo, waiting to come to maturity" (26). The formulation is now dynamic. In place of a proper self and its (unwanted) cotenants, there is a struggle of "mingled lives," which will come to prominence at different moments of the activity of self-formation, "before the absolute and total result of their several forces had found its equilibrium in the character by which she was to be known as an individual" (27).

The achievement of equilibrium will be a hard-fought battle, marked by danger: "The World, the Flesh, and the Devil held mortgages on her life before its deed was put in her hands; but sweet and gracious influences were also born with her; and the battle of life was to be fought between them, God helping her [presumably through her guardian angels] in her need, and her own free choice siding with one or the other" (27). Holmes insists that his formal statement be "borne in mind" by the reader and that he will not repeat it. So much for Boewe's thesis that Holmes wants to persuade the reader that Myrtle "is not responsible for her actions;" rather, Holmes makes it clear that, unlike Elsie Venner, Myrtle Hazard will be an exemplar of self-determination by working through her conflicting impulses—framed by a battle between good and evil—and will achieve a distinctive equilibrium (individuation) with the assistance of God / others and "her own free choice."

Whereas *Elsie Venner* was a *Romance of Destiny*, in which the (anti-)-heroine was sacrificed to the workings of the reflex arc, *The Guardian Angel* is a romance of liberty based on an (optimistic) humanistic psychology (of struggle) among impulses, desires, and motives that erupt into consciousness and plunge back into the underground workshop as the ego tries to harmonize them and decides on their order of priority in constituting the personality. In *Elsie Venner*, Holmes imagined a sacrificial victim; in *The Guardian Angel*, he imagines a free personality who comes to master herself.

Holmes reprises the issue of multiple personality and provides a second formulation of his thesis in a "Note by a Friend" (presumably Byles Gridley) that is appended to Myrtle's written account of a vision that she had on her ill-fated adventure down the river, in which she saw before her all of the personifications of the sides of her complex character. The friend speculates that the experience was "one of those visions, with *objective projection*, which sometimes come to imaginative young persons, especially girls, in certain exalted nervous conditions" (94). From the psychological point of view, the vision indicates a "struggle for mastery" between ancestral influences: ". . . by and by one or more get the predominance, so that we grow to be like father, or mother, or remoter ancestor, or two or more are blended in us, not to the exclusion, however, it must be understood, of a special personality of our own" (94). This is no longer a description of multiple personality disorder, but the statement of a dynamic psychology that is evinced in the adventures of all of the major characters in *The Guardian*

Angel and, in a more sketchy fashion, in most of the minor characters. Holmes's success in working his depth psychology into his characters and into the twists and turns of his narrative is the literary achievement of *The Guardian Angel*.

How Holmes makes good on evincing his doctrine of limited responsibility through a discourse of depth psychology can be shown through studies of the development of the three major characters in his novel. Byles Gridley exemplifies a paragon of goodness, maturity, and self-responsibility; Murray Bradshaw instances an ideal type of evil, for which he must bear responsibility; and Myrtle is the exemplar of how someone with a disordered volition can come into her own as a self-determining individual.

Mature Freedom

Holmes's project of redeeming moral freedom begins with Byles Gridley, who at the end of the novel will become the paradigm of a fully mature moral individual—a guardian angel. The text opens with a critical review of an issue of Oxbow Village's weekly newspaper, *The State Banner and Delphian Oracle,* conducted by Gridley, who is annotating it liberally with bilious observations that reflect his anti-rural prejudices. He comes off as a hopeless crotchet, singling out spelling errors for special censure.

The picture changes in chapter 4, which is devoted to descriptions of Gridley's physiognomy, character, and state of being. He is introduced as a Master of Arts with broad learning and a library that spans Holmes's interests in science, the humanities, and current affairs. A bachelor and once a university professor, Gridley has now retired to Oxbow Village to mark time until he dies, living among his books as a boarder in the house of the good widow Ammi Hopkins. In his prime, Gridley had written and published his masterwork, *Thoughts on the Universe,* which fell on a blind public. Chastened by his failure, he believes that his life has been wasted and that he is useless.

As Holmes sketches him, Gridley is a complex character. Not only is he a generalist ranging over all branches of knowledge; he has also developed an individuality that combines conflicting elements—a "strange union of trampling radicalism in some directions

and a high-stepping conservatism in others" (39). Through his decades of teaching, Gridley has acquired the ability to read character,
manage political situations, and deploy crafty strategies. He is in
good health and is endowed with "strong, squared features," a
"solid-looking head," a "positive and categorical stride," and measured speech. Gridley only lacks moral sentiment to rouse him
from his demoralized isolation. He has the means for moral action
and the leisure for it provided by an inheritance, but he does not
yet have sufficient impulse to undertake it.

That impulse has begun to grow under the influence of the Hopkins household. Ammi Hopkins is a paragon of human-hearted
virtue, doting on her son, the aspiring poet Gifted Hopkins; raising
and nurturing foundling twins who had been left on her doorstep;
and providing a warm environment for her young relative, Susan
Posey, who is attending the local ladies' finishing school. Gridley
has started to give Gifted mentoring and to engage the little twins
in play: ". . . it seemed as if some of the human and social sentiments which had never leafed or flowered in him, for want of their
natural sunshine, had begun growing up from roots which had
never lost their life" (47). In medical terms, the "grand-paternal instinct" had awakened in him (47).

Gridley is ready for his moral adventure, in which the moral impulses that are beginning to flower under the protection of a loving
household will carry him into successive battles with evil in the
cause of Myrtle Hazard's self-development. At each juncture that
Gridley is called upon to enter the fray, he is faced with a moral
choice—to engage in a distasteful confrontation or to retreat back
into isolation. His first act of service to Myrtle, in whom he has
taken a benevolent interest, is to reclaim her from the Lindsay
household where she is recuperating from her boat wreck. He suspects that she is there from a conversation on another matter with
Susan Posey and resolves to bring her back to Oxbow Village without allowing her reputation to be compromised in any way.
Gridley's motivation to undertake this initial rescue, which sets the
pattern for others to come, is not explained by Holmes, who gives
no indication about whether the act was free or determined.

Gridley's moral struggle begins in earnest as Myrtle continues
her recovery at home. Traumatized by her calamitous adventure,
she is in a state of hysterical shock, delusional and vulnerable.

Gridley has withdrawn from the scene, but he will continue to be called back to it to save Myrtle from evil in the form of predatory males. Each time the challenge will be more demanding, and each time Gridley will surmount it after a moment of moral conflict between his impulse to generosity and his tendency to withdraw into the isolation of his books and his habits. By refusing to succumb to "a longing for rest that it is baseness to indulge," Gridley will redeem the Professor's promise of moral freedom in *Elsie Venner*.

In her helpless state, Myrtle is being cared for by Dr. Fordyce Hurlbut, who has found that she seems to respond favorably to his "magnetic" touch. As his treatment proceeds, he becomes the only one who can enliven Myrtle, at the expense of her complete thralldom to him and the dissipation of her will. Murray Bradshaw, with his own designs on Myrtle, learns about the situation and, judging it imprudent to act himself, solicits Gridley's help, ironically bringing his adversary into play. Responding to the call, Gridley learns from the local wet nurse that Hurlbut is, indeed, on the verge of "gettin' a little bewitched" by Myrtle and his power over her (139). The nurse appeals to Gridley to "get the young doctor to stay away" and bring in his father, "the old Dr. Hurlbut" (139).

In response to the request, Gridley groans to himself: "He had come to this village to end his days in peace, and here he was just going to make a martyr of himself for the sake of a young person to whom he was under no obligation, except that he had saved her from the consequences of her own foolish act, at the expense of a great overturn of all his domestic habits" (139–40). He then concludes that, nonetheless, there is "no help for it"; he has to "perform the disagreeable duty" of telling Fordyce that "he was getting into a track which might very probably lead to mischief, and that he must back out as fast as he could" (140). Disagreeable as the duty is, it is not very difficult to perform. Gridley uses his fine sense of strategy to draw Fordyce into a discussion of medicine, turning the conversation to the Hippocratic Oath. The young doctor is basically good-willed and understands its application to himself immediately, realizing that he must withdraw from Myrtle's case. Gridley has secured his first triumph over himself through his adherence to his sense of duty, the moral imperative. He could have done otherwise and was at first inclined to retreat, but he overcame himself.

Having removed Fordyce Hurlbut as a threat, Gridley has opened

the way for Rev. Bellamy Stoker to try his hand at spiritually healing Myrtle. One of Holmes's evil Calvinist ministers, Stoker preaches
fire and brimstone in church, but woos his young female devotees
with erotic intimacies parading as religious talks. He neglects his
bedridden wife, leaving her in the care of his long-suffering daughter Bathsheba. Stoker has let the lustful and predatory side of his
disordered will take control of him and has beguiled Myrtle in a
series of close conversations.

Again ironically, Gridley learns of Stoker's danger from Ammi
Hopkins, who has been informed of Stoker's activities by Cynthia
Badlam, a relative living with Myrtle and her aunt Silence Withers.
Badlam has leagued with Murray Bradshaw in his designs on
Myrtle and uses Ammi to get Gridley to intervene and eliminate
another rival. When Ammi says to Gridley, "You've got to help
Myrtle Hazard again," the Master of Arts replays the conflict between action and abstention. No longer does he groan; he is already
beginning to "take a pleasure" in thinking that he is capable of
being useful" (174). Yet his old doubts surface: "For a whole generation he had lived in no nearer relation to his fellow creatures than
that of a half-fossilized teacher; and all at once he found himself
face to face with the very most intense form of life, the counsellor of
threatened innocence, the champion of imperilled loveliness" (174).
Gridley questions whether Myrtle's plight is any of his business, recalling a passage from his *Thoughts on the Universe: "Every man leads
or is led by something that goes on four legs"* (174). Then he remembers
"the grand line of the African freedman, that makes all human interests everybody's business" and feels "a sudden sense of dilation
and evolution" (174). This is the moment of Gridley's triumph over
himself, when he achieves moral freedom and responsibility explicitly and reflectively. Drawing again upon his beloved book, he re-
calls his thoughts on the aphorism, *"Some things may be done as well
as others"* (175). Thereupon, he decides to see what he can do by vis-
iting Myrtle Hazard.

Gridley's strategy is to show Myrtle, who is growing stronger,
that she faces a danger from Stoker. He sows doubts and suspicions
in her mind that will awaken her own misgivings. He tells her
about Stoker's reputation as a womanizer and succeeds in his purpose. This time he does not rush in to remove the threat directly,
but gives Myrtle the encouragement to do the job herself, which

she accomplishes after a dream in which she sees Stoker as an odious serpent. Gridley has not only achieved moral freedom for himself but also nurtured it in Myrtle.

The last challenge that Gridley faces is to save Myrtle from the danger posed by Murray Bradshaw and his ally Cynthia Badlam. Bradshaw, who has discovered a will that leaves the estate of Myrtle's uncle Malachi Withers to her, and has secreted it in Badlam's care until he is able to win Myrtle's hand, is perilously close to succeeding in his designs. Having surmised the plot, Gridley realizes that he has to get Badlam to surrender the will to him "voluntarily," which will cause her great pain. Here Gridley's struggle is not to overcome the temptation to withdraw (he has come too far to be prey to it), but to be able to cause suffering in the service of a greater good. Knowing that Badlam will resist giving up the document, Gridley must avail himself of incriminating evidence that he has against her, the nature of which is never revealed. He is reluctant to use it, but resolves to do so if he cannot achieve his aim otherwise: "'I think this will fetch the document,' he said to himself, 'if it comes to the worst. Not if I can help it,—not if I can help it. But if I cannot get at the heart of this thing otherwise, why, I must come to this. Poor woman!—Poor woman!'" (344).

Gridley's resolve is tested when he visits Badlam, a spinster, and sees that she hopes that he has come out of an affectionate interest in her. When he disabuses her of that illusion and asks for the document, she refuses, forcing him to play his card. This intimidates her into submission. Gridley tries to be as gentle with Badlam as possible, but she is devastated and in desperate fear of Bradshaw: "I am in the power of a dreadful man" (353). Having applied his "heart-screw" successfully, Gridley takes leave of Badlam and delivers the will to Lawyer Penhallow, who handles the Withers estate and is unaware of his junior partner Bradshaw's mischief. Gridley has performed what he sees as his duty at the expense of engaging in extortion, which he abhors.

Throughout his account of Gridley's moral struggles, Holmes never presents his hero as a victim or beneficiary of the reflex arc or any other form of determinism. Instead, the Master of Arts fights a battle between his generous and isolationist tendencies, his "lower" and "higher" natures. Rather than being the register of the balance of passion, Gridley deliberates about his choices and relies upon his sense of duty to motivate him to act morally. He is aware of the moral consequences of his conduct and is not carried away by emotion. He has a resolve that is progressively strengthened by his growing moral sense. It might be objected that Gridley's moral sense is simply dominant among the forces in his character and, consequently, that he is determined to his path of goodness. That is possible, but it is not the way that Holmes presents the case. The moment of freedom is not, by its very nature, representable, yet it can be indicated, as Holmes tries to do, through the experience of deliberation. Holmes presents Gridley as not only the Master of Arts but also the master of his will, overcoming the resistances to his commitment to a higher law of service that surely is supported by inclination, but is not mechanically determined by it.

Misdirected Strength

If Byles Gridley is Holmes's model of mature goodness, then Murray Bradshaw is his most complete and formidable villain. Almost all of the evil that is done in Holmes's works of imaginative prose is caused by characters who are victims of their constitutions and upbringings, too weak to withstand the temptations or impulsions of their lower natures, and to overcome them in the service of a higher obligation and attraction. For example, of the first two predators who assail Myrtle in the name of curing her, Dr. Fordyce Hurlbut is swept away by the power of his magnetic hands and the Rev. Bellamy Stoker, though guileful, submits to his lusts and has scant control over them. Bradshaw is a different case—he belongs to Holmes's class of natural aristocrats, with impressive powers of mind and body and an excellent education that has prepared him for a promising career in law and politics. Yet he turns his gifts to evil.

Bradshaw is introduced in tandem with Gridley in chapter 4, where his character is sketched. A former student of Gridley's, Bradshaw won the admiration of his professor for his quick mind and urbanity, but also aroused a suspicion that his student might be too crafty for his own and others' good. Holmes makes Bradshaw's basic duality plain at the outset of his character sketch: "Murray Bradshaw was about twenty-five years old, by common consent good-looking, with a finely formed head, a searching eye, and a sharp-cut mouth, which smiled at his bidding without the slightest reference to the real condition of his feeling at the moment" (44). His false smile, radiating "ingenuous good nature," is the emblem of his character, which is structured by his ability to split his presentation of self from his backstage cogitations (396). Unlike Gridley, who is moved by the solicitations of the world around him, Bradshaw has laid out a "plan of life" that will take him to the pinnacles of political power through a long march that begins in the provinces. With his goal of success firmly fixed, Bradshaw has delivered himself entirely to achieving it. He has devoted all of his gifts to practicality and acts only out of self-interest.

Bradshaw's smile and his ability to ingratiate himself are his major weapons in his struggle to scale the high reaches of society. He uses strategy in every social encounter, ingratiating himself to his interlocutors, always with an ulterior motive, if only to make them well disposed toward him. A consummate courtier, he is a master of winning the favor of women, making them feel that his attentions only indicate their objective virtues; he will need to marry into a fortune to achieve his aim, and part of success is to have a trophy wife. Having surrendered himself to his selfish program, Bradshaw is "not handicapped with any burdensome ideals," taking "everything at its market value" (45–46). He calculates his every move as would a chess player, assessing and charting "[e]very strong and weak point of those who might probably be his rivals" (46).

Holmes does not provide any explanation of Bradshaw's addiction to personal success in bourgeois society. He is constituted by his ethic of possessive individualism, which restricts his freedom of choice to prudential calculations based on cost-benefit analysis. He has great strengths, but he misdirects them to amoral purposes that will lead him into immoral action. Murray Bradshaw is, for Holmes, the epitome of what American manhood should not become—a bourgeois manipulator. Anne Dalke has fruitfully read *Elsie Venner* as a criticism of fortune-hunting in mid-nineteenth-century capitalist society.[6] Holmes brings that criticism to its fullest development in *The Guardian Angel* through Murray Bradshaw, who represents

6. Dalke, "Economics, or the Bosom Serpent," 57–68.

the antithesis of the ethic of richesse oblige that Holmes believed was the only way to redeem American society from a tawdry scramble for wealth, and that he exemplified in Gridley.

Although he has left undecided the question of whether or not Bradshaw made a conscious choice to be a possessive individualist, Holmes makes it clear that his villain has all of the requisites for the exercise of moral freedom, except moral sense and insight. Most importantly, Bradshaw is continually carrying on a deliberative interior monologue in which he systematically considers every possibility and strategy with cool rationality. He is even able to go out to others sufficiently to assess their motives astutely. Until the end of the novel, Bradshaw is able to maintain the self-control necessary to split overt self-presentation from covert judgments. His will and intellect are too strong for him to be a slave of passion as long as he retains hope for success. After being tricked into self-congratulation by his former student, Gridley dubs him "Niccolo Machiavelli Bradshaw" (54). The ambitious young lawyer is the bane of the liberal humanist—the intelligent, educated, and talented person who should know better than to be narrowly selfish, an exploiter of society's opportunity structure.

In contrast to Gridley's ascending trajectory in the text, marked by moments of self-overcoming, Bradshaw's is one of decline as he fights his losing battle to win Myrtle's hand against her growing strength and individuality, and her guardian angel's aid. As the story begins, he has been working on a disputed land claim that, if settled favorably, will bring a fortune to the heirs of Malachi Withers's estate. Although Malachi's will specifies Silence Withers as his beneficiary, Bradshaw has taken an interest in Myrtle, because of her beauty and the outside possibility that she will share in the wealth. When he discovers a later will that names Myrtle as the beneficiary, he secretes it and begins in earnest his pursuit of her, planning to have the document come to light after he has subdued her. During a visit to the law offices, Gridley has seen Bradshaw hiding the document, but he does not know its nature.

Holmes uses the episodes of Bradshaw's adventure to bring out the dimensions of his villain's character as he takes him through his downward spiral. When he learns that Myrtle has gone missing, Bradshaw is astute enough to surmise that she has run away to take a ship to India. Unaware of her accident, he runs off to the port with the intention of proposing to her. Believing that Myrtle is on a particular ship in the harbor, Bradshaw retires to his hotel room, summoning "all his faculties in state council to determine what course he should follow" (69). Holmes recounts Bradshaw's deliberations in great detail, showing how he considers every angle: "He worked out the hypotheses of the matrimonial offer as he would have reasoned out the probabilities in a law case" (70). Thwarted in his initial effort, Bradshaw returns to Oxbow Village where he continues to work on the land case and curries Myrtle's favor through frequent visits to the Withers household once Dr. Hurlbut and Rev. Stoker have been eliminated from the picture and Myrtle has recovered from the worst of her traumatic hysteria.

Having established that Bradshaw is an almost obsessive strategic and tactical calculator, Holmes displays another dimension of his character when the lawyer escorts Myrtle to a party in the village. Bradshaw has already met Clement Lindsay, but does not know that he had saved Myrtle. Believing that Lindsay is already committed to Susan Posey, Bradshaw decides to show Myrtle off to the young architect and sculptor with the motive of asserting his superiority: "He would bring this young man, neutralized and rendered entirely harmless by his irrevocable pledge to a slight girl, face to face with a masterpiece of womanhood, and say to him, not in words, but as plainly as speech could have told him, 'Behold my captive!'" (244). Bradshaw's "proud moment" is shattered when Myrtle encounters Lindsay and she falls into a faint, not recognizing him because she still suffers amnesia about the rescue. Bradshaw is stymied again; Holmes has revealed his will to power and his vainglory.

The villain's adventure reaches its climax when he again resolves to propose to Myrtle. In the interim, she has become aware of some of her virtues and powers, and has been sent to Boston to continue her education, under Gridley's sponsorship. She has already outgrown Bradshaw, but is still susceptible to his charms. Bradshaw has learned that the land claim has been settled in favor of the Withers estate and decides to make his decisive move. The action takes place at a posh party in the city, where Clement Lindsay and Byles Gridley are also in attendance. By this time, Bradshaw has fallen under Myrtle's spell; he knows that she will be harder to catch than ever, but now he wants her, and not only for her fortune.

Holmes uses this opportunity to show the limits of Bradshaw's capability to love: "[D]azzled with the brilliant effect of Myrtle in full dress," Bradshaw "could say *I love you* as truly as such a man could ever speak these words, meaning that he admired her, that he was attracted to her, that he should be proud of her as his wife, that he should value himself as the proprietor of so rare a person that no appendage to his existence would take so high a place in his thoughts" (315). Even at his most magnanimous, Bradshaw cannot exceed the limits of possessive individualism.

Using all of his courtly stratagems, Bradshaw succeeds in taking Myrtle to a corner where they can be alone: "It required all his self-mastery to avoid betraying himself by look or tone, but he was so natural that Myrtle was thrown wholly off her guard" (321–22). Sensing that she is ready to submit to him, Bradshaw prepares to pop the question when Gridley appears to reintroduce Clement to Myrtle. Foiled again, Bradshaw keeps up his surface equanimity, but the game is over; Myrtle will soon learn that Clement is her rescuer, after she has fallen in love with him.

When all of the characters return to Oxbow Village, Bradshaw makes one last attempt to win Myrtle. Already having pledged herself to Clement, she refuses to see him, but finally resolves to confront him. Desperate, Bradshaw is unable to sleep the night before his interview: "He paced his room, a prey to jealousy and envy and rage, which his calm temperament had kept him from feeling up to this miserable hour" (394). He even thinks of killing Myrtle if she rejects him ("he thought of everything"), but "cunning was his natural weapon, not violence," and he still preserves sufficient prudence to avoid the consequences of such a crime (395). With great effort he puts his face into his habitual smile and sets off on his mission.

When he is in Myrtle's company, Bradshaw takes up his flattering ways and even succeeds in momentarily beguiling her. But when he confesses his love for her, Myrtle stands her ground in her greatest moment of strength. In response to rejection, Bradshaw loses control of himself and falls into a rage that ends in his throwing into the fireplace a document that he believes is the will he had secreted, thinking that he has destroyed Myrtle's future. Gridley and Lawyer Penhallow have made sure the true copy is safe, so Bradshaw's gesture is in vain. Again he loses, but this time the loss is total: the very basis of his character—the ability to separate overt and covert selves—has collapsed, along with his self-mastery. He has become the slave of passions that he did not suspect he harbored: ". . . the bitterness of heart that lay hidden far down beneath his deceptive smile" had surfaced.

If the best that a possessive individualist can be is an admirer and steward of his property, the worst is a vindictive despoiler who attempts to destroy the good of others if he cannot have his way. Beneath cool calculation beats the nihilism of the thwarted child. Although he thought of everything that bore on his plans, Bradshaw had repressed his deeper emotions. Holmes shows here that the nihilistic will shadows the will to success and superiority over others. In his depth psychology, only the good are free. Amoral strength is deceptive, because it is only sustainable when there is still hope for success. Free to calculate, the possessive individualist implodes when calculation can no longer do any good.

Defeated, Bradshaw leaves Oxbow Village and enlists in the Union army, suffering a mortal combat wound in the Civil War—his punishment in Holmes's morality play. By chance, he is attended by Myrtle in his last moments and partly redeems himself by expressing gratitude that Byles Gridley had bested him: "And so the old man beat me after all, and saved you from ruin! Thank God that it came out so!" (419). Even Bradshaw finally acquires a moral sense, but it is not enough to spare him; he should have known better.

Serene Resolve

The basis of Holmes's depth psychology is the principle that there are suppressed and repressed potentialities in the personality, of which the conscious individual is not (fully) aware. Some of those potentialities are consistent with or definitive of a moral disposition and others subvert it. Mental health requires becoming aware of one's potential; affirming those possibilities that are consistent with or productive of morality, and eliminating or containing the others; and harmonizing the remainder in an individuated balance. The fruit of successful harmonization is moral freedom. Far from describing a reflex arc, Holmes's depth psychology defines a process of self-development impelled by difficult conscious work on the personality.

Byles Gridley presents a case of the release of suppressed morality. He does not have any aggressive, nihilistic, or destructive impulses, but only is subject to the sin of sloth and (mild) despair. When the guardian-angel side of his personality emerges, it is all to the good. In contrast, Murray Bradshaw is a case of the release of repressed immorality. The nihilistic will to revenge cannot be incorporated into a healthy personality. Both Gridley and Bradshaw are ideal types: their polar characteristics are highly structured and already formed, with only one more shoe to drop in each case. Myrtle Hazard is in a different situation; she is Holmes's great test of the doctrine of limited responsibility, where he shows how a character develops from disordered volition to moral freedom.

Myrtle Hazard is a composite of the personalities of her ancestors, especially of four women—the worldly beauty Judith Pride, the Protestant martyr Ann Holyoake, the medium Ruth Bradford, and the part–Native American Virginia Wild. The two most important of these women are Judith, who will take Myrtle in the direction of becoming a sex-subduer seeking to gain power over men with her charms, and Ann, who will exercise a restraining and protective influence over her will, and guide her sentiments toward moral freedom. Ruth Bradford gives Myrtle the gift of oneiric vision, and Virginia Wild appears at a dangerous moment, forcing Myrtle to confront her destructive side. Although the conceit of the novel is that the ancestors project themselves into Myrtle's present, they can also be understood as personifications of the sides of Myrtle's personality that she is challenged to harmonize or contain.

Under a favorable upbringing, Myrtle would not necessarily suffer from disordered volition, despite the diversity and tension within her makeup. She is healthy, beautiful, and intelligent, with the graces of good breeding and a strong will, but her development has not been nurtured. Orphaned as a young child when she was living in India with her mother and ship-captain father, Myrtle is brought to Oxbow Village to stay with her uncle Malachi Withers and his sister Silence. Raised by Silence, she is subjected to a particularly repressive regime of Calvinist child-rearing based on the proposition that children are inherently sinful and that any will they show toward self-determination should be broken. Endowed with self-will, Myrtle soon resists discipline by refusing to eat brown bread and demanding white. In response, Silence locks and ties her up in a forbidding spider-infested garret where she spends eighteen hours without food, until she is rescued by the family's Irish servant Kitty. Myrtle has been traumatized, but her will is unbroken, and she has won a victory and set up a pattern of opposition that will dominate her personality throughout childhood. Later, she is further traumatized when she is exploring the garret and comes upon Malachi, who has committed suicide by hanging himself.

When the novel opens, Myrtle is fifteen years old and in a state of depression from the confinement and dolorous ethos of the Withers household, which has repressed her vitality. Her beauty had become manifest at age twelve and she had attracted attention from boys, but "the dreary discipline of the household had sunk into her soul, and she had been shaping an internal life for herself, which it was hard for friendship to penetrate" (35). Her one opening to life has been a trove of Judith Pride's romance novels and letters, and a stash of gold and silver coins that she found on yet another adventure in the garret, which symbolizes the unconscious as the seat of beneficial as well as destructive possibilities.

Myrtle reaches the end of her tether one spring evening when she is singing hymns with Silence and Cynthia Badlam. Cynthia has already told her that there is "a worm in every young soul," and the hymns are filled with descriptions of the tortures of hell. Finally Myrtle has had enough: "I won't sing such words. . . . You can't scare me into being good with your cruel hymn-book!" (82). Retreating to her room, Myrtle faces a "moment of fearful danger to her character, to her life itself" (82). Seized with rebellion, she contemplates throwing herself out of the window into the river below to "dare the worst these dreadful women had threatened her with" (83). She is saved from defiant suicide by the sense of an invisible hand restraining her and the vision of a "fair woman," perhaps herself or her mother, surrounded by palm trees, reflected in the waters below. The vision incites the sense that the river, which she has explored and loved, could be a deliverer; she resolves to try to make her way back to India and escape from her vital and emotional imprisonment. From then on, Myrtle becomes "serene" around the household, as she plans her adventure.

Myrtle's trip down the river ends in a disastrous shipwreck that would have killed her but for Clement Lindsay's heroic rescue.

Nevertheless, the trip is essential to the liberation of her personality. Before the accident, as she floats past Witches' Hollow at night, she has the vision of the multitude of her ancestors milling on the bank, seeming to "want to breathe the air again in my shape" (92). As Myrtle regains self-possession, every one of the assembly becomes part of her, "by being taken up, one by one, and so lost in my own life" (92). Through "objective projection," all of the elements of Myrtle's character that she will be challenged to harmonize or contain have become manifest and have been admitted. She is ready to begin the struggle to become a free and whole person.

When Myrtle is brought back to the Withers household by Gridley, she plunges to the depths and extremities of disordered volition, falling victim to a severe case of hysteria. Suffering from amnesia about the wreck and physical trauma, returning to imprisonment after a failed escape, and having released the multitude of dispositions in her personality, Myrtle regresses to infantile rebellion, going through manic-depressive mood swings, feigning symptoms to intimidate her caregivers, and hiding food and eating it secretly while pretending to starve herself.

Under the influence of Fordyce Hurlbut's magnetic hands, Myrtle begins to lose the power of her will: "'I can't help it'—the hysteric motto—was her constant reply" (135). It is at this juncture that Holmes introduces the observation which forms the basis of Boewe's judgment that Myrtle is a plaything of the reflex arc: "And now the reader . . . who believes in the absolute independence and self-determination of the will, and the consequent total responsibility of every human being for every irregular nervous action and ill-governed muscular contraction, may as well lay down this narrative . . ." (131). Holmes is, indeed, making the point here that there are limitations on responsibility, notably in cases of mental illness. Yet he has made it clear that Myrtle had a will that she could lose temporarily, and he will allow her to regain it in a perfected moral form.

"Drifting without any self-directing power," Myrtle cannot save herself (137). After Gridley intervenes to remove Fordyce, she recovers from hysteria, but her personality is very far from being "poised in the just balance of its faculties" (155). The "defeated instincts of a strong nature were rushing in upon her, clamorous for their rights," and "she was not yet mature enough to understand and manage them" (163). It is at this dangerous juncture that the Rev. Bellamy Stoker enters the scene and establishes an erotic spiritual intimacy with her. As she falls under Stoker's sway, Myrtle is again threatened with the loss of her will. Again, she needs Gridley, but now only to suggest to her what she already knows but has not been able to make explicit to herself—that Stoker is a predator.

Once she acknowledges Stoker's depravity, Myrtle is faced with the first challenge to overcome herself: "The word had been spoken. She saw its truth; but how hard it is to tear away a cherished illusion, to cast out an unworthy intimate" (182). Myrtle is given the strength to reject Stoker by a dream in which the minister appears to her as a hideous serpent. The dream is presided over by Judith Pride and Ann Holyoake, both of whom oppose the serpent, but each of whom draws Myrtle in her own direction. She is faced with a moment of genuine "choice," and cedes to the "might of beauty": "Myrtle resigned herself to the guidance of the lovely phantom, which seemed so much fuller of the unextinguished fire of life, and so like herself as she would grow to be when noon should have ripened her into maturity" (185). Myrtle's underground workshop has given her both the imaginative power to resist and the options for her first deliberate choice. She is becoming her own person and has entered into normal adolescent self-experimentation.

After the dream and reverie, Myrtle goes up to the garret and finds a secret drawer in an old desk that Malachi had given her. She retrieves from it Judith Pride's golden bracelet, which becomes her amulet in the next of her series of adventures. From then on, she escapes the discipline of Silence Withers and Cynthia Badlam. Her horizons expand along the erotic path and she eventually becomes the beauty of Boston. Enamored by the "power of beauty," she feels that she has found her "destiny": "It was to please, and so to command, to rule with gentle sway in virtue of the royal gift of beauty,— to enchant with the commonest exercise of speech, through the rare quality of a voice which could not help being always gracious and winning, of a manner which came to her as an inheritance of which she had just found the title" (277). In many ways, she is a female counterpart of Murray Bradshaw in this phase of her development— a practitioner of the arts of ingratiation in the service of power.

Indeed, immediately after sensing her destiny, Myrtle is forced to confront her aggressive side. Playing the role of Pocahontas in tableaux at the annual school party, she nearly surrenders to the impulse to plunge a knife into a jealous classmate who had trampled on a wreath that had been thrown to her from the audience. This impulse marks the appearance of Virginia Wild, the part-Indian woman. Her incitement is suppressed by the same restraining impulse of Ann Holyoake that had earlier saved Myrtle from suicide—her inner guardian angel. Unlike Bradshaw, Myrtle's personality is not structured by reactive hostility, so she repudiates this "passion such as her nature had never known, such as she believed was alien to her truest self" (281). She has passed another test in her struggle for self-integration and is free from repression.

Myrtle is now ready for her final stage of self-development, in which she surrenders the pride of power for the higher value of the love of Clement Lindsay. After Gridley saves her from her remaining vulnerability to Murray Bradshaw, by interposing Lindsay between them, Myrtle forgets "herself and her ambitions,—the thought of shining in the great world" (387). A new "vision" takes hold of her "of a future in which she was not to be her own,—of feelings in the depth of which the shallow vanities which had drawn her young eyes to them for a while seemed less than nothing" (387). Ann Holyoake has triumphed over Judith Pride, though Myrtle Hazard will not be a martyr; she will preserve her beauty and vitality, will be happily married to Clement, and will show herself capable of selfless service. When Bradshaw makes his last move and surrenders to vengeful rage, Myrtle is not threatened; resisting him is simply a distasteful task and she meets his most furious canards with "a slight contemptuous movement" (401). She has harmonized her personality with the help of an internal and external support network, and has achieved the strength of self-determination.

When Myrtle follows Clement to war and becomes a battlefield nurse, the last "dross of her nature" burns away: "The conflict of mingled lives in her blood had ceased. No lawless impulses usurped the place of that serene resolve which had grown strong by every exercise of its high prerogative" (417). When she cares for Bradshaw in his final moments, Myrtle maintains a "perfect calmness of voice and countenance," holding "her feelings firmly down" and hoping that his last words of repentance are tokens of a real transformation (418). She has achieved moral freedom and has herself become a guardian angel.

The serene resolve of a harmonized personality is Holmes's definition of sanity and moral goodness, a blend of humanism and perfection of the will that suggests the practices of Zen Buddhism, the Karma yoga of the Bhagavad-Gita, and twentieth-century existentialist conceptions of resolute choice—not mechanistic reflex psychology. The doctrine of limited responsibility passes Holmes's test.

Chapter 6

The Rise of the Specialist and the Eclipse of
the Humanist at the Poet's Breakfast Table

When Oliver Wendell Holmes published his third table-talk book, *The Poet at the Breakfast-Table,* in 1872, he awoke to the modern mass industrial society that had grown up in the United States after the Civil War. Before the great conflict to save the Union, Holmes had been an optimistic believer in the progress of American civilization, which he thought was destined to create a world civilization based on freedom of conscience and expression. In his second table-talk book, *The Professor at the Breakfast-Table* (1860), his romantic hero was the Young Man from Maryland, an engineer primed to conquer the West by planning great infrastructural works. Material and scientific progress went hand in hand with the triumph of liberty, tempered and humanized by the feminine contribution to life and a broad human-centered Christianity. The new society shattered Holmes's comfortable formula and caused him to doubt the promise of American life, creating a rupture in his social thought that is registered in *The Poet.*

Holmes makes references to the advent of a new and troubling era throughout *The Poet.* Addressing the reader, the narrator—Holmes's poet persona—asks: "Do you recognize the fact that we are living in a new time?" (*The Poet,* 267). Contemplating the distance of his present from the times when the first table-talk books were written, he reflects: ". . . my own eyes moistened as I remembered how long it was that friend [the Autocrat] of ours was sitting in the chair where I now sit, and what a tidal wave of change has swept over the world and more especially over this great land of ours, since he opened his lips and found so many kind listeners" (284).

For Holmes, the essence of the new time is the advance of science, which has two effects beyond its instigation of material progress: religious dogmas that are inconsistent with scientific truth are eroded away, and the structural-functional differentiation of society, including the scientific community, becomes hyper-specialized and loses a common perspective and discourse. Before the Civil War, Holmes had fought the battle against Calvinist dogma, confident that science harnessed to a Christian humanist ethic was unequivocally progressive. In *The Poet,* he grasps that the internal development of science harbors a destructive tendency of fragmentation that threatens social solidarity. Acknowledging that destructive tendency leads to Holmes allowing himself to question whether science is altogether progressive. *The Poet* is a work of doubt and problematicity that appear in both its plentiful and extended cultural-critical discourses and its romantic plot.

The vehicle for Holmes's inquiry into specialization is the Scarabee, an entomologist who is consumed with proving that a tiny bee parasite is the larval form of a beetle. In reviewing *The Poet* for his 1882 preface to that work, Holmes writes that he noticed "one character, presenting a class of beings who have greatly multiplied during the interval which separates the earlier and later Breakfast-Table papers,—I mean the scientific specialists. The entomologist, who confines himself rigidly to the study of the coleoptera, is intended to typify this class" (v). Signaling the theme that will dominate the work, Holmes follows with a juxtaposition of rampant specialization to the attempt to preserve the possibility of "encyclopaedic intelligences," represented by *The Poet*'s major character, the Master of Arts. The intellectual structure of the work is the Master of Arts's struggle against the disintegrative tendencies symbolized by the Scarabee, with the Poet narrator functioning as a tempering critical moderator.

In a further reflection on *The Poet* for his 1891 preface, Holmes emphasizes the character of the specialist, bringing forward the core of his cultural criticism: "The movement is irresistible; it brings with it exactness, exhaustive knowledge, a narrow but complete self-satisfaction, with such accompanying faults as pedantry, triviality, and the kind of partial blindness which belong to intellectual myopia" (viii). Anticipating Jose Ortega y Gasset's description of the "specialized barbarian" as the "self-satisfied man," Holmes remarks: "I have never pictured a character more contented with himself than the 'Scarabee' of this story" (viii). As a social and cultural critic, Holmes is one of the forerunners of mass society theory, with its undercurrent of cultural pessimism based on the premise that the price of progress is the destruction of the full personality and social solidarity. In *The Poet*, Holmes strives to overcome cultural pessimism and never gives way to it, yet he is unable to transcend his doubts.

Although their citations concentrate on *The Poet*, the commentators on Holmes's cultural criticism have failed to recognize the well-marked rupture in his thought, with the result that they have projected his earlier optimistic and complacent views into that work. Writing within the period between the two world wars, the commentators interpreted Holmes within the dominant democratic welfare-liberal paradigm, casting him as a progressive in his defense of science against Calvinist dogma and as a conservative in his reluctance to part with the genteel tradition of the Boston Brahmin aristocracy.

Reflecting his Jeffersonian perspective, Vernon Parrington established the undisputed line of interpreting Holmes as social critic, dubbing him the "Yankee Victorian": "Unfortunately his Brahminism sealed pretty tightly certain windows of his mind that might better have been kept open. A radical in the field of theology where personal concern brought him to serious grappling with the problem, a tolerant rationalist in the realm of intellect, he remained a cheerfully contented conservative in other fields." Parrington surmises that Holmes was "unconsciously insulated against the currents of social and political thought flowing all about him." Of particular concern to Parrington is Holmes's deprecation of "all proletarian appeals" and his complacent acceptance of "economic inequality."[1]

1. Vernon L. Parrington, *The Romantic Revolution in America*, 448.

A later generation of liberals attempted to revise Parrington's thesis to Holmes's advantage, but preserved the basic distinction between his progressive and conservative sides. Acknowledging that Holmes was "gratefully a participant in the democratic experiment" and that his defense of good breeding "does not mean that he was hopelessly old-fashioned," Hayakawa and Jones still call him "the ancient relic of Augustan New England" and criticize him for being blind to the new society and its problems of immigration, economic exploitation, and political graft. Echoing Parrington, they conclude that Holmes's "true weakness was that he failed to understand Boston—the Boston that was undergoing profoundly significant social changes under his very eyes."[2]

Harry Hayden Clark, Holmes's most sensitive and sympathetic commentator, continues the line of established criticism, juxtaposing Holmes as "spokesman of the relatively reactionary, traditional and Federalistic point of view in social, political and literary thought" to Holmes as "spokesman, in religious and philosophical terms, of an attitude which might be described as at once rational, scientific, progressive, and humanitarian, and partially monistic and deterministic." Although Clark acknowledges Holmes's animus against "reformers, masquerading as apostles of brotherhood" and "stirring class hatred," he points out that Holmes's naturalistic critique of original sin anticipates twentieth-century liberal reforms in criminal justice, based on paradigms stressing psychological and social causation of crime.[3]

The commentators are all correct as far as they go. Holmes did not much concern himself with the problems of industrial capitalism that dominated their perspectives, and he clearly did not sympathize with labor agitation and economic egalitarianism, as the few passages to that effect in The Poet demonstrate. As a critic of social economy, Holmes's view is summarized concisely by Parrington: "Wealth as a means to power he would have none of, but wealth as a means to leisure, and leisure as a means to cultivated living, he was fond of extolling."[4] Yet to criticize Holmes for neglecting the economic agenda is to fail to understand that he was

---

2. Hayakawa and Jones, "Introduction," xv–xviii.
3. Harry Hayden Clark, "Dr. Holmes: A Re–Interpretation," 19, 21, 34.
4. Parrington, The Romantic Revolution in America, 448.

demonstrably aware of the changes going on around him and was concerned primarily with one of them—specialization—that was not on his commentators' agendas, but that would be highlighted in twentieth-century theories of social structure and collective psychology. Far from being cocooned in an antebellum conservative ideology that made him complacent and protected him from the conflicts roiling around him, Holmes was open to the world, disquieted by it, and motivated to get to the bottom of his discontent by formulating a diagnosis of his times.

The Inter- and Non-Locutors

The Poet is the most mature and accomplished of Holmes's table-talk books, in which he brings all the literary skills and intellectual clarification that he had gained from his first works of imaginative prose to bear on perfecting his signature genre. He is able to thematize the form reflectively and to make it rich and dense with the play of ideas, to populate it with many characters, each of whom contributes to illuminating the dominant theme, and to tightly interweave plots and subplots to conform with his leading ideas.

The Holmes table-talk book is a "dramatized essay" or problem-romance in which the clarification of an existential / cultural issue is pursued on the level of intellectual discourse among one or two major rhetors, and through a romantic plot in which a person leading a life of quiet desperation is rescued for a life of love, happiness, and prosperity. In Holmes's first table-talk book, *The Autocrat of the Breakfast-Table,* the title character was the only major rhetor, and the rescue romance was only faintly sketched. The form began to take on its mature characteristics in *The Professor at the Breakfast-Table.* Holmes introduced there two major rhetors to play off against each other—one of them, Little Boston, expressed extreme opinions that drove some of the author's premises to their logical conclusions, and the other, the title character, exercised a moderating influence, on the whole sympathetic to his interlocutor. The romance was fully developed and complex, with the object of rescue, a young female art student, making decisive interventions into the narrative to illuminate its intellectual theme of reconciling liberty and social solidarity.

The Poet follows the pattern of *The Professor* while placing greater emphasis on intellectual discourse and eliminating adventitious conversational filler, yet allowing the romance to function to enlighten the theme and giving minor characters roles that contribute to enhance and reinforce the work's meaning. Holmes now has a repertory troupe of recognizable players who have appeared in his previous works of imaginative prose and play familiar parts. Those parts are not fixed in all respects and are not stereotyped; the characters are similar over the different works, but the power with which they are endowed varies, reflecting Holmes's assessment of the issue that he is addressing.

The greatest difference between *The Poet* and the two previous table-talk works is that all of the characters are problematic. The Autocrat (Holmes's conversational persona) and the Professor (Holmes's medical-professor persona) were arbitrators declaring final judgments and resolving issues; Holmes's poetic narrator-character is much more a mediator and moderator, with an attitude of gentle skepticism rather than certainty. Similarly, the rescuer in *The Autocrat* was the title figure and, in *The Professor*, it was the full-blooded, well-bred Young Man from Maryland; in *The Poet*, the rescuer is the young Astronomer, a scientific specialist with existential agonies and an uncertain future. Indeed, all of the characters in *The Poet* are plagued by doubts and/or woes, except for the new addition to the troupe, the self-satisfied Scarabee, who is the problem.

Early in the text, the Poet introduces the dramatis personae, providing character sketches of the fourteen of them and even a seating chart of the breakfast table. The Poet initially sits between the Master of Arts and the Scarabee, symbolizing his mediating role in the intellectual discourse. The order will later change when the young Astronomer displaces the Scarabee and becomes the junior member of the front opposing the excesses of specialization.

Holmes's most grotesque creation, the Scarabee resembles the beetles that he studies, with slender limbs, a stoop, and a creaky voice, and he is dressed in a shiny black coat. His apartment is filled with cases of insects impaled by pins and has no other decoration. The Poet attempts to get to know the Scarabee by asking him about a local election that is the talk of the town. The specialist misunderstands the question, believing that it concerns the coming contest for the presidency of the Entomological Society. When the Poet asks the Scarabee if he is an entomologist, the latter insists that anyone who would claim that title would be a dilettante and an impostor; at most, the Scarabee is a Coleopterist, but even that is too much. He studies the genus Scarabaeus exclusively: "Call me a Scara-beeist, if you will; if I can prove myself worthy of that name, my highest ambition will be more than satisfied" (50).

In contrast to the hyper-specialized Scarabee, the Master of Arts is the quintessential generalist, who takes all knowledge as his province and whose proximate aim is to understand how it all fits together. He is a "sturdy-looking personage of a good deal more than middle age, his face marked with strong manly furrows, records of hard thinking and square stand-up fights with life and all its devils" (6). Capable of satire and evasiveness, the Master of Arts is fundamentally honest and does not try to fool his interlocu-tors.

The Master of Arts had already made his appearance in Holmes's imaginative prose in the person of Byles Gridley, the title hero of *The Guardian Angel*, the novel that immediately precedes *The Poet*. As guardian angel, the Master of Arts roused himself from his "thoughts on the universe" to apply his wisdom, knowledge, and sagacity to perform good works of rescue. In *The Poet*, he is back to his speculations and is not the model of mature intellectual and moral manhood that Gridley was. When the Poet probes him about his interests, the Master, who "has a certain air of authority which none of us feel inclined to dispute" and "good solid prejudices," as well as sometimes "fanciful" and "fantastic" opinions that he "pro-mulgates at table somewhat in the tone of imperial edicts," replies that his "specialty" is "contemplation of the Order of Things" (41). Further questioning, however, reveals that the Master is not even satisfied with that broad a field. He would really like to achieve ab-solute truth "without reference to the empirical arrangements of our particular planet and its environments. I want to subject the formal conditions of space and time to a new analysis, and project a possible universe outside of the Order of Things" (27). Perhaps, he opines, he will realize that aim in heaven—"if I ever get there" (42).

This specialist in the general will bear the burden of providing an alternative to the fragmentizing and isolating tendencies of hyper-specialization, yet he is flawed from the outset by his proclivity to dogmatize his opinions and by his vain wish to transcend the world, mirroring the Scarabee's isolation. Although the Poet prefers the Master's "telescopic" mind to the Scarabee's "microscopic" one, both mentalities run to excess and alienation from the world around them. In a telling initial confrontation, the Master remarks that a boy at the table, who has imitated the Scarabee by amassing a collection of flies, has probably done as much of significance in the Order of Things as the Scarabee with his "Museum of Beetles" (51). The Poet "cannot help thinking that perhaps That Boy's questions about the simpler mysteries of life might have a good deal of the same kind of significance as the Master's inquiries into the Order of Things" (51).

Functioning as a mediator and moderator between the Master and the Scarabee, with a qualified bias in favor of the former, the Poet is not Holmes the man, but his poetic persona: "I am talking, you know, as a poet, I do not say I deserve the name, but I have taken it, and if you consider me at all it must be in that aspect" (11). Far from a dogmatist, the Poet recognizes his limitations: "I am afraid I am becoming an epicure in words, which is a bad thing to be, unless it is dominated by something infinitely better than himself" (46). The virtue of the Poet is to inspire life with crystallized expression of its possibilities, especially the goods of the past that are being lost in the onward rush of industrialized society. That vocation is made clear in the long evocation of Holmes's boyhood home that substitutes for the narrator-character's self-introduction: "I know I have rambled, but I hope you see that this is a delicate way of letting you into the nature of the individual who is, officially, the principal personage at our table" (47).

As a representative of a conservative and moderating principle, the Poet plays a role within the economy of the text, rather than standing above it and dictating its meaning. Poetry will not be the solution to the dysfunctions of hyper-specialization and the Poet will not be a saving figure or visionary pathfinder; he will be the voice of reasonableness who checks excess with good-humored skepticism without pretending to provide solutions. He is more connected to the world around him than any of the other characters, and less determined and decided.

A second important mediating figure is the young Astronomer, who partakes of the Scarabee's specialization and the Master of Arts's broad vision. The most complex character in the cast, he bridges the intellectual discourse and the rescue romance, composing a series of philosophical poems and saving a young lady in distress from her life of quiet desperation. He also goes through a process of maturation, from troubled anguished isolation in his observatory to member of the Poet's and Master's discussion group, and lover. Yet he never becomes the romantic male hero whose destiny is to build the new American nation that Holmes idealized in his earlier works of imaginative prose. The Astronomer is as isolated and unworldly as the Scarabee and the Master at the work's outset. The Master comments to the Poet: "But that young man lives in a world beyond the imagination of poets. . . . The daily home of his thought is in illimitable space, hovering between two eternities. In his contemplation the divisions of time run together, as in the thought of his Maker" (58). He enters his observations, says the Poet, "in the diary without beginning and without end" (59). Although the Astronomer is primed to abandon his specialty at the end of the book, his future is undetermined.

The Young Girl, whom the Astronomer will rescue, is also an isolated and troubled figure. Showing hysterical tendencies, she is oppressed by her job of writing romances for the *Weekly Bucket*, a popular newspaper. A hack writer with glimmers of originality and a simple humanist faith, she has been trapped by circumstance into a life as separated from community as those of the other major characters. Her world is one of "ever-ending and ever-beginning stories," in which she tries to vary "the dead monotony of everlasting narrative"—the world of the modern culture worker (53). Unlike the Astronomer, Scheherezade, as the Poet dubs her, does not participate in a process of personal growth, but simply is freed from her grinding tedium, leaving her with her incipient talents and her good-willed humanist faith. Her future is as uncertain as the Astronomer's.

At the beginning of the story, the Young Girl's only friend is another boarder, The Lady, who has lost her wealth but has preserved the fruits of her good breeding and her refinement. A minor character who plays an integral part in the development of the intellectual discourse, The Lady does not speak, but writes a letter to the Poet in the middle of the book that introduces a plea that the Master and the Poet respect the sensibilities of traditional faith in their speech at the table. Her letter opens up a second front in the cultural conflict—the humanist-generalists have to confront the claims of religious tradition as well as scientific specialization. The Lady is isolated by her poverty and appears to support herself by painting and crafts. Reflecting his own conserving tendencies, the Poet says: "I mean to stand up for this poor lady, whose usefulness in the world is apparently problematical. She seems to me like a picture which has fallen from its gilded frame and lies, face downward, on the dusty floor" (58).

The other minor characters are also imprisoned in their own hermetic worlds of specialized activity. The boarding-house table is a gathering of social isolates, each of whom deploys a discourse that the others either do not comprehend or do not care to comprehend. Except for the Poet, the major characters are strikingly portrayed as having abandoned history and a common life for some kind of specious eternity. Taking his name from the Scarab—the ancient Egyptian symbol of eternity—the Scarabee pursues final and perfected knowledge of a tiny detail of the universe. The Master wants most of all to transcend the universe through absolute knowledge of a Platonistic or perhaps supra-Kantian sort. The Astronomer is lost in fathomless cosmic time and space. The Young Girl is swamped in an eternal recurrence of the mass commercial imaginary. Even the Poet is in danger of cocooning himself in nostalgia. What is at stake in *The Poet* is the possibility of a shared public culture and a solidary society in a mass industrial age. In his set-up of his problem-romance, Holmes provides scant promise of a favorable resolution.

Scientific Humanism

As the work in which Holmes perfected the table-talk genre, the intellectual narrative of *The Poet* is tightly bound into an intelligible pattern of inquiry that is not so much an argument as a reconstruction of a developmental process of reasoning. The major rhetor is the Master of Arts, who is charged with finding a way to ward off the threat to solidarity posed by hyper-specialization and the individual isolation in hermetic spheres of activity that attends it. In the first half of the book, through a series of mini-essays, he evaluates the Scarabee's life-project, considers the claims of the old professions to constitute a public culture and finds them wanting, offers his own scientific-humanist solution, and defends it so zealously that he evokes The Lady's counterattack, at which point he must redirect his attention from the problem of hyper-specialization to the claims of traditional faith. Following the pattern of *The Professor*, the first half of *The Poet* is dominated by the masculine principle of liberty and the second half by the feminine principle of sympathetic inclusion.

The reflection begins when the Scarabee refuses to attend an outing to the Astronomer's observatory, pleading the need to pursue his research. Mystified by someone who would prefer to peer at a bee parasite through a microscope than to wonder at the starry heavens, the Poet decides to visit the Scarabee and see what is so attractive about the *pediculus melittae*. The Scarabee welcomes the request, and the Poet sees his eyes for the first time taking on "a real human look": ". . . he had not seemed to me much like a human being, until all at once I touched the one point where his vitality had concentrated itself and he stood revealed a man and a brother" (75).

Despite this auspicious beginning, the visit turns out to be a whimsical dialogue of the deaf, showing the mutual incomprehension of the poetic and experimental science perspectives on life and value. When the Poet learns that the *pediculus* is a bee parasite, he launches into a fanciful silent rapture about how the microscopic larva must be a happy being, flying through the air, feeding upon the fruits of the bee's labors and appreciating the bee's "music." When the Scarabee wants to know if he thinks that the *pediculus* is the larva of the meloe (the question to which the specialist has devoted his life), the Poet responds: "Oh, I don't know much about that, but I think he is the best cared for, on the whole, of any animal that I know of; and if I wasn't a man I believe I had rather be that little sybarite than anything that feasts at the board of nature" (77). The Scarabee responds, "as if he had not heard a word" that the Poet had said: "The question is whether he is the larva of the meloe" (78). He adds that if he can settle the question, he will trust his "posthumous fame to that achievement" (78). The Poet leaves the Scarabee with the sense that the experimentalist is an "enthusiast" who "does certainly know one thing well" and "does not pretend to form a judgment of anything but beetles"; he feels "not only kindly but respectfully towards Him," but decides to find out what the Master has to say on the matter (78).

For the Master, the Scarabee, like all specialists, is a "coral-insect" building the reef of civilization, the fate of which cannot be known (78). For the old guard, like Newton and Leibniz, science opened the way to holistic vision, but in the new era, ". . . you have a Society, and they come together and make a great mosaic, each man bringing his little bit and sticking it in its place, but so taken up with his petty fragment that he never thinks of looking at the picture the little bits make when they are put together" (79). Concerned that "science is breeding us down too fast into coral-insects," the Master poses his Renaissance humanist approach to life and culture as an alternative: "I had rather be a voyager that visits all the reefs and islands the creatures build, and sails over the seas where they have as yet built up nothing" (78–79). Yet he does not claim that the generalist can supplant or even dominate the specialist, reaching the Poet's conclusion that "any man who knows one thing well is worth listening to for once" (82). Indeed, the Master cannot "fill out" his "programme of the Order of Things" without getting "the half-notes and flats and sharps of humanity" into his scale, and many of those are provided only by specialists.

The issue remains unresolved; the Master is ambivalent: the proliferation of specialization turns human beings into coral-insects with no vision of totality to guide and harmonize them, and renders the integral visions of the past anachronistic; yet specialization seems to be the necessary consequence of the pursuit of scientific truth. If tradition cannot supply integrative vision, is there another discourse that can? The Poet asks the Master if he is a Darwinian. He replies evasively and ironically, "with that twinkle in his eye," saying that he accepts Blair's biblical chronology, preferring to remain on the ship of tradition than set out on Darwin's raft. When the Poet asks what the Master would do if the ship sprang a leak, he answers that he would see whether the crew was "gaining on the leak or not" (83). The discussion ends there when the Master orders the Poet to find out what is troubling the Young Girl, initiating the drama of her rescue.

The reflection moves to its next moment when the Poet asks the Master to assess the current status and prospects of the old professions—law, medicine, and the ministry—as sources of cultural leadership. The Master dismisses lawyers immediately, because "there is nothing humanizing in their relations with their fellow-creatures" (124). Lawyers are "quicker witted" and "abler men generally" than other professionals, but they "go for the side that retains them," whether guilty or innocent. The Master concedes that they are justified in doing so because "every side of a case has a right to the best statement it admits of"; nonetheless, "it does not tend to make them sympathetic" (124). Doctors, in contrast, are sympathetic, but in the new era, they do not have "half the general culture of the lawyers, nor a quarter of that of the ministers" (126). The latter should be the cultural leaders, but the rising tide of science has left them behind and increasingly irrelevant: "They used to lead the intelligence of their parishes; now they do pretty well if they keep up with it, and they are very apt to lag behind it" (125). Indeed, ministers are "coming down every generation nearer and nearer to the common level of the useful citizen" (125). They are locked into dogmas about human nature that have been effectively challenged by science and have lost their leadership role; they have become the "wheel-horses" of "the great coach and team that is carrying us fast enough, I don't know but too fast, somewhere or other" (128).

The failure of the ministry to provide cultural leadership has serious consequences. Human beings, according to the Master, are "cowards . . . and are driven by fear as the sovereign motive"; "idolators" who "want something to look at and kiss and hug," or soothing words: ". . . we couldn't get on without the spiritual brotherhood, whatever became of our special creeds" (127–28). The challenge, as yet unmet, for the Master of Arts is to proffer a discourse of solidarity adequate to the conditions of the new era.

The Master takes up the challenge in the next moment of his reflection when he announces his program for "comparative theology," anticipating culture studies and placing them in the service of a humanist vision: "You can't know too much of your race and its beliefs, if you want to know anything about your Maker" (149). He announces that he belongs to "the Human sect," inspiring the Poet to ask him whether he includes cannibals within it. Beginning his polemical campaign against the failed traditional orthodoxies that must be scrapped to make way for his new vision, the Master compares cannibals favorably with historical Christianity: ". . . the eating of one's kind is a matter of taste, but the roasting of them has been rather more a specialty of our own particular belief than of any other I am acquainted with" (150). "If you broil a saint," you might just as well eat him, the Master concludes, at which point, at the secret instigation of the Young Girl, That Boy fires his popgun at the Master, putting an end to his excess.

The Master is not to be denied, and soon after the embarrassing incident he takes up the cudgels again in the most determined way. Attacking "all the spiritual pessimisms which have been like a spasm in the heart and a cramp in the intellect of men for centuries," he adopts the evolutionary perspective, proclaiming the "RISE of man" in place of the Fall (182). Repeating his call for "the study of theology through anthropology," he argues that "until we have exhausted the human element in every form of belief, . . . we cannot begin to deal with the alleged extra-human elements without blundering into all imaginable puerilities" (183). Following the logic of his argument remorselessly to conclusions that would only become current in the twentieth century, the Master claims that all religions "come to us through the medium of a preexisting language; and if you remember that this language embodies absolutely nothing but human conceptions and human passions, you will see at once that every religion presupposes its own elements as already existing in those to whom it is addressed" (183).

Since "all human words tend . . . to stop short in human meaning," the Master has effectively barred the presumption of any discourse to a logocentric status transcending language. Pursuing his perceived advantage, he contrasts the arrogance of traditional theology with "the utter humility of science," showing how the painstaking advances of the latter have always eventually overcome theological dogma that is inconsistent with them. He ends with a defense of free inquiry that anticipates the positions of Charles Sanders Peirce and John Dewey: "What we have gained is not so much in positive knowledge, though that is a good deal, as it is in the freedom of discussion of every subject that comes within the range of observation and inference" (185).

This is the Master's high point. Tradition must be cleared away—deconstructed of its pretensions—to make way for a humanism based on the cultural sciences. The question remains whether the Master's paradigm will ever be able to address "the alleged extrahuman elements," since his theory of language would seem to render them beyond "the range of observation and inference." It is also questionable whether his version of the scientific-positivist religion of humanity will be able to provide the idols that human beings cannot and will not live without. Keeping the door open for inquiry is inherently iconoclastic. The Master of Arts has not provided an alternative to an anachronistic religion, only a scientific project. When the Master ends his speech, the Poet remains silent: "I was thinking things I could not say" (186).

The Counter-Attack of Faith

In driving his scientific humanism remorselessly to its logical conclusion that the way to transcendence is blocked by the limits of language, the Master of Arts awakens an intellectual rejoinder from The Lady, who defends faith against reason in a letter to the Poet admonishing him to try to limit free discussion at the table so that the pieties of the more sensitive boarders will not be destroyed, leaving them pained and adrift. The Poet had pledged to "stand up for this poor lady," and Holmes fulfills the promise. Her response is thoughtful, philosophical, and well reasoned. A well-bred Brahmin, The Lady is conversant with modern rationalist culture and sympathetic to its insights; she is not threatened by the Master of Arts and long ago learned that the discoveries of science only increase the sense of mystery about the cosmos and its Creator. She is cosmopolitan, not traditionally provincial; her concern is for those who are not strong enough to maintain their faith under the assault of doubt, especially the Young Girl.

As is always the case with Holmes, the position of social solidarity is represented by a woman with wider concerns than logic. Acknowledging and affirming "the fullest liberty of calling to account all the opinions which others receive without question," she adds that "one ought to be very careful that his use of language does not injure the sensibilities, perhaps blunt the reverential feelings, of those who are listening to him" (190). She is suspicious of following out "a train of thought until it ends in a blind *cul de sac,* as some of what are called the logical people are fond of doing" (190).

The Lady bases her case for limiting discussion on an idealistic philosophy of religion, rather than a particular creed. Anticipating Josiah Royce's "loyalty to loyalty," just as the Master of Arts anticipated the pragmatist's theory of inquiry, The Lady argues that "the sense of dependence on Divine influence and the need of communion with the unseen and eternal" are transhistorical contents of human nature, and that experimental science will not "take away the need of the human soul for that Rock to rest upon which is

higher than itself" (190–91). She does not, however, drive her idealism to the point of advocating a purified spirituality of reverence to
stand as a modern religious alternative to scientific humanism.
Instead, she embraces a reverence for particular reverences: "I want
to beg you to handle some of these points, which are so involved in
the creed of a good many well-intentioned persons that you cannot
separate them from it without picking their whole belief to pieces"
(191). The "fever of doubt which it cannot be denied is largely prevailing in our time" is not to be abetted, but contained so that the
"standard of reverence for all sacred subjects" might "grow and ripen
into the devotion of later years" (195–96).

Just as the Master of Arts acknowledged that most human beings
need their idols, The Lady insists that they need their creeds.
Neither a purified humanism nor a purified spirituality can serve as
the cultural basis of the new era. The issue has been joined—iconoclasm confronts reverence, both sides fighting in the name of humanity, and neither one capable of discerning the direction that the
racing carriage of specialization, science, and civilization is trans-
porting it. The Lady does not provide a solution to the problem of
solidarity; she exerts a restraining influence aimed at preventing
damage to individual souls. Her criticism works negatively, chal-
lenging the blind optimism of the Master's scientific humanism. By
changing the value sign of need and weakness from idolatry to reverence, she raises the stakes of iconoclasm and focuses on its
blindspot precisely.

Scientific Humanism Slackens

The Lady's letter is the turning point of the intellectual narrative
of *The Poet*; from here on, the Master's star will fall as he suffers humiliation at the hands of the Scarabee and devastating criticism
from the Poet, ending with concessions of his position and confession of defeat. The process of taking the Master down begins with
his visit, accompanied by the Poet, to the Scarabee's apartment. The
Master turns out to have been a serious student of entomology, having discovered a species of house fly and having become proficient
at laboratory technique. He decides to challenge the Scarabee with
an entomological query that he is sure the specialist will not be able

to answer. Instead, the Scarabee responds to the question by announcing that he had solved that very problem "by a series of dissections six-and-thirty in number, reported in an essay" (242). Realizing that he has been defeated, the Master does not fall into a pique, but takes "a pride" in the Scarabee's "superiority."

The Scarabee is now the undisputed standard bearer of modern knowledge, but he remains a coral-insect, a social isolate incapable of humor and void of social sentiment. His only "friend" is a large gray female spider; the only human friend he once thought he had stole a discovery from him years ago: "Since that time I have liked spiders better than men. They are hungry and savage, but at any rate they spin their own webs out of their own insides" (250). He has "no scruple," however, in letting the Master explore his laboratory: "I have never had any complaint to make of amatoors" (250). This final unintentional cut devastates the Master, but he preserves his equanimity. After they leave the Scarabee, the Professor tells the Poet: "If I had not solemnly dedicated myself to the study of the Order of Things . . . , I do verily believe that I would give what remains of my life to the investigation of some single point I could utterly eviscerate and leave finally settled for the instruction and, it may be, the admiration of all coming time" (251).

The Master's humiliation and The Lady's letter have put the efficacy of the generalist and his humanist and integrative conception of knowledge in jeopardy. In the next moment of the intellectual narrative, the Poet assesses their consequences in a reflection directed to the reader, apart from the table talk. Confessing the defeat of Holmes's own pretensions to be a conversational Autocrat, the Poet declares the end of the Dynasty of the great "conversational dogmatists," such as Samuel Pepys, Samuel Johnson, and Thomas Carlyle. In the new era, if a generalist "is in intelligent company he will be almost sure to find someone who knows more about the subjects he generalizes upon than any wholesale thinker who handles knowledge by the cargo is like to know" (263). It is no longer possible to "believe things because considerable people say them, on personal authority, as intelligent listeners very commonly did a century ago. The newspapers have lied that belief out of us" (266). General statements are convenient, but a "wise man . . . bows to the authority of a particular fact": "It is the province of knowledge to speak and it is the privilege of wisdom to listen" (264). The Master of Arts is an anachronism.

What, then, becomes of the practical fruits of the Master's studies and reflections—his scientific humanism? When the Poet turns to consider the challenge posed by The Lady, he recurs to the Master's position and vigorously defends freedom of expression and comparative theology. Although he cannot "help honoring the feeling which prompted her" to write the letter and respects "the innocent incapacity of tender age and the limitations of the uninstructed classes, it is quite out of the question to act as if matters of common intelligence and universal interest were the private property of a secret society, only to be meddled with by those who know the grip and the password" (271).

The dogmas must fall. The new world is "manly" and calls for self-respect, without which reverence is "good for nothing" (270). Specifically, self-respect involves respect for justice "between the Infinite and the finite," which has been perverted by the doctrines of human depravity and original sin. The "half-civilized banditti who have peopled and unpeopled the world for some scores of generations" have "so utterly dehumanized, disintegrated, decomposed and diabolized" justice for the human creature that "it has become a mere algebraic x, and has no fixed value whatever as a human conception" (270). The only path forward is to restore the natural conscience, "which from the dawn of moral being had pointed to the poles of right and wrong only as the great current of will flowed through the soul" (268). In order to repolarize conscience, "we must study man as we have studied stars and rocks" (268). The result, anticipating Nietzsche's transvaluation of values, will be an aristocratic ethic—the model of the "noble man" in contrast to the "sickly monomaniac" who projects the image of God as the "Infinite Invalid" (272).

In the new era, technology is weaning people from "all superstition" about power. As human beings progress in their ability to control "the mob of elemental forces," they no longer need and are stifled by a punishing God with arbitrary power. With his embrace of technological progress, the Poet has simply swept aside the danger of a world of coral-insects and the claims of the idolators. His praise of the noble life that "reverences truth, . . . loves kindness, . . . respects justice" is utopian in light of the conditions to which it is addressed. The transvaluation is only for the select few; the Poet provides no indication of how the few might come to direct society or of how nobility might be democratized. He has nothing to offer of substance, in fact, but the program of human(ist) science, a project with an ethic. A masculine program without feminine supplementation cannot stand.

The last word on The Lady's letter is provided by the Master when he reads to the Poet from his book on the order of things. Continuing the advance of the humanist front, he embraces Darwinism because it "restores 'Nature' to its place as a true divine manifestation" and "lifts from the shoulders of man the responsibility for the fact of death," promising a "Revival of Humanity" through its perspective of ascending rather than fallen life (305). Sin must be studied as "a section of anthropology," as a "vital process" (moral pathology), and "we must not allow any creed or religion whatsoever to confiscate to its own private use and benefit the virtues which belong to our common humanity" (306). Moralized scientific humanism has again reached a high point, but there is another shoe to drop. The Master draws back and acknowledges that "the real difficulty of the student of nature at this time is to reconcile absolute freedom and perfect fearlessness with that respect for the past, that reverence, for the spirit of reverence where ever we find it, that tenderness for the weakest fibres by which the hearts of our fellow creatures hold to their religious convictions" (308). Only then will "the transition from old belief to a larger light and liberty" be "an interstitial change and not a violent mutilation" (308).

The Lady's objections have been acknowledged, but to what effect? The Master offers no suggestion about how free inquiry and reverence are to be harmonized. His concession of full-strength humanism leaves the issue undecided. In a telling juxtaposition that concludes his reflection, he wishes that people would understand the obvious historical fact that "humanity is of immeasurably greater importance than their own or any other particular belief" and immediately adds that "we are all tattooed in our cradles with the beliefs of our tribe; the record may seem superficial, but it is indelible" (327–28). The coral-insects will go on building blindly, and the carriage will continue to race to its undetermined destination; there is no new synthesis of culture to guide and direct the new era.

As *The Poet* draws to a close, the Master is about to tell the Poet and the Astronomer his "final intuition"—"*The one central fact in the Order of Things which solves all questions*" (339). He does not get to relate his wisdom, because the Landlady abruptly intrudes to tell them that she is closing the boarding house, ending the reign of the conversational dogmatist. When the Poet later asks him to continue the conversation, the Master refuses: "That which means so much to me, the writer, might be a disappointment, or at least a puzzle, to you the listener" (343). The Poet privately reflects that the Master is probably not so sure that his formula "hold[s] water" (344).

After the Landlady's announcement, the boarders quickly find other quarters, except for the Scarabee and the Master who will remain to await the establishment's new owner, the one with his specimen cases and the other with his library; the man of the future and the man of the past, isolated from the present and from each other—the coral-insect and the anachronism. The intellectual narrative of *The Poet* begins and ends with problematicity and undecidability; the Holmes of *The Poet* is infected with the "fever of doubt," far from Parrington's "tolerant rationalist in the realm of the intellect" and "cheerfully contented conservative in other fields."

Doubts about Identity

Intellectual narrative—the development of ideas abstractly through the discourse of characters—dominates *The Poet*. As Holmes writes in his 1882 preface, the work's dramatic narrative—its characters' deeds and performative utterances and silences—is "slight," showing off "a few talkers and writers, aided by certain silent supernumeraries" (v). That said, *The Poet*'s dramatic narrative is tightly related to the work's intellectual narrative, mirroring and varying it through a parallel story of doubts about identity and, as always for Holmes, romantic rescue. Having presented his diagnosis of the times, Holmes now assesses the promise and projects of youth in the new era.

In the typical Holmes rescue romance, a person leading a life of quiet desperation is saved by a strong figure who delivers the object of rescue from danger or tedium into a future of love, wealth, happiness, and high social position. In keeping with the problematicity that pervades *The Poet*, neither of its romantic pair is a strong figure—both the Young Girl and the Astronomer are troubled youths, isolated by their specializations, leading lives of quiet desperation and uncertain of their identities. Both have been raised with Calvinist theology, and both are endowed with basic good natures that will be given full play when they overcome their discontents. Both are writers—the Young Girl for the popular press and the Astronomer for his personal clarification. The Young Girl is poor, forced into her oppressive specialty by circumstance. The Astronomer is wealthy and has chosen to spend his life in the ascetic pursuit of scientific discovery. The Astronomer will save the Young Girl, not because of his initial character traits, but because he has the material resources to do so. Indeed, the two save each other, with some discreet help from the major rhetors, the Poet and the Master of Arts.

The romance begins at the breakfast table when the Poet opines that if he wanted to use the image of double stars—"those loving celestial pairs"—in a composition, he would check out its accuracy with the Astronomer. The young man responds by taking the initiative and inviting the boarders to come to his observatory to see anything in the heavens that they wish. The Young Girl is thrilled with the idea of seeing a double star. The trip is arranged.

The terms of the romance are sealed at the visit of the party of boarders to the observatory when both prospective lovers reveal their emotional individualities. As the Young Girl looks through the telescope, she becomes overexcited with delight and starts expressing fanciful conceits about what might transpire on heavenly bodies in "a rattling, giddy kind of way"—the manic side of her hysteria (139). "[Q]uite astonished" with the Young Girl's "vivacity," the Astronomer shows her the double stars and explains their "complementary colors" (139). She speculates that double stars are fortunate not to be alone in empty space; they can shine their light on each other rather than wasting it in "the monstrous solitude of the sky" (140). The Astronomer responds that a single star is "not more lonely than I am myself" (140). Silence follows, as the Young Girl feels the tender "pity that a kind-hearted young girl has for a young man who feels lonely" (141). Soon the Astronomer will be giving the Young Girl astronomy lessons and will propose to her when he has fought through to strength of character.

The two troubled young people are not fit to make a lasting match with each other at the outset of the romance—the Young Girl is a semi-hysteric, and the Astronomer is in the throes of doubts about his identity. She, however, does not have to work through her symptoms, because they have been imposed on her by circumstance; she must wait to be saved by the Astronomer, who must do the interior work of defining himself as he ponders the meaning of life and his place in it. Each has a separate story to fill the interim between their first connection and their final commitment.

The Young Girl is the occasion of one of Holmes's most devastating attacks on the injustice of the new specialized capitalist society; whatever his views on labor agitation and socialism, Holmes is clear that his heroine is a victim of predatory economic forces beyond her control. She is intelligent, creative, vital, compassionate, sweet, modest, good-natured, and good-willed. She has rebelled against her strict Calvinist training by affirming love and the goodness of the world against the depravity of the human condition. Her rebellion runs to humor, which she expresses in satirical poems rather than rancor, and she has achieved a simple, humane faith. Yet the Young Girl is ground down by her thankless job of writing a romance every week for *The Bucket*, which consumes almost all her time, burns her out emotionally and creatively by forcing her to keep repeating the same formula with ever new variations, pays her a pittance, and exposes her to the vicious torment of an anonymous critic who heaps sarcasm on her, anticipates her plots, and sends her every negative comment on her writing that appears in print. The Young Girl's only friend is The Lady, who listens to her stories sympathetically, puts her poems to music, and gives her encouragement. Her youth is being stolen from her, she has lines on her face, and her isolation—enforced by the grind—has kept her from experiencing "love, the right of every woman" (54).

The Young Girl has responded to the stress imposed on her with hysterical symptoms. She has trained That Boy to use his popgun on secret command whenever one of the rhetors bores her. The Poet comments, as one such incident unfolds, that, given "a little touch of hysteria," nothing "can lie and cheat like the face and the tongue of a young girl"—"'Machiavel the waiting-maid' might take lessons of her" (147). Subject to manic-depressive mood swings, the Young Girl goes from transports of fancy at the observatory to the breakdown of her ability to write coherent stories as her attraction to the Astronomer grows. By the time that the Astronomer is ready to save her, she has gone over the brink, unwittingly reviving a character in one of her stories that she had already killed off.

The Poet is clear that the Young Girl is not to blame for her symptoms. She yearns for love and happiness, but has found that she has been allotted "a seat on a wooden bench, a chain to fasten [her] to it, and a heavy oar to pull day and night" (54). The Young Girl does not grow through her romance; her basic good nature is liberated when the Astronomer reciprocates her love for him and removes the need for her to continue her brutally tedious and frustrating job. The disorder in her volition is purely induced by the society's economic and gender structure, not by genetic factors, early childhood experience, or even repressive Calvinist culture. In her case, isolation in her unwanted specialty is a brutal imposition.

The Astronomer, in contrast, has chosen to exile himself from the world and others. He has displaced Calvinist rigor to "asceticism in the cause of science, almost comparable to that of Saint Simeon Stylites" (59). He returns from his nights in the observatory, where he isolates himself in pursuit of discovery, looking "so pale and worn, that one would think the cold moonlight had stricken him with some malign effluence" (59). No happier than the Young Girl, the Astronomer is also sensitive, intelligent, and good-willed. His discontent is not imposed on him, but is the product of his own self-doubts, which he expresses in a series of philosophical poems in blank verse that he composes when clouds obscure the heavenly bodies and that he gives to the Poet for redaction and eventually begins writing without the Poet's aid and reading to a company of the Poet, the Master, The Lady, and the Young Girl. The series of seven poems entitled by the Poet "Wind Clouds and Star-Drifts"—the most ambitious of Holmes's poetic projects—chart the Astronomer's struggle for identity, his story of intellectual, moral, and existential development from unhappy consciousness, through experimentation with perspectives, to affirmation of love—a phenomenology of the adolescent spirit.

The Astronomer's first poem, which describes his unhappy consciousness, appears immediately after the visit to the observatory. As it turns out, rather than sacrificing himself to pure science, the Astronomer has been motivated by the fame, the social immortality, of discovery, of having his name linked to a heavenly body. This ambition, however, contends with a sense that it is vain and unworthy: "The noblest service comes from nameless hands" (146). Taking up the image of the coral-insect, he wonders whether he must "leave his sign" (145). The conflict deepens in the second poem when fame becomes a "jealous nightmare" (172). The Astronomer makes his first step to self-revelation when he abandons the alternative of the coral-insect—the hyper-specialist like the Scarabee—

and confronts his discontent at losing himself in the "ethereal void" (173). He longs "to walk with eyes unraised above my fellow-men" and to "change the myriad lifeless worlds / I visit as mine own for one poor patch / Of this dull spheroid and a little breath / To Shape in word or deed to serve my kind" (173).

The Astronomer, however, is not ready yet to commit himself to the world and others. The third poem is a lengthy autobiography relating how the hero apprenticed himself to an old astronomer, eventually became his master and caregiver, and, finally, when his mentor died, was plunged into existential abandonment, feeling "the dread stillness around him" when he "leaves the slumbering earth / To watch the silent worlds that crowd the sky" (200). Launching his existential adventure, the Astronomer pledges not "to hate the meaner portion of myself / Which makes me brother to the least of men," and to make his life "a challenge, not a truce!" (201). He will dare "to ask / More than [God's] wisdom answers," trusting that God will not hold him "in scorn" (201).

The fourth poem drives the Astronomer's incipient defiance to full-fledged assertion that adopts the Master's and the Poet's iconoclasm and leads to the most extreme conclusion. Attacking the "jealous God" of tradition, he demands that God be worthy of worship. The Astronomer's defense of the manly freedom proclaimed by the Master and Poet ends with the reversal of the traditional relation between man and God, just as The Lady feared that it would: "Ye are gods! Nay, makers of your gods, / Each day ye break an image in your shrine / And plant a fairer image where it stood" (233). The Astronomer's proclamation of free play with idols is the logical conclusion of creative freedom, as Nietzsche understood. By this time he is reading to the small company of appreciators, and the Master responds to the poem dryly: "That is the kind of talk the 'natural man,' as the theologians call him, is apt to fall into" (234). The Master contents himself with saying that the natural man—unblessed by grace—"is worth listening to now and then" (234). It is after reading this defiant poem that the Astronomer offers the Young Girl lessons in his specialty and she blushes and accepts. He begs The Lady to pardon him for his harshness, explaining that he has had to think his way out of the "old theologies" and "superstitions" with which he had been raised. His rebellion is positive and good-willed, not reactive and resentful.

Yet the Astronomer cannot hold his high ground. The next poem finds him in dialogue with God, claiming the "rights of weakness" (238). Placing himself in Job's position, he challenges a God that gives human beings no control over anything, imprisoning them in circumstances that can crush them at any time, and then leaving "that mighty universe the Soul, / To the weak guidance of our baby hands" (260). The injustice of being set "adrift with our immortal charge" in a world of temptation and evil leads the Astronomer back to iconoclasm; he will "set the stubble-fields" of dead and deadly dogma "ablaze," preparing the way for the "young reapers" who will "flash their glittering steel / Where later suns have ripened nobler grain!" (261). He has fallen from Nietzsche's playful child to the adversarial roaring lion. The Master judges the ideas to be old hat.

The Astronomer's slide takes him to the bottom in the sixth poem, where he carries the Master's mordant observation about the proclivity of human beings to worship idols to its most bitter conclusion. He supposes that God smiles when He "sees us with the toys / We call by sacred names, and idly feign / To be what we have called them" (288). In the years between infancy and old age, human beings go through their charade and end up retreating to "the simple life we share with weed and worm," back in "cradles, naked as we came" (288). No comment is recorded from the Master in response to the Astronomer's world-weariness and cynicism, which comes at the same time that the Young Girl is losing her concentration and control—the moment of negation right before affirmation.

Affirmation comes in the last poem with an abrupt turn, in which the Astronomer abandons self-pride and defiance, leaves his isolation, and embraces the need for the feminine contribution to life. The way to God is through women's unstinting, selfless love: "Would that the heart of woman warmed our creeds" (312). The world needs "Mary's Gospel": "Love must be still our Master; till we learn / What He can teach us of a woman's heart, / We know not His, whose love embraces all" (312). Again the Astronomer has driven an idea to its extremity. Rather than the Master's lukewarm concession to the female sensibility, the Astronomer has embraced the female virtue of solidarity absolutely.

In response to the reading, the Young Girl nearly has a "hysterical turn," "her heart heaved tumultuously, her color came and went," and she avoids "a scene by the exercise of all her self-control" (313). The Astronomer takes her out for a lesson, asks her to save him from his "unwholesome scorn of life" and "endless questionings" leading nowhere, and proposes to her. She accepts, and they become, as promised, twin stars.

When the Landlady announces that she is closing the boarding house, the young couple is left to face the future. They have proved capable of overcoming their isolation through love, but their future is uncertain—the romance has not resolved any of the problems posed by modern society and culture. Unlike Holmes's earlier romances, in which the future is bright and prefigured, here it is a blank. The Young Girl is freed from her wage slavery, but how she will use her talents is an open question. The Astronomer has been called back to earth and will probably abandon his specialization, but no new vocation opens up for him. He will wrestle with the questions that have preoccupied him through "the duties, the cares, the responsible realities of life drawn out of itself by the power of newly awakened instincts and affections" (346). There is promise, surely, but it has no public dimension. The coral-insects continue to build, the carriage keeps racing—with uncertain purpose and direction.

Chapter 7

Morality in the New Society in *A Mortal Antipathy*

In 1885, at the age of seventy-six, Oliver Wendell Holmes opened, as he explains, "The New Portfolio."[1] Holmes is insistent on his use of the definite article. A portfolio—a collection of fragmentary writings that compose the resources for more structured works—is very personal for Holmes. As a creative reservoir, each portfolio is an expression and objectification of the author's present mind; it is consubstantial with the author's personality. Each portfolio is the one for its time in the author's life: "the cradle in which I am to rock my new-born thoughts, and from which I am to lift them carefully and show them to callers, namely, to the whole family of readers belonging to my list of intimates, and such other friends as may drop in by accident" (*Mortal Antipathy*, 1). A new portfolio announces a change in the author's mentality and sensibility. Holmes reports that he had opened his second portfolio when he began writing imaginative prose in 1857, because the materials in the first one from his youth were no longer alive for him. The middle-age man does not have the perspective of youth, and the old man no longer judges things as the middle-age man did.

1. Holmes, *A Mortal Antipathy*.

The New Portfolio opens with Holmes's last novel, *A Mortal Antipathy*, which like the two preceding it is a rescue romance "medicated" by intellectual discourse on existential, cultural, and scientific themes. It marks, however, a sharp break with the others in its form. Although it is recognizably a novel in the conventional sense that it has characters involved in a plot, that plot is advanced and the characters defined far less by deeds than by a dizzying array of documents—papers presented to a provincial discussion society, letters, scientific reports, and private journal writings—taken out of the portfolio and spread before the reader in an intelligible order. Holmes had inserted "documents" into his five previous works of imaginative prose, but he had never before made the documentary approach to exposition the basis of a work. Standing between Holmes's table-talk books, in which mini-essays on the themes he is addressing are woven together by a sketchy plot, and his earlier novels, in which the essays are embedded in the plot, the documentary novel is a synthesis of the two forms—the essays are dominant, but they are integral to the plot by moving it along. In *A Mortal Antipathy*, Holmes invented the form that best suited his literary purpose of dramatizing ideas. Personal documents, in particular, fuse character and ideology, evincing the former through the latter.

When Holmes wrote *A Mortal Antipathy*, he had just completed his long memoir of Ralph Waldo Emerson, which had been requested of him. Writing the memoir had been a problematic and intense experience for Holmes, as he reports in the extended autobiographical introduction to *A Mortal Antipathy*. Not only was Emerson a celebrity, adored as a prophet by many of his followers and derided by his critics, but Holmes was divided between the two camps. Holmes admired Emerson for being a "pure and high-souled companion": "After being with him virtue seemed as natural to man as its opposite did according to the old theologies" (*Mortal Antipathy*, 19). Yet Emerson also displayed a "union of prevailing good sense with exceptional extravagance" (18). Holmes could not abide Emerson's transcendentalism, which tended toward an unscientific mysticism that discounted "the promises of a remote future long before they were due" (18). Emerson's utopianism, as Holmes saw it, had encouraged his more eccentric and unbalanced followers to embrace unrealistic reforms such as feminism, communal living, political radicalism, and the return to nature, all of which threatened the functioning of normal society.

Despite his ambivalence, Holmes reports that he threw himself into his subject, carrying himself into Emerson's personality and finding himself thinking his subject's thoughts, using his phrases, and writing in his style, to the point that he sometimes completely identified with him (19). Holmes is grateful for the opportunity "to share the inmost consciousness of a noble thinker," but he also remarks that it is a "misfortune" to borrow the "tones and expressions and habits which belonged to the idiosyncrasy of the original" (19). *A Mortal Antipathy* is Holmes's recovery of himself after empathizing with Emerson, under the influence of that experience.

In his careful study of Holmes's response to Emerson, Len Gougeon argues that Holmes resolved his ambivalence by separating Emerson and his good sense from the excesses of his followers. Gougeon's case is persuasive, but in the process of making it, he identifies Holmes as a romantic idealist in contrast with the new realists, such as William Dean Howells, who appropriated Emerson for his breaches of polite convention and his democratic impulses. For Gougeon, Holmes represents "an increasingly effete romantic idealism," dedicated to maintaining a separation between elevated themes appropriate for literary art and the dirty details of life. As evidence for his claim, Gougeon quotes Holmes's denunciations of the French "ultra-realism" of Flaubert and Zola, who bring the "slop-pail" into print. The opposite of ultra-realism, however, is not necessarily romantic idealism—as Gougeon seems to imply—but might also be a moderate realism or some combination of realism and idealism. Advertently or not, Gougeon acknowledges an alternative to his thesis when he quotes Holmes on Zola: it is "time for the decently immoral to interfere with the nauseating realism of Zola and the rest."[2]

As Gougeon recognizes, his thesis fits into the main line of Holmes criticism that places him in the "genteel tradition" of New England letters, nostalgic for preindustrial Federalist order and decency, and suspicious of any challenge to traditional culture.[3]

2. Len Gougeon, "Holmes's Emerson and the Conservative Critique of Realism," 114–15.
3. Ibid., 108.

Holmes's idealism is thought to be evidenced by his romantic conservatism and his unwillingness to deal with society's dirt. *A Mortal
Antipathy* is an appropriate test of Gougeon's thesis, because it comes
on the heels of the Emerson memoir, when Holmes was thinking
about the debates of literary theory, having been plunged, as he
writes, into ". . . the vortices of uncounted, various, bewildering
judgments, Catholic and Protestant, orthodox and liberal, scholarly
from under the tree of knowledge and instinctive from over the
potato hill; the passionate enthusiasm of young adorers and the
cool, if not cynical, estimate of hardened critics, all intersecting each
other, as they whirled, each around its own centre" (18).

As Holmes's self-recovery after the Emerson memoir, *A Mortal
Antipathy* is both continuous with his previous works of imaginative prose and a break from them. It follows the same form of rescue
romance that structures all of Holmes's imaginative prose, in which
a person leading a life of quiet desperation is saved by a heroic figure, only now the rescuer is, for the first time, a strong heroine and
the object of rescue a young man. On the intellectual plane, the work
continues the development of three of Holmes's longstanding
themes: the new mass democratic society, the nature and virtues of
women, and the proper practice of medicine, with emphasis on the
promise of scientific psychology. The break here comes in the ab-
sence of the ideological target of Calvinist theology and its doctrine
of original sin, and its substitution by reformist humanism, represented by feminism and the suffragist movement.

Holmes, who had first turned his attention to the new society in
the work immediately preceding *A Mortal Antipathy*—*The Poet at the
Breakfast-Table*—is now firmly focused on it and ready to deal with it
realistically. Nonetheless, *A Mortal Antipathy* is not a simple example of realism. Holmes's earlier works of imaginative prose had all
been organized around a single guiding theme; that is not the case
here—each major concern is developed autonomously through relevant documents, the intelligible connections among them being
made at strategic junctures of the plot. Autonomous development
serves as the vehicle for Holmes to resolve one of his themes—the
new society—realistically ("the decently immoral")—and the other
two—the woman question and medicine—idealistically. Like *The
Poet, A Mortal Antipathy* is a work of problematicity, an example of
neither romantic idealism nor commonsense realism. Holmes is too

keen and sensitive a critical observer of his circumstances to over-
look disquieting social circumstances, yet he is unwilling or unable
to surrender his romantic myth of gender and his idealist defense
of scientific medicine. His New Portfolio finds him unreconciled.

Character(s)

An extremely heterogeneous text in a formal sense, *A Mortal
Antipathy* gains complexity through its characters and not through
its plot. The novel's plot is the simplest that Holmes conceived,
containing only two major events with a straight line between them
filled mainly by documentary evidence. In his earlier novels, Holmes
had proliferated subplots and minor characters, expanding his range
of topics and reflecting his major themes. *A Mortal Antipathy* has no
subplots and few and poorly sketched minor characters; it is a character study of its five major figures whose personalities are developed through documentary evidence and evinced in telling deeds.

The spare but highly concentrated and tightly configured plot of
A Mortal Antipathy centers on a young stranger of good breeding
and means—Maurice Kirkwood—who has taken up residence in
Arrowhead Village, a resort town on Cedar Lake in western Massachusetts that is being subjected to change from the new urban-
industrial society in the form of wealthy tourists. Kirkwood is a
mystery to the town's residents because he keeps himself apart
from almost all social relations. His Italian servant Paolo only gives
the cryptic explanation that Kirkwood suffers from an "antipathy."
The plot creates a force field around Kirkwood, formed by the attempts of the other major characters and the community in general
to solve the mystery of the stranger and, in some cases, to cure him
of his antipathy and restore him to community life. Those efforts include local law enforcement breaking into Kirkwood's house when
he and Paolo are gone, a hack journalist interviewing him, the local
doctor studying his case and helping him benevolently, a brilliant
young feminist woman trying to outdo the doctor and save Kirkwood in a gesture of humanitarianism, and her friend—a perfect
young woman with poise, modesty, great beauty, good judgment,
firm self-control, iron will, and extraordinary powers—rescuing
him in an act of selfless service. The four major characters who intrude and/or intervene in Kirkwood's life are polarized in a line

of opposition—the journalist and feminist are invaders of privacy, and the doctor and the Brahmin Amazon are benevolent and tactful facilitators of cure. The invaders represent the new society and the facilitators the old society; realism characterizes the treatment of the former and idealism the treatment of the latter.

The two events that crystallize, concentrate, and structure the plot are a great boat race and a devastating house fire. The race is the first-of-its-kind duel between the rowing teams of the local men's college and the Corinna Institute, a girl's finishing school that Holmes probably named after Germaine De Stael's 1807 novel *Corinne: Or Italy,* one of the first texts to address the conflict between female liberty and the traditional deferential role of women. Instigated by Lurida Vincent, the first scholar and committed feminist at the Institute, in the name of proving that women are as good as men at anything, the contest is won by the Institute's crew through the combined efforts of Vincent's Amazonian friend Euthymia Tower—the team's captain—and Vincent—the coxswain—who throws a bouquet of flowers to the men's crew just as they are about to overtake the women. The contrast between Euthymia's healthy strength and Lurida's compensating strategy sets up their characters and foreshadows how they will respond when Maurice falls into peril. The entire community of Arrowhead Village attends the boat race, including Maurice, who watches it from afar in his birchbark canoe through opera glasses. His attention is focused on Euthymia, but he cannot approach her.

The boat race comes in the spring at the end of the school year. Lurida and Euthymia graduate and are vacationing for the summer, and the village is abuzz with rumors about the mystery man: Is he a spy? A political exile? What is this antipathy of his? The local physician, Dr. Butts, has taken a humanely intellectual interest in the case and is reading up on antipathies. Lurida is contemplating the study of medicine, comes to Butts for guidance, and resolves to solve the mystery. At the same time, she assumes the position of secretary of The Pansophian Society, the local discussion group, and energizes it with a lecture program. A correspondent for a cheap newspaper comes to town and is persuaded by Lurida to interview Maurice while she continues her research. The Interviewer fails to pry the truth out of Maurice, and Lurida writes a letter to the stranger appealing to him to accept her as a charitable confidante. Lurida's letter is never sent, because Maurice falls ill with typhoid fever, requiring the care of Dr. Butts, to whom he confides that his antipathy is to young women, stemming from a childhood trauma in which he fell off a balcony when his older cousin was negligently bouncing him in her arms.

The plot is moved along mainly by documents—papers by Maurice (anonymous), the Interviewer, and Dr. Butts, presented to the Pansophian Society; letters from Lurida to Maurice; a private journal writing on his case, shared with Butts, by Maurice; and a scientific report on Maurice's case appended to his journal writing. Each document brings out the character of its writer and does not build up to the climactic event. The sequence of documents and the sparse events surrounding them set up an indecisive situation, which is only resolved by an abrupt cataclysmic fire at Maurice's house, while he is unattended and prostrate from his fever. With the rest of the village, Lurida and Euthymia rush to the scene, whereupon Lurida faints and Euthymia charges into the flames with no thought of herself and rescues Maurice against all odds in an act of supreme heroism. Her bravery and devotion result in a "repolarization" of Maurice's personality; he is cured of his antipathy and goes on to marry his rescuer. Euthymia is the only major character who has not written a document and the only one capable of taking action.

The characters and the issues that they represent grow around the simple narrative. The Interviewer is the repository for Holmes's damning criticism of the new society, Lurida and Euthymia epitomize his judgments on female character, and Dr. Butts is his ideal healer. These characters are defined primarily by their relations to the passive Maurice, and to a far lesser degree by their relations to one another; they are fixed types, constituting autonomous vectors in the force field around the mysterious stranger. They interact with each other but do not undergo personality change through their relations. *A Mortal Antipathy* is a study of social character-types in the new society, some of them real and contemporary, and others idealized and nostalgic.

Loss

The New Portfolio is necessary for Holmes, because he is an old man. He had opened his second portfolio in his late forties, when he was at the height of his powers and had the vital surplus to embark on an ambitious literary career, which began with the great success of his first work of imaginative prose, *The Autocrat of the Breakfast-Table*. Thirty years later, his popularity has diminished and he has been firmly planted in the "genteel tradition"—a relic—by the rising tide of realism, represented by his admirer William Dean Howells. He has also lost any hope of success and writes for his "list of intimates" and anyone else who might drop in by "accident."

Old age is a time of loss and displacement of the immediate (living presence) by memories. Holmes had outlived most of his peers and was on the verge of becoming "the last leaf" of his famous poem of youth. He had witnessed the change from the old commercial-agricultural order to the new mass industrial-capitalist society with mixed emotions, affirming scientific and technological progress, but acknowledging the threat to social solidarity caused by the hyperspecialization that attended them. His hopes for a bright America that harmonized liberty of conscience and expression with benevolent service (the female principle) were memories, pushed into the past by industrial capitalism and mass democracy, which valued neither term in Holmes's formula very highly.

The long autobiographical introduction to *A Mortal Antipathy* is figured by loss. First, there is the loss of Emerson, which cost Holmes dearly and rewarded him richly when he struggled through his memoir. In *A Mortal Antipathy*, Holmes settles decisively his position on transcendentalism—the philosophical theme of his generation—which he had left open in *The Poet at the Breakfast-Table:* "When you see a metaphysician trying to wash his hands of [space and time] and get rid of these accidents, so as to lay his dry, clean palm on the absolute, does it not remind you of the hopeless task of changing the color of the blackamoor by a similar proceeding? For space is the fluid in which he is washing, and time is the soap which he is using up in the process, and he cannot get free from them until he can wash himself in a mental vacuum" (*Mortal Antipathy*, 26–27). At least philosophically, Holmes is not an idealist; he embraces "accident," without which the mind would be vacant.

Holmes has also lost his imaginary companion, Samuel Johnson—born a hundred years before him. Holmes had compared himself to Johnson at every point in his adult life, noting the similarity of their development and gaining confidence and kinship thereby. Now he had outlived Johnson, sealing the judgment that he had made in *The Poet* that the generalist—the "conversational dogma-tist"—was an anachronism. He is on his own in the new society.

The loss that grieves Holmes the most is the destruction of his beloved ancestral home—the old "gambrel-roofed house" in Cambridge—to make way for the expansion of Harvard University. In the introduction to *A Mortal Antipathy,* he rues the "slaughter" of the house—albeit a "justifiable domicide"—and relates his memories of life in it in a concrete Proustian way. Holmes writes about the house to represent the "great numbers of men and women who have had the misfortune to outlive their birthplace" (33). That misfortune is the loss of a concrete and immediate link to one's past and a confirmation of one's identity: "But the house . . . where [one] one day came into the consciousness that he was a personality, an *ego,*—a little universe with a sky over him all his own, with a persistent identity, with the terrible responsibility of a separate, independent, inalienable existence,—that house does not ask for any historical associations to make it the centre of the earth for him" (31). Holmes's existentialist declaration again places him on the side of a realism focused on being-in-the-world. Without the touchstone of his house, he loses an anchor to his vital past; more and more he becomes a shade, a tissue of memory.

The New Society

Despite the displacement of presence to memory that Holmes suffers in old age, he places *A Mortal Antipathy* in his present. Following his evocation of the gambrel-roofed house, he remarks that the American is a nomad "who pulls down his house as the Tartar pulls up his tent-poles" (31). The phase of the novel devoted to the character of the new society uses that mobility and placelessness to diagnose and criticize the life of his times. The vehicle of Holmes's diagnosis is The Interviewer who comes to Arrowhead Village to find whatever material that he might use for the columns and notices that he writes for *The People's Perennial and Household Inquisitor,* a popular weekly newspaper. He is "careless" of his appearance, smokes cigars, dresses tastelessly, and is "curious" about everything. The Interviewer's character is revealed when he encounters Lurida at the library and offers that he does not like to read books and will sometimes read a magazine, but prefers to read newspaper articles summarizing magazine articles. Lurida, who is curious about The Interviewer, soon finds that he has turned the tables and is pumping her for information on the Pansophian Society, lacing his questions with flattery. She recovers and gets him to describe his work; he is a "correspondent" from "anywhere,—the place does not make much difference" (132). Indeed, he writes from all over the world, but never leaves America, using a gazetteer, newspapers and guide books to compose his stories: ". . . you can get the facts much better from them than by trusting your own observation" (132–33).

The Interviewer gives his description of his practice to Lurida without the slightest trace of embarrassment or irony; he is fully self-satisfied, a mass man with no sense of civilized standards—an exemplar of the "decently immoral." His mentality is abstract; he has no sense of concrete place; his articles are simulacra of simulations, which he holds to be superior in their truth to perceptual presence. Recently, he has turned to interviewing, which he finds to be a "very pleasant specialty," as "good sport as trout-tickling, and much the same kind of business" (133). Confident of his virtues, he offers to present a paper on his practice to the Pansophian Society.

The paper recounts how The Interviewer got a story out of a famous author. He is uneasy about undertaking the assignment because he is not sure that the author will welcome him, but his editor tells him: "It isn't our business whether they like it or not, . . . the public wants it, and what the public wants it's bound to have and we are bound to furnish it. . . . what you've got to do is pump him dry. You needn't be modest,—ask him what you like; he isn't bound to answer you know" (133–34). With his marching orders to get all of the information that he can from his subject and a journalistic ethic of subject beware, The Interviewer visits the author and proceeds to seduce him with flattery, playing on his vanity, all the while pretending to be simply an admirer. When the conversation turns to literature, The Interviewer shows his cultural illiteracy, but the author is pleased to fill in the blanks. A perfect courtier, The Interviewer finally gets the author to confess his distaste for his admirers who bedevil him with correspondence and ask him to read their manuscripts. Having gotten what he wants—the dirt that his subject would have wished to have kept hidden—The Interviewer goes off to publish the revelations. Summarizing his practice, The Interviewer compares himself to an oysterman: "Mark how the oysterman's thin blade insinuates itself,—how gently at first, how strenuously when once fairly between the shells!" (136).

As a specialist in prying, The Interviewer uses his subjects purely as means—he extracts and sells information to a commercial enterprise dedicated to satisfying its readers' taste for gossip. All of the elements of the new society are here—the supremacy of capitalist market value, the rise of unenlightened mass taste, and the specialist who cannot see beyond his function within the pluto-democracy and is incapable of solidary relations with others. Holmes is brutally realistic here, not in the sense of describing a normal or average situation, but in creating an ideal-typical character who brings into high relief the structure of social relations that constitute the mass information media in the new society. His picture has become familiar through generations of social, cultural, and media critics.

Despite the obvious (decent) immorality of The Interviewer's practice, Lurida tries to interest him in pumping Maurice, playing on his professional vanity and moral sense. Euthymia, who sees through The Interviewer and fears for her friend's reputation, takes Lurida out of the picture by sending her brother to The Interviewer to convince him that it is worthwhile to get at Maurice, another seduction: "It would be just the thing for a sensational writer" (150). "[A]lways in want of a fresh incident, a new story, an undescribed character, an unexplained mystery, it is no wonder that The Interviewer fastened eagerly upon this most tempting subject for an inventive and emotional correspondent" (150).

Having learned that Maurice is a coin collector, The Interviewer visits him on the pretext of having him examine some old and distressed Roman coins that he had picked up at a toll booth. This time the results are the opposite of what they were in the interview with the author. All of The Interviewer's flattery has no effect on Maurice, who soon turns the tables, exposing The Interviewer's cultural illiteracy and conducting an inquisition into his practice, to which he cannot help but submit. Maurice has even read The Interviewer's article from Rome, knows the guide book from which it was taken, and criticizes the facts on the basis of his personal observation. The encounter reaches its climax when Maurice asks The Interviewer to justify the invasion of his privacy: "What has the public to do with my private affairs?" (158). The Interviewer appeals to democracy: "You are a minority of one opposed to a large number of curious people that form a majority against you" (158). Maurice calmly answers: "There is nothing left for minorities, then, but the right of rebellion . . . I rebel against your system of forced publicity" (158–59).

As a representative of the old Brahmin elite who is only blocked from finding his proper scope by his antipathy, Maurice can stand up to The Interviewer and master him. Here Holmes's realism is tempered dramatically by a nostalgic romantic idealism, but it remains the case that he faced up to the decent immoralities of the new times, rather than taking refuge in the past; at most, his idealism is that of a Brahmin who is aware that he is untimely. The new society combines market value and mass democratic taste in predatory relations in which the ends of profit and consumer satisfaction justify the means to them, in this case, a system of forced publicity. Holmes understands that, disapproves of it, and describes it with sly and mordant satirical wit. The stray Brahmin can still defend himself, but he is not the wave of the future.

Holmes acknowledges the rise of a new ruling class—a plutocracy—in a series of letters that form an appendix to the novel. Writing to Euthymia, who has moved to the big city after her marriage to Maurice, Dr. Butts comments on the changes that have come to Arrowhead Village. It is now a watering hole for the super-rich who have been engaged in a wave of gentrifying and rebuilding, creating an antagonistic gulf between themselves and the local population, which experiences jealousy and class resentments. The new rich are a "mob of millionaires who come together for social rivalry" (298). They have nothing in common with their neighbors and no solidarity with them. The social distance is so great that religion, "which ought to be the great leveler, cannot reduce these elements to the same grade" (299). The only hope is that "society will stratify itself according to the laws of social gravitation" (298).

Holmes's prescription for the new society—for making the laws of social gravitation operative and restoring solidarity—is romantic and utopian, but not backward-looking and traditionalist. Instead, he advocates a new direction for the plutocracy, following which its members would create estates scattered throughout the land rather than exclusive preserves—a form of industrial feudalism. The ideal member of the new pluto-aristocracy would be "the providence of the village or the town where he finds himself during at least a portion of every year" (32). Having slackened his commitment to civil-libertarian democracy that characterized his early works of imaginative prose, the elderly Holmes is now focused on the peril of impending class warfare: "Our dangerously rich men can make themselves hated, held as enemies of the race, or beloved and recognized as its benefactors" (32). In a final appeal to prudence, Holmes warns that "the safety of great wealth with us lies in obedience to the new version of the Old World axiom, *RICHESSE oblige*" (32). The substitution of an ethic of service for predatory means-end market relations was always already a dead option, but it is at least a response to the new society rather than a retreat to an irrecoverable old order. In old age, Holmes refuses to bury himself in the past; he is not an "effete" romantic idealist, but a realistic critic with a utopian program in which a new ruling class creates its own traditions, guided by a Christian ethic.

The Woman Question

When Holmes turns to consider the second of his major concerns in *A Mortal Antipathy*—the woman question—he does so in the context of the new society. Represented by The Interviewer, that society is abstract, populated by nameless and placeless people who have lost trust in direct experience, and who perform functions within the capitalist system, enmeshed in its simulacra. For Holmes, abstraction is the curse of the new society, the polar opposite of the human-heartedness that he believed to be the root of the good and moral life, and that he identified with women. As a manifestation and symptom of the new society, feminism threatened to overturn Holmes's most cherished prejudices.

Holmes had been preoccupied with female temperament and its social consequences from the beginning of his venture into imaginative prose. In *The Professor at the Breakfast-Table*, he had distinguished between "brain-women" and "heart-women," comparing the intellectualism and lack of emotional responsiveness of the former to the good sense and capacity for love of the latter (*The Professor*, 147). *A Mortal Antipathy* brings that distinction into high relief through the characters of Lurida Vincent and Euthymia Tower, and their friendship. Lurida, the brain-woman, is a committed feminist; Euthymia, the heart-woman, knows her place. Lurida is a symptom of the new society; Euthymia represents Holmes's romantic utopia of modernized tradition. Lurida, though drawn extremely as a caricature, is treated realistically, in the sense that her disorder is diagnosed unsparingly; Euthymia is an impossible super-woman. Lurida is a case—Holmes medicalizes her through his own descriptions and through the judgments of Dr. Butts. Euthymia is a model.

Holmes presents the relation between Lurida and Euthymia as a bosom friendship of mutual admiration.[4] Each one is exceptional in her own right: Lurida, the "Terror" of the Corinna Institute, is a brilliant first-scholar who can outdo anyone in book knowledge; Euthymia, the Institute's "Wonder," has magnificent physical prowess, elegant beauty and carriage, good judgment, and goodwill. They are "the natural complements of each other," and each one values the accomplishments of the other more than her own, wishing that she could exchange places with her friend (*Mortal Antipathy,* 122). Yet their relation is fundamentally unbalanced. Euthymia looks up to Lurida "on all common occasions," but when "the graver questions of life" arise, Euthymia keeps her own counsel, fends off Lurida's abstract fancies, and brings "her calmer judgments to bear on them" (145–46). Euthymia is also a gifted scholar, excelling particularly in field sciences such as botany, whereas Lurida lacks physical strength and grace. Euthymia is insensible to Lurida's attempts to convert her to feminist positions, whereas Lurida defers to Euthymia's judgment and orders at critical times. When their friendship enters the novel's sparse narrative, Euthymia is always trying to save Lurida from the consequences of her delusions with the help of Dr. Butts.

In her study of the relation between Euthymia and Lurida, Lillian Faderman remarks that Holmes does not depict Lurida as a "morbid" figure, but presents her, instead, "as a charming young

4. Lillian Faderman has persuasively argued that efforts to interpret the friendship between Lurida and Euthymia as a lesbian relationship ignore the prevalence of romantic attachments between young women in the nineteenth century that were not understood as having sexual import and would dissolve as soon as one or both of the intimates married. See her "Female Same-Sex Relationships in Novels by Longfellow, Holmes, and James."

woman, despite her involvement in the nineteenth-century feminist movement, which he disparaged."[5] Although it is true that
Holmes endows Lurida with many positive qualities—she is tire-
less in her quest for knowledge, vitalizes the Pansophian Society
through her intelligence and initiative, admires excellence in others,
and does not have malevolent intentions—she has a disordered
will that is made manifest in overexcitement, (unconscious) dis-
ingenuousness, hysterical symptoms, constitutional imbalances,
monomania, an impulsive imagination, delusion, and performative
contradiction. Her feminism is a symptom of her disorder, an intellectual superstructure that reflects and rationalizes it, rather than a
system of ideas to be engaged on its own merits. Holmes performs
a psychological criticism of feminism in his portrait of Lurida, making her ideology an element in her complex; she is a case, and there
is much about that case that is far from charming.

Lurida is introduced at the beginning of the novel as the leader of
the "advocates of virile womanhood" at the Institute who had carried their thinking to the extreme of asserting "the physical equality
of woman to man," on the basis of epic heroines such as Semiramis
and Boadicea, and the Amazons (40). Holmes finds it ironic that
Lurida should have assumed her leadership position, because she
is "far better equipped with brain than muscles" (25). She is "large-
headed, large-eyed, long-eyelashed, slender-necked [and] slightly
developed," appearing childlike (sexless) (40). Indeed, for "Lurida
sex was a trifling accident to be disregarded not only in the interests of humanity, but for the sake of art" (255). She has a "penetrat-
ing head-voice" and has a man's handwriting. She would gladly
give up her title as the "Terror" who has been "fatal" to all acade-
mic rivals "if she could go through the series of difficult and graceful exercises in which she saw her schoolmates delighting" (51).

When Lurida goes to Dr. Butts to seek his recommendations
about the best resources that she can use in her project of studying
medicine, she demands that he treat her as a man: "You must talk
to me as if I were a man, a grown man, if you mean to teach me anything" (124). In a letter to Euthymia written after the action of the
novel is over, her rivalry with men has hardened into hatred: "On
the whole, I don't think I want to be married at all. I don't like the

5. Ibid., 322.

male animal very well (except for such noble specimens as your husband). They are all tyrants,—almost all,—so far as our own sex is concerned, and I often think we could get on better without them" (284).

Unable to assert herself and her will directly, due to her physical and emotional constitution, Lurida resorts to guile and cunning. The "Machiavellian young lady" wins the boat race with the men's college for the Institute by the stratagem of tossing a bouquet she had secreted for such an occasion. In her quest to solve the mystery of Maurice's antipathy, she conceals her aim from Dr. Butts, telling him that she needs his help to find out whether she wants to study medicine. When she mounts her final plans to invade Maurice's privacy, she attempts to hide her letter to him from Euthymia, her intimate friend. At the same time, Lurida is aware of her own nervous temperament and of the weakness of women (164). She simply cannot and will not control herself.

Lurida's intellectualism and strategizing disposition coalesce around the defining element of her complex—monomania. Intrigued by the mystery of Maurice Kirkwood, she becomes possessed by the desire to get to the bottom of his antipathy and is eventually seized by the conceit that she can save him and restore him to normal social life, which Butts and Euthymia fear will lead to the destruction of her reputation. Butts tells Euthymia: "You know as well as I do what a complete possession any ruling idea takes of her whole nature. I have had some fears lest her zeal might run away with her discretion" (190).

Lurida's feminism and its relation to her thwarted will to power is encapsulated and integrated into the novel's narrative through the long letter that she writes and plans to send to Maurice imploring him to accept her as a confidante and sister of charity. Ostensibly an offer of selfless service to a suffering "brother," the letter evidences her misrecognition of her motives and her tissue of delusions and contradictions. Through her research into nervous diseases, Lurida believes that she has found the cause of Maurice's antipathy in tarantula poisoning and, according to Euthymia, wants to test her hypothesis. Euthymia warns Lurida that she is acting at least partly out of curiosity rather than unmixed benevolence, but she will not listen—she is possessed and also refuses to understand that except for Butts and Euthymia, nobody in Arrowhead Village, including

Maurice, will see her intervention as anything but a brazen imposition actuated by suspect (erotic) motives, if it becomes known.

Lurida understands enough about prevailing social norms to realize that her approach to Maurice is unconventional, so she begins
the letter by stating that she is aware of the "very common feeling
that it is unbecoming in one of my sex to address one of your own
with whom she is unacquainted, unless she has some special claim
upon his attention" (194). She overcomes that obstacle by affirming
her commitment to the "service of humanity": "And should I carry
out that idea, should I refuse my care and skill to a suffering fellow-
mortal because that mortal happened to be a brother, and not a sister?" (195). The letter then veers away from Maurice altogether and
into an impassioned defense of women's equality, crediting Maurice
with enlightened views concerning equal educational and occupa-
tional opportunity, and belief in the physical equality of women
and men, citing Euthymia as a case in point: "My brother! Are you
not ready to recognize in me a friend, an equal, a sister, who can
speak to you as if she had been reared under the same roof?" (196).

Realizing that she has been "led away into one of my accustomed
trains of thought," Lurida starts to offer her services as a sympathetic confidante, but is again diverted by a reflection on her own
disorder, under the pretext of sympathy: "I myself have known
what it is to carry a brain that never rests in a body that is always
tired. I have defied its infirmities and forced it to do my bidding.
You have no such hindrance, if we may judge by your aspect and
habits" (197).

When she finally gets to Maurice's problem, Lurida presents a
disquisition on antipathies, based on her research, ending with an
appeal to him to confide in her with the promise of cure if he lets
her "into the hidden chambers" of his life (198). Unwilling to let ill
enough alone, Lurida concludes her letter by restating her humanist-
feminist credo: "I will never suffer myself to be frightened from the
carrying out of any thought which promises to be of use to a fellow
mortal, by a fear lest it should be considered 'unfeminine.' I can
bear to be considered unfeminine, but I cannot endure to think of
myself as inhuman. Can I help you, my brother?" (198).

All of Lurida's complex is present in the letter—her compensation for physical inferiority, her concern to prove herself equal to
men, her abstract humanist rationalization of her motives, and the

feminist ideology that mediates between her self-serving and self-inflating motives and her rationalization. The letter is about herself and not about Maurice. In Lurida's case, feminism is a strategy for inflating a weak ego and compensating for a frail constitution. Lurida is a damaged product of the new society, as abstract as The Interviewer in her own way. The Interviewer used Machiavellian guile in the service of gathering any salable information; Lurida uses the same guile—disingenuously—in the cause of an intellectualized humanism. Neither of them has sufficient emotional responsiveness to feel and practice benevolent sympathy.

When Euthymia persuades a reluctant Lurida to show her the letter, she puts her foot down and tells her friend that she *"must"* accompany her to see Dr. Butts before she delivers it: "There was no resisting the potent monosyllable as the sweet but firm voice delivered it" (201). The visit never takes place because Butts is attending to Maurice, who has fallen ill with typhoid fever. Lurida has to shelve the letter, which has served the purpose of revealing the structure of her character and ideology.

The superficiality of Lurida's feminism is disclosed starkly when Maurice is trapped in a house fire and Euthymia gets ready to dash into the flames to save him. Appalled at the probable loss of her friend, Lurida shrieks: "Not you! Not you! It is a man's work, not yours! You shall not go!" (270–71). When Euthymia goes ahead with her selfless deed, Lurida faints.

In the series of letters following the action that Holmes stages as "After-Glimpses," Lurida gives up any plans to study medicine, falls briefly into anti-male sentiments, takes up more purely intellectual pursuits, and finally has a courtship with a young minister with whom she shares an interest in mathematics. She comes to terms with her limitations and is ready to take her place in provincial life, retaining her feminist ideology, but abjuring feminist practice. She will now be socially protected from the dangers of her complex, which is the best that can be expected—she will no longer be subject to the temptation to be decently immoral. She nurses the ambition, nonetheless, to "indoctrinate Maurice with sound views" on the woman question. Lurida has been taken out of the new society and placed into the old order, a kind of halfway house.

In contrast to Lurida's "impoverished organization," which makes her "appear, in the presence of complete manhood and womanhood, like a deaf mute among speaking persons," her friend Euthymia is the perfection of complete womanhood, a wonder woman who could only exist in the imagination (256). The accent is on "complete." Lurida and Euthymia are presented by Holmes as complementary, but their complementarity is asymmetrical. Lurida has a disordered mind-body; she is a genius of book learning, capable of every movement of thought—like a martial-arts expert—but she is subject to impulsive enthusiasms and has a defective body that cannot tolerate her nervous mental energy and does not ground her in sensory reality. She depends on Euthymia to provide the justification for her feminist view that women are equal to men, even physically; she lives vicariously through Euthymia, and she relies on Euthymia to save her from herself when she contemplates embarking on rash projects. Euthymia does not need Lurida in the same way. She admires Lurida's intellectual prowess and would exchange her own physical virtues for it, but Lurida is not her ego ideal. Euthymia defers to Lurida "on every-day matters," but not on any important subjects. Euthymia has her own fine mind that is integrated with her remarkable body. Her own perfection excludes Lurida's intellectual penetration, which comes at the price of draining too much energy to the brain from the rest of her body. Euthymia's mind does not have to force her body to serve it; her mind and body are harmonized to serve her person.

A model of health, Euthymia has a muscular, but perfectly proportioned, body; ". . . her organization was one of those carefully finished masterpieces of nature which sculptors are always in search of, and find it hard to detect among the imperfect products of the living laboratory" (41). She is a remarkable athlete and can overmatch most men in strength, agility, courage, and concentration; yet she is also the "sweet soul" suggested by her name, taking care to be gentle toward the weak and modest about her virtues and accomplishments. She is intelligent and well educated, and has good judgment. She is the only female character that Holmes created who is "born and bred . . . to command of herself as well as others," though he never gives her the opportunity to rule (240).

The essence of Euthymia is her integrity; Holmes never gives any indication that she experiences dissociation, splitting, alienation, or imbalance: "With Euthymia the primary human instincts took precedence of all reasoning or reflection about them" (260). Unlike

Lurida, Euthymia does not calculate: "Unconsciousness belonged to her robust nature, in all its manifestations. She did not pride herself on her knowledge, nor reproach herself for her ignorance" (145). Euthymia represents a perfect balance between nature and civilization. She roams the woods alone like a panther, but is sensitive to others, poised and spontaneously generous and sympathetic. Having no conflicts in her personality, she does not experience existential or moral choice; she is free in the sense that her being is expressed completely in every one of her acts. Euthymia does not have to be saved from herself and has no need for an ego ideal; her mind, body, and temperament are ordered in such a way that she affirms herself and life with full confidence, uncut by self-defeating tendencies.

Euthymia is the only major character in *A Mortal Antipathy* who is not revealed in a document. She cannot have one, because she does not need one; she does not have to explain herself. Instead, Holmes describes her and gives her the starring role in the romantic rescue of Maurice when she saves him from the house fire in an act of courageous and selfless service, and is then rewarded with his love. Euthymia's character is evinced in her deed, unreasoned, but sure and decisive.

The clearest rupture, opposition, and imbalance in Euthymia's friendship with Lurida is ideological. Whereas Lurida makes Euthymia the exemplar of her feminism, Euthymia is not a feminist. In a conversation with Dr. Butts, Lurida reports that Euthymia does not share the opinion that women should be physicians; rather, she believes that "the same woman who would be a poor sort of doctor would make a first-rate nurse . . . I can't argue her ideas out of her" (164). The duality constructed by the two friends is not one of mind and body, but of brain and heart. As a heart-woman, Euthymia is focused on concrete experience and its solicitations and demands; she accepts the traditional definitions of gender roles and evinces her personality within their boundaries. As the only woman to whom Holmes gave the role of romantic rescuer, Euthymia is also his idealized solution to the woman question. She has "health, beauty, strength," but she bends them to service in the traditional order. She recoils from The Interviewer's and Lurida's attempts to invade Maurice's privacy, and she takes offense, in the name of modesty, at Lurida's suggestion that she should have her bust sculpted in the cause of art. Euthymia has extraordinary ego strength, but no trace of self-will and self-assertion. She is not preoccupied with men and romance, but she is ready to give and accept love when a man who is up to her standards offers himself.

After Euthymia's rescue of Maurice, who is an exemplar of complete manhood but for his antipathy to young women, "repolarizes" his personality and makes him fit for love, Dr. Butts persuades her to visit the recovering patient to stabilize his cure. When Maurice gets healthy enough to fend for himself, Euthymia determines that her visits threaten to become compromising to her proprieties. She has feelings for Maurice, but will not impose herself on him. When she tells him that henceforth he must visit her, Maurice proposes to her and she accepts. Euthymia will become the wife of a wealthy Brahmin scholar and consummate athlete who will take her to the city where she will be able to shine as the "queen" that Lurida and most of Arrowhead Village thought that she should be. Perhaps Maurice will become a great diplomat and she will be a great lady.

The model woman, Euthymia exercises her gifts and maintains her dignity within a disposition of deference to social order and a generous and spontaneous will to serve. She neither cares about nor needs gender equality, because she can realize herself fully within traditional norms. She is destined to carry the old society into the new. Yet Euthymia and Maurice are throwbacks to the noblesse oblige of the Brahmin caste, not harbingers of the richesse oblige hoped for by Holmes from the new capitalist class. They will do nothing to leaven the new society in any lasting way; they are idealizations of romantic reaction. The Interviewer is still out there and will not disappear; there will be more Luridas. For all of her vitality and magnificence, Euthymia Tower is a nostalgic construction, a model drawn from the past, not a contemporary case or a promise of the future.

Medicalization

Medical practice, *A Mortal Antipathy*'s third major theme, was one of Holmes's longstanding concerns. As an eminent professor of medicine and a practicing physician, Holmes drew upon his knowledge and experience to craft doctors as characters in his imaginative prose and to "medicate" his novels explicitly with the thesis that actions and dispositions that are interpreted theologically as sinful should be understood as psycho-physical disorders and treated rather than censured or punished. As Charles Boewe shows, Holmes grounded his novels in an extension of neurological theories of reflex action into the domain of psychology, using the works as vehicles to speculate on the possibilities for psychological science.[6] At least in terms of the polemical aim and theoretical foundation of Holmes's novels, they are realistic, neither excluding nor sublimating the unpleasant facts of mental disorder.

Holmes acknowledges his realism in an abrupt interruption to the narrative of *A Mortal Antipathy*, before he introduces Lurida's translation of an Italian medical report on the relation of antipathy to tarantula poison. Realizing that he is trenching on the slop-pail or at least the bed pan, he distinguishes himself from Swift and Zola, who have "outraged all the natural feelings of delicacy and decency," arguing that it is justified to write about "curious medical experiences which have interest for every one as extreme illustrations of ordinary conditions with which all are acquainted" (*Mortal Antipathy*, 177).

A Mortal Antipathy presents the only case that Holmes analyzed that has contemporary scientific interest. In *Elsie Venner*, the cause of the title's character's dual personality was snake venom and in *The Guardian Angel*, the cause of Myrtle Hazard's multiple personality was inheritance of ancestral character traits. In *A Mortal Antipathy*, Maurice Kirkwood suffers from a familiar kind of post-traumatic phobia that functions as a defense mechanism whenever the condition of the trauma—the close presence of a young woman—triggers panicked apprehension that the event of his being thrown off a balcony in his early childhood will be repeated. Maurice experiences symptoms of acute anxiety and angina pain when his phobia is activated. Through scientific "documents," Maurice's report of his problem, and Dr. Butts's reflections, Holmes presents a speculative neurological diagnosis of Maurice's antipathy based on reflex physiology. His physiology is crude and he does not have recourse to the conceptual armory of the various schools of depth psychology, but his identification of the causal efficacy of traumatic shock is still current.

6. Boewe, "Reflex Action."

A Mortal Antipathy is a doubly medicated novel, because its authority figure and mediator is a physician. Doctors had played those roles in Holmes's other works of imaginative prose, but had shared them with clergymen or humanist scholars and conversational dogmatists. In the new society, religion and general humanist knowledge are no longer, for Holmes, possible cultural bases for social solidarity, and only medical science is left. *A Mortal Antipathy* is a doctor's novel.

Like Euthymia, Dr. Butts is a complete character, a model of mature professional manhood. The "leading medical practitioner" in the entire region surrounding Arrowhead Village, he is "an excellent specimen of the country doctor, self-reliant, self-sacrificing, working a great deal harder for his living than most of those who call themselves the laboring classes" (*Mortal Antipathy,* 82). "Soberminded, sensible [and] well-instructed," Dr. Butts's essential trait is a harmonious blend of "sagacity" and "learning" (174, 82). In contrast to Euthymia's instinctive integrity, Butts's is thoughtful. In contrast to The Interviewer's abstraction and absorption into functionality, Butts is close to concrete experience and infuses his practice with a medical ethic that leads him beyond the mere application of technique.

Dr. Butts is as idealized a figure as Euthymia, with no faults and an unstinting goodwill, romantically moralizing a realist discourse; rather than being a throwback to the old society, he synthesizes the new scientific medicine with traditional values, evincing Holmes's utopian aim of blending past and present. When Butts learns about Maurice's antipathy, he begins a study of that phenomenon, not because he is "infected by the general curiosity" about the stranger, but because of human-hearted concern: "He could not look upon this young man, living a life of unwholesome solitude, without a natural desire to do all that his science and his knowledge of human nature could help him to do towards bringing him into healthy relations with the world around him" (87). Yet Butts respects Maurice's privacy and autonomy, and abstains from taking any initiative except study to prepare himself to serve if Maurice solicits his aid. His relation to the subject of his other case— Lurida—is similar; he gives her access to his books and wisdom even though he does not believe that she would make a good doctor and only tries to thwart her plans, and then tactfully, when they imminently threaten to harm her. Butts is respectful and patient toward his patients and sees them whole—as mind-bodies—in a particular social and cultural environment. He is a total healer and life counselor, and a militant opponent of the system of forced publicity.

Butts's ethical medical practice is grounded in a philosophy of medicine that is exposed in a paper that he presents to the Pansophian Society. He begins by defending the nearly universal concern for care of the body by recurring to a persistent philosophical conception in Holmes's work—personal consciousness is the core of a series of wrappers that enclose it: "...all the accidents of our lives,—the house we dwell in, the living people round us, the landscape we look over, all, up to the sky that covers us like a bell glass,—all these are but looser outside garments which we have worn until they seem part of us" (166). The body is the most intimate of the wrappers, and it is continually vulnerable to disease and disorder. The aim of physicians is "to remove [their] subjects from deadly and dangerous influences," and to control or arrest their effects, yet their efforts are necessarily imperfect; "the agency of nature's destroying agencies" is ruthlessly "uniform," as actuarial tables demonstrate (171).

Butts's response to the inexorable power of nature's destructive forces is humility, which leads to a general disposition to caution. Given the centrality of the body to human beings and their distress when it fails them, physicians are tempted to seize upon slim evidence of success to pursue unfounded cures: "Thus the physician is entangled in the meshes of a wide conspiracy, in which he and his patient and their friends, and nature herself, are involved. What wonder that the history of Medicine should be to so great an extent a record of self-delusion!" (172). That last comment is an indirect warning to Lurida, but it also links closely with Butts's ethic of respect; here respect is for the destructive forces, which have their own patterns, must be observed closely, and can only be contained or abated by prudent intervention. Holmes learned this patient disposition when he was a medical student in Paris and the old assaultive remedies were being abandoned and scientific medicine was in its infancy, leaving observation and inquiry as the preferred strategies and leading to new insight into the natural history of disease and self-healing of the body. Holmes carries this early modern approach into the new society through Butts; it is not traditional, but it was already being superseded by scientific discoveries. In this respect, he is a forerunner of holistic medicine, which revives the early modern moment along with unconventional therapies of which he would be deeply suspicious.

Butts's treatment of his cases is in strict conformity with his theoretical approach to medicine. He quickly diagnoses Lurida's disordered volition and then lets her test the waters of medicine, making it plain to her that he believes most women are too subject to imaginative flights on slim evidence to be judicious doctors, and that she would be better off leaving Maurice alone. He is afraid that her overexcitement will break her weak constitution and that her monomania might lead to severe damage to her reputation, but he leaves her alone until he suspects that she is about to make her move on Maurice, at which point he enlists Euthymia's aid. He realizes that Lurida will not heed orders, but has to learn from experience; he only leaps in when she is immediately endangered. He is free in his admiration of Lurida's intellectual prowess, but is acutely aware of her suspect motivations. His fine balance of respect, criticism, and intervention exemplify ethical practice.

Butts's treatment of Maurice is also exemplary. When he is called to treat Maurice for typhoid fever, Butts modulates his care in light of the natural history of the disease and waits for his patient to broach his antipathy. When Maurice gives Butts his self-report on his condition and a scientific document about it, Butts ponders the case and realizes that it is only an extreme form of the fear that many young men have of women—gynophobia (246). Although there is no medical cure for the condition, Butts speculates that an abrupt encounter with a young woman in a favorable circumstance might provide a counter-shock to reverse the polarization resulting from the initial trauma. He does not pursue that possibility practically, because he knows that it might also cause an extreme reaction and even death from heart failure. Instead, he lets Maurice express his desires for normal relations with women and for love, allowing him to build his confidence. After Euthymia applies the counter-shock and repolarizes Maurice's personality, Butts convinces her to visit him to assist in his recovery. He had already thought before the accident that it would be good for both of them to test their affections for each other, but, again, he would not "meddle where I am not asked for or wanted" (184). He lets Maurice and Euthymia discover each other, mediating and facilitating, rather than invading.

Dr. Butts never directly effects a cure, but maintains his vigilance and deftly arranges the conditions for one. His respect for privacy and autonomy, the time that he applies to studying the case, his humility, his patience, and his concern for the entire particularized life—physical, mental, and social—of the patient are in stark contrast to the medicine of his time and contemporary practice. He represents a romantic ethical ideal that, if nothing else, defies capitalist economics, technological specialization, and the moral climate that they engender. As a replacement for the clergyman and the humanist, Butts succeeds ideologically, but, for all his realist methodology, his model is impractical. He is the romantic antagonist of the embedded yet rootless Interviewer.

A Mortal Antipathy is the only of Holmes's novels not to pit his concrete humanism against Calvinist theology. Religion plays no role in the work and is replaced by the gossiping mob swayed by fancy and abetted by the greedy system of forced publicity and the misguided projects of abstract humanitarian reformers. Even the "Broad Church" Christian humanism of Holmes's earlier writings gives way to a strictly medical humanism. In the after-glimpse letters that form the appendix to the novel, it turns out that Butts receives an invitation to teach medicine at a major university and is persuaded by an insistent Lurida to remain in Arrowhead Village, where his wisdom, expertise, and experience can be put to good use in alleviating the suffering of his patients. Butts will remain a country doctor, tempering the effects of the new society's invasion of the village. His practice has a defensive implication and will not be transformative of the new society. Holmes understands the new society and is unreconciled to it, yet finds no way beyond it. A blend of realism and romantic idealism, *A Mortal Antipathy* is positioned in its problematic present, not in a promising future or primarily in a nostalgic dream of the past.

Chapter 8

Over the Teacups as an Account of
Senescence and a Last Testament

In Oliver Wendell Holmes's final work of imaginative prose,
Over the Teacups, written when he turned eighty and his health was
failing, he reviewed his major intellectual and artistic concerns for
the last time, framing them in a reflection on life and death. A quintessential modern (male) individual, for whom religious faith had
become problematic, Holmes approached his impending death
through meditations on old age and how its perspective and horizon disclose the problem of how to value life and the world.

Over the Teacups is the most troubled and tortured of Holmes's
works of imaginative prose. Not only are its substantive themes
unresolved, but Holmes has profound doubts about whether he
should have written it at all and released it to the public. After he
has already introduced the book in the first chapter and started getting into substance, Holmes opens the second chapter with a communication to the reader, expressing his fear that he might be an
anachronism. Imagining what critics of the book might say, Holmes
exposes his own misgivings: "We don't want literary *revenants,* superfluous veterans, writers who have worn out their welcome and
still insist on being attended to . . . You are not in relation with us,
with our time, our ideas, our aims, our aspirations" (*Over the Teacups,* 21). Holmes can only respond to the criticism modestly, say-

ing that he has "some things which he would like to say" for "a limited class of readers" (22). Even if he cannot "beat his record,"
Holmes will not be "lazy and cowardly" and "shrink from exerting
his talent, such as it is" (22).

Then Holmes suddenly veers off and reflects on the gain to critics
from his effort, which they will be able to compare unfavorably to
his earlier works: "It is a pleasure to mediocrity to have its superiors
brought within range, so to speak; and if the ablest of them will
only live long enough, and keep on writing, there is no pop-gun
that cannot reach him" (22). Holmes finds his reflection to be "unamiable" and drops it because "I am at this time in an amiable
mood" (22). *Over the Teacups* is in great part an attempt to sustain an
amiable mood in the face of unamiable judgments.

Near the end of the text, Holmes takes up the sense of his anachronism again, in another communication to the reader, acknowledging that "if the world of readers hates anything it sees in print, it
is apology" (293). Yet he cannot help himself, confessing his inability
to resist the temptation of writing, "notwithstanding that the terrible
line beginning 'Superfluous lags the veteran' is always repeating in
his dull ear!" (294). To whom is he writing? If his audience is his
generational peers, it is minuscule. Yet he cannot expect to win a
new public from younger readers who "have found fresher fields
and greener pastures" (294). Holmes's meditation leads him finally
to ask: "Ought I not to regret having undertaken to report the do-
ings and sayings of the members of the circle which you have
known as The Teacups?" (295–96). He has no answer to the question
but a personal one: "For myself, the labor has been a distraction,
and one which came at a time when it was needed" (296). *Over the
Teacups* is written under the sign of cultural death; Holmes cannot
deny that he is a cultural anachronism—he does not believe in his
historical immortality; old age is loss of relevance and loss of vain
hope. He cannot fully affirm his last project.

Over the Teacups is one of Holmes's table-talk books, which he defines in the text as "studies of life from somewhat different points of
view" (308). Their form is "a series of connected essays," in which
continuity is provided by a group of major and minor rhetors who
discourse around a set of themes and become involved in romantic
plots and subplots. The essays are "largely made up of sober reflections," with the "gilding of a love-story" (308).

The viewpoint of *Over the Teacups*—old age—is made plain in its title. Holmes's three earlier dramatized essays centered on the breakfast table of a boarding house, whereas his last one revolves around evening teas. Holmes compares the vibrant stimulation of coffee drunk when the sun is rising and the "labors of the day" are still ahead, with the "benign stimulant" of tea, which brings up "many trains of thought which will bear recalling" (6–7). The withdrawal from the world at tea time is reinforced by Holmes's cast of characters; in the earlier books the interlocutors formed a variegated party of boarders thrown together by accident, whereas here they are a refined circle of friends and acquaintances—an "unorganized association"—brought together in the home of the Mistress.

Acquiescing in the constraints of infirmity, Holmes admits to relaxing his literary reins in the organization of *Over the Teacups:* "Various subjects of interest would be likely to present themselves, without definite order, oftentimes abruptly and, as it would seem, capriciously" (6). He cautions readers to accept his "patchwork quilt" on its own account and not to compare it to the breakfast-table books unfavorably, hoping only that they find "anything" to "profit from" (6). He warns that his "slight project" will repeat the themes and judgments of his past work, remarking that if "he has anything to say worth saying; that is just what he ought to do" (9). Holmes also drops the conceit of masking himself in personae, such as the Autocrat, the Professor, and the Poet, who were the major rhetors and narrator-characters in his breakfast-table books. In *Over the Teacups,* he calls himself the Dictator (recurring to the Autocrat), but makes it plain that he does not intend to conceal or differentiate himself from that subject position: "I have not tried to keep my own personality out of these stories. But after all, how little difference it makes whether or not a writer appears with a mask on which everybody can take off" (20). Holmes has no strength or will to play games and will be free to indulge himself.

At the outset of *Over the Teacups,* Holmes is not even sure how much he will write. He reserves the right to stop the series at any time, write at any length he pleases, and leave the cast of characters indeterminate (8). By the middle of the book, he claims that he is still not sure of what it is. He had planned to "report grave conversations and light colloquial passages," containing "a not wholly unwelcome string of recollections, anticipations, suggestions, too often perhaps repetitions, that would be to the twilight what my earlier series had been to the morning" (134–35). Yet the tea room has insensibly become a "tinder-box" of romance: "Now, the idea of having to tell a love-story,—perhaps two or three love-stories—when I set out with the intention of reporting instructive, useful, or entertaining discussions, naturally alarms me" (136). Holmes is, of course, disingenuous—*Over the Teacups* has to be gilded with romance; he simply has not yet found the way to do it.

Holmes's last table-talk book is the perfect complement of his first. *The Autocrat,* Holmes reports, "was begun without the least idea what was to be its course and its outcome. Its characters shaped themselves gradually as the manuscript grew under my hand" (304). It came from Holmes's "mind almost with an explosion, like the champagne cork; it startled me a little to see what I had written, and to hear what people said about it" (307). *Over the Teacups* also develops with uncertainty about its course and outcome, but it is not a pleasantly surprising explosion filled with promise; it is a sigh of exhaustion in "the least promising season of life" (i). As *The Autocrat* was the imaginative construction of Holmes's existential doubts in his middle age, *Over the Teacups* records his struggle with senescence.

Despite all of his warnings, doubts, and caveats, Holmes's last work of imaginative prose is as tightly focused intellectually as his earlier table-talk books and novels. The problem with the work—if it is one—is not laxity, but inconclusiveness. Conscious of writing his last extended work, Holmes is unable to get a final unitary reading of personal life and is unable to settle the public concerns that had occupied him for the three decades spanning *The Autocrat* and *Over the Teacups*. Holmes's doubts about his relevance and concessions of literary rigor are symptoms of deeper existential and cultural ambivalences, agonies, and discontents.

Senescence

For Holmes, old age is a stage of the life process that is defined primarily through a perspective on time. Although Holmes was an eminent physician and medical professor who embraced mechanistic conceptions of the body and even extended them to the psyche, he does not interpret old age physiologically. Biological mechanism is presupposed in old age—the active powers of the body to engage in the world effectively decline, the body suffers from diseases and infirmities, and death is imminent and continually known to be so. Yet there is also the historical death of losing one's peers and understanding oneself as an anachronism, and, most importantly, the loss of hope in the possibilities of the future: old age is the least promising season of life; there is little or nothing more to hope for from the world.

The challenge of old age, for Holmes, is to preserve equanimity in the face of physical death; amiability when assailed by pain, infirmity, and incapacity; and generosity toward a future in which one will play no part and will probably be forgotten. If one does not meet the challenge successfully, the consequences are despairing madness, irritated pique, and resentful bitterness. In a discussion that comes in the middle of the text on the major divisions of human temperament, Holmes contrasts the "Ifs" and the "Ases." The former "go through life always regretting, always whining, always imagining," whereas the latter take things "just as they find them, they adjust the facts to their wishes if they can; and if they cannot, then they adjust themselves to the facts" (121–22). Holmes is determined not to be a whiner pining over what was, might be, or could be ("if only . . ."); *Over the Teacups* is his effort to adjust himself to the inconvenient facts when he can no longer hope to adjust the facts to his desires.

Holmes's first attempt to adjust himself to the adverse conditions of old age comes early in the text in a paper that the Dictator presents to the society of Teacups. The document is a rambling discussion of various aspects of life's final stage, focused on all of the ways it can be made supportable. Holmes notes the advantages of retirement from the press of action, the improvements in comfort wrought by material and medical progress, the saving grace of habit, hope for release from world weariness, greater tolerance of one's own limitations and others', and awareness of the service one renders to the young by being an example of longevity. Yet when he describes the "cheerful equanimity" of the remnant of his Harvard class at its last reunion, Holmes acknowledges that the major compensating factor in old age is biochemical; in one's sixties, Nature begins to administer a narcotic: "More and more freely she gives it, as the years go on, to her grey-haired children, until, if they last long enough, every faculty is benumbed, and they drop off quietly into sleep under its benign influence" (30).

Under the influence of Nature's narcotic, "[o]ld age is like an opium-dream. Nothing seems real except what is unreal" (22). Memory in particular becomes more vivid: "Nature has her special favors, and this is one which she reserves for our second childhood" (39). Acceptance of old age means acquiescing in the "favor" of withdrawal from the world into imagination, and enjoying the play of memory. Throughout his previous works of imaginative prose, Holmes had affirmed individual self-determination as his highest value, but now "every act of self-determination costs an effort and a pang" (38). The greatest concession of old age is the surrender of self-determination to the play of subjectivity; one no longer participates in the creation of the future and retreats into the imagined past, ensuring that one is an anachronism.

The retreat into dream and the reversal of the primary mode of temporality from future to past that provide old age with its phenomenological structure are at the root of Holmes's doubts about whether he should have written *Over the Teacups.* The opium-dream is solipsistic; it takes one out of real time, regardless of what others think: it makes one a living relic, habitually repeating oneself.

In the discussion that ensues at the table after the Dictator has read his paper, the Mistress wonders why he has not addressed the religious attitude of old age. The Dictator refuses to comment on the subject, pleading that "the relations between man and his Maker grow more intimate, more confidential, if I may say so, with advancing years" (45). Then he abruptly repeats his main point: "More and more the old man finds his pleasures in memory, as the present becomes unreal and dreamlike, and the vista of his earthly future narrows and closes in upon him" (46). The promises of faith have no place in Holmes's discourse on old age, which is locked into the modes of mundane temporality.

Near the middle of the text, Holmes again takes up the discussion of time, now in a horror story reminiscent of Edgar Allan Poe's tales that is read by Teacup Number Five, the major female rhetor at the table. "The Terrible Clock" is a cautionary tale about what happens when one dwells on the passage of time. The story concerns a man who inherits a large clock with an exposed mechanism and becomes obsessed with its ticking and striking of the hours, until he can do nothing but listen and is driven mad. As he becomes absorbed in the "infernal machine," he becomes convinced that it is speaking to him, uttering "Quick" with each tick and "Gone" at each striking of the hour: "So on through the darkening hours, until at the dead of night the long roll is called, and with the last Gone! the latest of the long procession that filled the day follows its ghostly companions into the stillness and darkness of the past" (171).

Time as mechanically registered passage is antithetical to both the dreamlike present-directed-to-the-past of old age and the plenitude of promise of mature adulthood. Gutting out concrete possibility from the future, the intentionality of abstractly marked passage carries with it a torturing, purposeless goad to action and a despairing sense of irretrievable loss of what is nevertheless meaningless. In the least promising season of life, dwelling on passage is the accursed alternative to the opium-dreams of memory. Holmes does not relate his story directly to his discourse on old age, but it stands as a warning against quitting the dream when one's temporal horizon "closes in upon him." For the healthy adult, time is the medium for making the future; for the resigned old person, it is the medium for recollecting the past; for the madman, it is the revelation of the present as anxiety and loss, empty frustration and frustrating emptiness.

Soon after the reading of "The Terrible Clock," Holmes makes his second and last attempt to come to terms with old age in a chapter devoted to answering questions that have been posed to him by his readers. Of those questions, the most frequent ask for advice on how to achieve longevity, and Holmes responds with medical wisdom and the commonsense maxim of "nothing too much" (181–82). As his reflection proceeds, it opens to the problematicity of the desire for longevity. Holmes warns that middle-age people who want a long life fail to realize that they will find themselves alone without coevals and will be subject to well-intentioned but humiliating consideration from others: "The world was a garden to me then; it is a churchyard now" (191).

When one of the Teacups reminds the Dictator that he claims to look at "old age cheerfully," and to welcome it "as a season of peace and contented enjoyment," he answers that his tears are not "bitter" and "scalding," and once again he recurs to memory and imagination. Old age is "melancholy," but it also has a "divine tenderness" born of "the sad experiences of human life," and a deeper level of "tranquil contentment and easy acquiescence," a plodding patience that is counterpointed by imagination taking wing: "The atmosphere of memory is one in which imagination flies more easily and feels itself more at home than in the thinner ether of youthful anticipation" (192). Holmes's transvaluation of the modes of temporality is his answer to the crisis of senescence, how he adjusts to the fact of vanishing promise.

Is life, then, a process of gathering up experiences to feed meaning in old age? From the viewpoint of the muscular vitalism of Holmes's early works of imaginative prose, which anticipated Nietzsche's reflections, the claim for the superiority of memory is an instance of *ressentiment,* inverting a healthy order of values and elevating a compensatory value to a final good. Equanimity comes at the cost of acquiescing in devitalization and at last affirming it. Yet Holmes has made the move intelligible as a mode of the will to power, the best that can be done when the horizon closes in and one prescinds from transcendence. Beneath both healthy adulthood and resigned old age is the terrible clock, which renders both of the former absurd and signals the collapse of humanly constructed time into agonizing and meaningless process.

Self-Deconstruction

An irony of *Over the Teacups* is that although Holmes counsels retreat into the opium dream of memory in his reflection on senescence, the text is not a series of reminiscences and rehashings, or even a settling of scores from the past, but is set within the time of its writing and is replete with new directions and topics. The reflection on senescence itself breaks fresh ground for Holmes; he continues to present studies of life from the perspectives on it that emerge as it changes, and does not freeze himself in the perspectives of his past.

Holmes also expands on his theory of the multiple self in light of the studies of his student William James on multiple personality. Considering any claims to distinction that he might make in the field of metaphysics, Holmes mentions "my studies of the second member in the partnership of I-My-Self&Co." (166). The second member—the emotional-volitional physical person who is directed by the executive ego—is the seat of character, of the individual's substance; in addition, it includes the idea that one has of oneself—one's official self-definition. The possibility of multiple competing second members of the self was explored by Holmes in depth fictionally, through the character of Myrtle Hazard in his novel *The Guardian Angel*, but he had not theorized the idea. In *Over the Teacups*, he adds "& Co." to the partnership of "I" and "me," allowing for a deconstruction of the official self-definition in terms of an alternative posed by a competitor for second member. He turns the insight on himself and ends up with a perspective that challenges his retreatism, making his final stance toward existence undecidable.

Having dropped his masks of Autocrat, Professor, and Poet (the subject positions of the differentiated engagements of his official self), and using the Dictator persona as an honorific title acknowledging longevity, rather than a distancing mechanism, Holmes, in *Over the Teacups*, introduces multiplicity into the text through the character called Number Seven, the "squinting brain," who is not assimilated fully into his official self-definition. The squinting brain is a counter-self, a disturbing influence, yet not an enemy, indeed, someone who is essential to the total personality. Remarking that a writer's characters "must, in the nature of things, have more or less of himself in their composition," Holmes finds proof for the principle in "the one whom I have called Number Seven, the one with the squinting brain" (299).

The squinting brain, another of Holmes's self-described claims to distinction in metaphysics, is defined by its "obliquity of perception"—the tendency to experience life at an angle that reveals insights that a balanced, straight-up perception cannot apprehend, but that also leads to ungrounded and unreasonable flights of fancy: "What extravagant fancies you and I have seriously entertained at one time or another! What superstitious notions have got into our heads and taken possession of its empty chambers,—or, in the language of science, seized on the groups of nerve-cells in some of the idle cerebral convolutions" (299–300).

One of the major rhetors at the tea table, Number Seven, the seventh son of a seventh son, is introduced as "the possessor of half-supernatural gifts," displaying "a certain confidence in his whims and fancies" (53). He is an exceedingly complex character with decided opinions and a dogmatic air who is assailed by self-doubt and awareness that he is a ridiculous figure: Only "an amount of belief in himself . . . shields him from many assailants who would torture a more sensitive nature" (82). At bottom, he is humble, dividing reality into higher and lower worlds: "The lower world is that of questions; the upper world is that of answers. Endless doubt and unrest here below; wondering, admiring, adoring certainty above" (117). When Number Seven expresses the desire to rule the cosmos for a brief time so that he can enforce a rigorous policy of eugenics, he does not include himself among the survivors of the purge.

Anticipated by the crippled Little Boston in *The Professor at the Breakfast-Table* and the Master of Arts in *The Poet at the Breakfast-Table*, Number Seven resembles his predecessors by being the mouthpiece for Holmes's more controversial views, but goes beyond them by presenting an entire view of life that stands alongside the narrator-character's perspective, rather than supporting part of it. Holmes is clear that the squinting brain deserves a place at the table and in the company and counsels of the self: "A mind a little off its balance, one which has a squinting brain as its organ, will often prove fertile in suggestion. Vulgar, cynical, contemptuous listeners fly at all its weaknesses, and please themselves with making light of its often futile ingenuities, when a wiser audience would gladly accept a hint which perhaps could be developed in some profitable direction, or so interpret an erratic thought that it should prove good sense in disguise" (96). Holmes does not give himself over to his squinting brain, but takes from that counter-self whatever can enrich his more balanced official perspective. The counter-self is not abolished in the process of appropriation, but remains autonomous and active, a genuine pluralization of the self.

Number Seven's major contribution to the table is a paper in which he presents a stark alternative to the embrace of the opium dream of memory. In his paper on old age, Holmes-Dictator had divided humanity into "Ifs" and "Ases," taking his stand among the latter. Number Seven is Holmes's supplement, an If personality who has his own division of humankind that cuts across the Dictator's and establishes a distinct structure of time. For Number Seven, the opposing human types are the "Eyes" and the "No Eyes." The No Eyes find "nothing to admire, nothing to describe, nothing to ask questions about" in the world, whereas the Eyes find "objects of curiosity and interest" everywhere (207). Placing himself among the Eyes, Number Seven describes a trip he took in the countryside and all of the things that he found to admire and meditate about—an old well sweep, the wheel of a wrecked wagon, and an arch over a river. In each case he marvels at the design and beauty of the artifacts, places them in historical context, and shows how their form follows their function. His discourse, up to this point, pleases the Teacups, but then Number Seven veers off into fancy, describing trees as the tails of "polypus-like" underground organisms, and Niagara Falls as the nation's tongue, which should be examined to determine the country's health. Finally, he marvels at the electric trolley, powered by "force stripped stark naked,—nothing but a filament to cover its nudity,—and yet showing its might in efforts that would task the working-beam of a ponderous steam-engine" (215). Contrasting himself with the majority of "fish-eyed bipeds" who do not care "a nickel's worth about the miracle which is wrought for their convenience," Number Seven expresses gratitude that "in our age of cynicism I have not lost my reverence" (215).

Whether they are old or new, Number Seven admires things and wonders at them, dwelling in a fulfilled and complete present in which direct perception is enhanced first by intellectual imagination and then by fancy. He is aware that his ideas might appear to be "odd," but he pleads that they render experience "wonderfully interesting": "I've got a great many things to thank God for, but perhaps most of all that I can find something to admire, to wonder at, to set my fancy going, and to wind up my enthusiasm pretty much everywhere" (214–15). After the paper is presented, the female Teacups are moved to tears; Number Seven, "too often made the butt of thoughtless pleasantry, was, after all, a fellow-creature, with flesh and blood like the rest of us. The wild freaks of his fancy did not hurt us, nor did they prevent him from seeing many things justly and perhaps sometimes more vividly and acutely than if he were as sound as the dullest of us" (216). Holmes leaves the matter there, without reservations.

Number Seven's affirmation of the world—his half-supernatural gift—is in bold opposition to the retreat into memory. It is not presented as an option for old age, but it is at least a reminder of the deprivation of the last period of life, which is not here figured as promise and possibility, but as presence. Number Seven's "If" does not partake of the "could be" or the "might have been," but of present imaginative association that transfigures the "As" into poetry. Perceptual experience is welcomed, yet not as a resource for the play of fancy; that play is a response to and enrichment of an intensely attractive perceptual experience that remains dominant over imagination, its context and not merely its stimulus. Number Seven has reverence for the perceived world that clothes experience so abundantly that the ticking of the terrible clock is muffled by a plenitude of quality. The most positive moment in the course of *Over the Teacups* comes from the squinting brain, which ends up producing a vision of life as a whole that is constructed out of insightful and fanciful obliquities, yet is not itself oblique. Holmes does not attempt to relate Number Seven's vision to his vindication of memory, nor does he try to synthesize the two discourses; he leaves the issue undecidable and his stance toward existence unresolved.

Women and Romance

Irresolution breaks out even more deeply when Holmes turns to another of his persistent concerns, gender relations. Throughout his imaginative prose, Holmes was preoccupied with female temperament, (romantic) love, and the role of women in a well-constituted society. Although he claims that romance is a gilding to add dramatic interest to a sober intellectual discourse, the rescue romances that are staples of Holmes's imaginative-prose works evince his more abstract ideas, dramatizing his connected essays. They are the vehicles by which women are brought into his reflections and their differences from men, special virtues and defects, and contributions to social order are discussed. In *Over the Teacups*, Holmes finds it almost impossible to get his romances going. More than three-quarters of the way through the text, he has still not been able to put a romance together and realizes that he is in trouble: "A whole year of a tea-table as large as ours without a single love passage in it would be discreditable to the company. We must find one, or make one, before the tea-things are taken away and the table is no longer spread"

(244). Holmes's difficulties do not indicate a simple literary failure, but problematicity in his attitude toward women.

Holmes makes two attempts to gild the text with romance in its concluding chapters, one of them purely contrived and successful, and the other serious and failed. The successful romance pairs two minor characters, a young doctor committed to family practice and the serving maid at the table, who turns out to be the first scholar at her women's college and who is endowed with good breeding, a beautiful voice, and striking beauty. Holmes does not develop the personalities of his two lovers, and their courtship takes place behind the scenes. Each one is a sketchy idealization; the doctor represents resistance to the overspecialization of medicine that disquieted Holmes, and the serving maid, nicknamed Delilah for cutting the Professor's hair at the table, is Holmes's model of young American womanhood—consummately skilled and gracious, but content to spend her adult life as a good wife. Unlike Lurida Vincent, the first scholar in Holmes's first imaginative-prose work of old age—*A Mortal Antipathy*—Delilah does not suffer from an imbalance of brain over heart, but is perfectly equilibrated. Unlike any of Holmes's other romances, the liaison between the doctor and Delilah is not based on rescue; it is a normal alliance of two capable people who have an affinity for each other, the most uninteresting romance that Holmes imagined—a halfhearted concession to the requirements of the genre that he invented.

Holmes's other attempt to formulate a romance in *Over the Teacups* is not pat and slight, but is tortuous and deeply embedded in the meaning-structure of the text. At its center is Teacup Number Five, the other major rhetor at the table alongside Number Seven and the Dictator. Her trajectory through the text reveals Holmes's struggle with his disposition toward women. *Over the Teacups* is an imaginative depth psychology, Holmes's most direct revelation of the structure of his psyche.

Number Five is introduced early in the text as Holmes's ideal of mature womanhood. For Holmes, throughout his works of imaginative prose, women are the keepers and protectors of the social bond, healing the conflicts caused by male self-assertion with sympathy and benevolence. Number Five is the only member of the tea parties with the "tact" to handle "every social emergency" (50–51). She stops the conversation from becoming too personal and shifts topics when another speaker gets boring. She is a gifted writer who has no care for fame and is an exceptionally discerning reader; indeed, the Dictator claims that he often cares more "for Number Five's opinion than I do for my own" (51). Yet Number Five is unmarried, and Holmes opines that perhaps "she has found nobody worth caring enough for" (51). He wishes that "she would furnish us with the romance which, as I said, our tea-table needs to make it interesting" (51).

In the first half of *Over the Teacups,* Number Five does not make a romantic move. Instead, her virtues are further described and evinced in her behavior. She gets her name from a line in the poem "Woodnotes I" by Ralph Waldo Emerson: ". . . nature loves the number five" (53) where that number represents the "star-form" that is repeated throughout nature. When the Dictator criticizes amateur poetry, Number Five admonishes him not to "be cruel to the sensitive natures who find a music in the harmonies of rhythm and rhyme which soothes their own souls, if it reaches no farther" (87). When Number Seven rails against the "hullabaloos" of modern music, she advises that everyone should take a "music-bath" weekly to cleanse the soul: "Every one of us has a harp under bodice or waistcoat, and if it can only once get properly strung and tuned it will respond to all outside harmonies" (98). When Number Seven proposes his radical program of eugenics, Number Five takes him down gently by remarking that Noah's ark was not an entirely successful experiment. Indeed, she is the only one who can "handle Number Seven in one of his tantrums" (96). Even when Number Seven is ludicrous, she finds something in what he says to redeem him and heads off ridicule from others with her gentle and tactful laugh that expresses her "kind heart": she is his "champion" (96). When the serving maid Delilah steps out of her place and cries over a letter from Helen Keller that the Dictator has read, Number Five crosses the social boundaries and quiets "the poor handmaiden as simply and easily as a mother quiets her unweaned baby" (143).

Holmes's unrelieved encomia to Number Five's wisdom, sympathetic appreciation, and kindness end abruptly at the midpoint of the text when he reveals a possible flaw in her character. She visits the Professor's laboratory and has him burn a diamond for her. The Professor reports that "Number Five said she didn't want a diamond with a flaw in it, and that she did want to see how a diamond would burn" (144). Number Five is a perfectionist.

Number Five's problem is revealed in a poem that she reads at the table immediately after the Professor's report to the Dictator on the laboratory visit. The poem is not written by her; she takes it from the vase in which the members of the tea gathering put their anonymous poetic productions. Entitled "I Like You and I Love You," and probably written by a young philosopher-poet at the table, the Tutor, the poem recounts a meeting between the two figures in the title: I LOVE YOU wants to pair with I LIKE YOU, but the latter rejects the proposal: "I LIKE YOU bared his icy dagger's edge, And first he slew I LOVE YOU,—then himself" (145). Number Five reads the poem "with a certain archness of expression, as if she saw all its meaning" (144).

From then on, the balance of the text shifts from the exposition and praise of Number Five's virtues to her effect on the people around her, especially men. Probably close to the cusp of middle age, she has "reached the wisdom of the ripe decades without losing the graces of the earlier ones" (167). The Professor remarks that "there is no such thing as time in her presence." She makes people forget their cares and they "throng about her" and "forget their own ages" (167). Number Five is an attractor.

Soon after she reads "The Terrible Clock," which recounts the horrors of obsession with time, Number Five begins a relationship with the young Tutor who comes to her for advice about whether he should form a romantic attachment to either one of the two young women at the table, an English and an American girl, whom Holmes calls the Annexes. Number Five says that he should select the one he loves, but the Tutor wants her to choose for him. She laughs without amusement and refuses to "take responsibility," telling the Tutor that "[t]here are several young women in the world besides our two Annexes" (179). The way is now open to Holmes's attempt at a serious romance. Will Number Five be able to love the Tutor or can she only like him, as she likes so many others?

As Holmes sets him up, the Tutor is an ideal object for one of his romantic rescues. He is well-bred and a formidable scholar, "born for a philosopher,—so I read his horoscope,—but he has a great liking for poetry and can write well in verse" (50). "[E]xcitable, enthusiastic, imaginative, but at the same time reserved," the Tutor is also "heart starved," and will likely "die early" if his need for love is not fulfilled. Although he is younger than Number Five, Holmes makes it clear that they could overcome their age differential. It is up to Number Five to overcome herself.

A perfectionist and an attractor, Holmes now pictures Number Five as "a kind of Circe who does not turn the victims of her enchantment into swine but into lambs" (217). Everyone adores her, especially men; she has time and goodwill for everyone at the table. The Doctor and the Counsellor (the lawyer at the table) consult her on difficult cases, the Dictator and the Professor depend on her for literary judgments, and the Musician plays duets with her on the piano. She seems to have so much love that Holmes wonders whether any man could withstand having all of it lavished on him (218). Yet "it is so hard to be her friend without becoming her lover" (238). Through her life, Number Five has been an enchantress, collecting her flock of lambs, many of whom are "graduates," who "have made love to her and would be entitled to her diploma, if she gave a parchment to each of them who had the courage to face the inevitable" rejection (243). She is a man-tamer: "So completely does she subjugate those who come under her influence that I believe she looks upon it as a matter of course that the fateful question will certainly come, often after a brief acquaintance" (243). Holmes now poses the question at the heart of his problem with Number Five: "She is the best of friends, they say, but can she *love* anybody, as so many other women do, or seem to?" (243).

The Tutor is a serious prospect. He has already come to Number Five for romantic advice, their acquaintanceship has become an intimacy through their private studies of Petrarch, which she initiated, and they have come "to depend upon their meeting over a book as one of their stated seasons of enjoyment" (242). Yet as the text nears its conclusion, Holmes is afraid that he will have to give up Number Five "as the heroine of a romantic episode," because so far she is only a "half-maternal friend to the young Tutor" (244).

Inevitably, the Tutor proposes to Number Five, and her response, which is not favorable, goes unreported. Afterwards, she is "rather more silent and more pensive than she had been" (263). Although the possibility of a romance is still not excluded, Holmes's doubts about Number Five have deepened. As the Tutor has progressively been "captivated" by her, she treats him as a favored nephew for whom she has a "special liking" (266). Now rather than it being a question of whether any man could withstand her love, it is a question of whether she can even recognize love in herself if she has it: "[S]he was so used to having love made to her without returning it that she would naturally be awkward in dealing with the new experience" (266).

As the text comes to a close, Holmes is unable to consummate the romance. Number Five has been sufficiently affected by the Tutor to have started dreaming about him and thinking of him more "than she was willing to acknowledge" (286). It should be "plain sailing for Number Five and the young Tutor," but that would be to misunderstand Number Five. She has rings of attraction, but once these have been crossed the prospective lover encounters "an atmospheric girdle, one of repulsion, which love, no matter how enterprising, no matter how prevailing or how insinuating, has never passed, and, if we judge of what is to be by what has been, never will" (286–87).

Seeming to have settled matters definitively, Holmes is unwilling to leave his failed romance alone. In his after-thoughts, once the tea table has been disbanded, he expresses hope that the Tutor and Number Five will form a loving pair in the imaginary future. He does not want to believe that the Tutor will die of "heart-failure" and that Number Five will be deprived of the "best inheritance of life" (308). If they do not consummate a romance, she will live on, with her lambs who "have been shorn very close, every one of them, of their golden fleece of aspirations and anticipations," "feeling all the time that she has cheated herself of happiness" (309). Number Five, who began as a genuine model of female virtue, is now a tragic figure who has armored herself against her potential to love.

The failed romance in *Over the Teacups* reveals Holmes's ambivalence toward women. There is nothing about Number Five that would have prevented Holmes from allowing her to dissolve her girdle of repulsion; she comes to the Tutor for enlightenment and ends up dreaming and thinking about him—she is capable of intimate attachment. Yet Holmes cannot forgive her for her perfectionism. Her graduates are burned diamonds who were not good enough for her—their passion has been carbonized. Number Five—the number loved by nature—has to be punished, though Holmes cannot bring himself to plunge his icy dagger into her all the way. One can feel the pain and anger of a child who believes that he can never do enough to be loved. At the core of Holmes's preoccupation with women is his own sense of unworthiness, leading to an attitude that mingles idealization with resentment and leaves him unresolved.

Liberty, Equality, and Forthputting

Throughout his adult life, Holmes maintained an interest in society, culture, and American national identity. Before the Civil War, he defended the promise of a society based on complete liberty of conscience, material progress, and human civility against the imposition of Calvinist orthodoxy in private and public life. A political optimist, he believed that dispelling the ignorance of the past would leave the way open to his notion of the direction of progress. After the war, a new society grew up in the United States that in many respects undermined Holmes's vision. Calvinism had been conquered, but it had been replaced with the reign of the dollar, class warfare, incivility, and elements of barbarism. Holmes shifted his polemical emphasis to the new society, criticizing overspecialization in *The Poet at the Breakfast-Table* and the invasion of privacy by the mass media in *A Mortal Antipathy.* He was no longer a confident optimist, but became doubtful that his vision would be realized. In *Over the Teacups,* Holmes presents his most general reflections on the new society through a series of scathingly sarcastic essays that focus on the central theme of egalitarianism, its contradictions and its dangers. He continues to defend liberty, but now against equality, its dialectical opposite in the modern formula, without achieving victory or conceptual resolution.

Always an ardent proponent of scientific and technological progress, Holmes begins his series of reflections on the new society with wondering praise of the rising level of material life brought about by industrial technology: "It seems as if the material world had been made over since we were boys" (31). Most importantly, communications media like the telegraph, telephone, phonograph, and photograph have created a "complete nervous system, a spinal chord beneath the ocean, secondary centres,—ganglions,—in all the chief-places where men are gathered together and ramifications extending throughout civilization" (32). The level of life has risen for all classes, due to "these unparalleled developments of the forces of nature" (31). Holmes can only ask: *"What next?"* (32).

Wonder turns to doubt when Holmes moves from technology to the society that it is transforming. Anticipating the negative utopias of the twentieth century, Holmes presents a vision of a totalitarian society based on the premise of absolute equality through a dream reported at the table by Number Five. The great attractor, she is also the bearer of grim stories such as "The Terrible Clock." Her dream is of a visit to the planet Saturn where her angelic guide shows her and tells her about the social life of its inhabitants. The "dullest, slowest, most torpid of creatures," because they breathe an atmosphere of nitrogen, the Saturnians have had a revolution that has installed the principle: "All Saturnians are born equal, live equal, and die equal" (62). They are "born free,—free, that is to obey the rules laid down for the regulation of their conduct, pursuits, and opinions, free to be married to the person selected for them by the physiological section of the government, and free to die at such proper period of life as may best suit the convenience and general welfare of the community" (62–63). With a rudimentary economy, the Saturnians have no luxury goods or trifles, and display no differences in personal taste, but they are proud that none among them goes hungry or without clothes. Dreading inequality more than anything else, they eat from common troughlike bowls and turned back an attempt to inject a modicum of privacy by putting separations in them. They are still in the process of postrevolutionary change with societies for the promotion of left-handedness and crawling (which would actualize the equality of the limbs).

Life on Saturn is deadly boring, so much so that its chief recreations are intoxication from the few springs of oxygen on the planet and suicide; "self-destruction becomes a luxury" in "a life which cuts and dries everything for its miserable subjects, defeats all the natural instincts, confounds all individual characteristics, and makes existence such a colossal *bore*" (65–66). This is the gray and gloomy picture of socialism painted by its twentieth-century critics—a state of stifling social entropy, void of freedom, individuality, benevolence, and generosity, and motivated by the reactive will to repel any attempt by individuals to distinguish themselves. The Saturnians drive the principle of equality to its absurd and gruesome conclusions with their squinting revolutionary brains; their life is the negation of everything that Holmes values and the utter corruption of a conscious being's dignity, even more oppressive than

Calvinism's malign reign of original sin, which leaves some space for distinction. The Dictator responds to Number Five's dream by remarking that a "great state" needs differentiation, through which varied social types are arrayed as on a chessboard, "looking for their proper places, and having their own laws and modes of action" (66). Between the directionless hyper-specialization that he criticized in *The Poet* and entropic, suicidal uniformity, Holmes seeks a just middle.

As Holmes sees the America of his time, it bears little apparent resemblance to Saturn; the revolution has not yet occurred. Indeed, America seems to be the opposite of that dull and deadly planet. Addressing his contemporary times, Holmes focuses on their vulgar ostentation and pride. Along with technological wonders has come the "materialization of the American love of superlatives" through the penchant to build ugly and obtrusive monuments, most notably the Washington Monument, which Holmes is glad has been surpassed as the tallest structure on earth by the Eiffel Tower: "We do not want to see our national monument placarded as 'the greatest show on earth,'—perhaps it is well that it is taken down from that bad eminence" (104). The sources of boorish vainglory are the "forthputting instincts of the lower" side of human nature, which need to be kept down by "the higher civilization" (104).

The forthputting instincts are the agents that subvert any possibility of achieving a harmonious balance between liberty and equality, substituting themselves for the former and rationalizing themselves by the latter. They are merely vulgar when they dominate architecture; they are far more dangerous when they penetrate social relations. Holmes links forthputting to egalitarianism in a damning satire on labor unionism related by the Dictator as a story told to him by a friend. Having hired Hiram, a staunch, independent New Hampshire Yankee, to dig post holes for him, the friend and his employee are accosted by two members of the Knights of Labor—Mike Fagan and Hans Schleimer—who have walked over to the work site from a nearby tavern. Drunk and speaking in heavy dialect, the Knights question Hiram about his wages, and when he refuses to give them the information, Fagan counters: "We're Knights of Labor, we'd have yez know, and ye can't make yer bargains just as ye loikes" (219). The friend intervenes, heaping sarcasm on the intruders by honoring their titles as he says in the same breath that he wonders how Lady Fagan is getting on as a washerwoman and hopes that Schleimer and his Lady have gotten over their domestic dispute that ended up in police court. Confused, but angered, the Knights make a grab for a shovel that Hiram had purchased from a store that the union is boycotting, at which point the friend and Hiram down their adversaries with well-placed blows.

With the Knights helpless on the ground, Hiram and the friend proceed to lecture them on liberty of contract. Hiram is the straightforward representative of the Yankee working class: "Ef I can't work jes' as I choose, for folks that wants me to work for 'em and that I want to work for, I might jes' as well go to Sibery and done with it" (221). The friend repeats the right-to-work line and gives the Knights a lesson in democracy: "If they didn't like the laws, they had the ballot box, and could choose new legislators. But as long as the laws existed they must obey them" (221).

Passing over Holmes's facile reduction of industrial relations in a corporate society to bargains among individuals, his nativism, and his caricaturing of unionists as drunken, pretentious oafs, his tale leaves the way open for his adversaries to have their way through democratic procedures. Forthputting, if done according to the rules, might bring about the dreaded reign of equality. In the context of Saturn's negative utopia, the Knights of Labor are the bullying forces of egalitarianism: forthputting is the prelude to totalitarian entropy. Holmes gives those forces an opening.

In his commentary on the story, the Dictator focuses on the travesty of the American fascination with titles: "It is a curious fact that with all our boasted 'free and equal' superiority over the communities of the Old World, our people have the most enormous appetite for Old World titles of distinction" (222). The "ambition for names without realities" that "do not stand for ability, for public service, for social importance, for large possessions; but, on the contrary are found in connection with personalities to which they are supremely inapplicable," is unworthy of a republic. Again, he calls for the higher civilization to curb ostentation and observes hopefully that "it is in that direction that our best civilization is constantly tending" (223).

The road to Saturn is blazed, for Holmes, by groundless and empty forthputting, which invades privacy and levels distinction by universalizing it, ending in an inversion of values that elevates the base above the noble. Holmes culminates his criticism of ostentation with the story of Timothy Dexter, a turn-of-the-nineteenth-century merchant who declared himself America's first nobleman. With his fortune, Dexter built himself a garish mansion, put statues of himself on its grounds, and hired a poet laureate to praise him. An early member of the line of populist megalomaniacs, Dexter "boldly took the step of self-ennobling, and gave himself forth—as he said, obeying 'the voice of the people at large'—as Lord Timothy Dexter" (232).

Holmes uses the figure of Dexter as his weapon to attack the democratization of American literature that had made Holmes an anachronism. Dexter's megalomania carried him into literary pursuits in which he defied every convention to the point of rampant misspelling and dispensing with punctuation, all with naive belief in his genius. Declaring himself "the greatest philosopher in the Western world," Dexter wrote meaningless emotional effusions: "it is the voice of the people and I cant Help it" (235).

Holmes makes it plain that Dexter is Walt Whitman in extremis: "If the true American spirit shows itself most clearly in boundless self-assertion, Timothy Dexter is the great original American egoist" (232). Whitman, as Holmes observes, "calls himself 'teacher of the unquenchable creed, namely egotism'" (234). Whitman refuses to distinguish among values and proclaims that "no one thing in the universe is inferior to another thing" (234). Whitman plays fast and loose with convention. Whitman celebrates himself, "but he takes us all in as partners in his self-glorification" (234). The difference between Whitman and Dexter is that Whitman is familiar and insists on using the short form of his first name, which, for Holmes, is simply the other side of the coin from giving oneself titles; both positions fail to recognize "simple manhood and womanhood as sufficiently entitled to respect" (236).

Holmes is not confident that American letters will find a just middle: "I shrink from a lawless independence to which all the virile energy and trampling audacity of Mr. Whitman fail to reconcile me" (237). Yet Holmes again draws back from a pessimistic conclusion. He reflects that "there is room for everybody and everything in our hemisphere" and compares "young America" to an unsaddled colt "sprawling in the grass with his four hoofs in the air; but he likes it, and it won't harm us. So let him roll,—let him roll" (238). Although he acknowledges the danger of forthputting to the civilized respect for liberty and its presupposition—privacy—that he holds dear, Holmes is not willing to forgo hope that American ostentation is a passing phase rather than the raucous preparation for totalitarian egalitarianism, the egotism that can only assert itself when it is rationalized as the voice of the people—totalitarian democracy. The saturnalia of self-assertion disturbs Holmes, but he wards off its most dreadful possibilities by distancing himself from them, preserving a good humor that he fails to justify; again, his text is unresolved.

In his final words on the new society that appear in his afterthoughts, Holmes is unable to maintain his good humor. As his reputation grew, he was besieged by requests from strangers for poetry, interviews, autographs, and advice, and, most irksome, by appeals to him to read and comment on manuscripts by aspiring writers. He became a public property, felt that his privacy was invaded and found it difficult to refuse, yet he could not keep up with the correspondence and had to defend himself. In *Over the Teacups*, he finally gives way to pique, remarking that "[t]he hypocrisy of kind-hearted people is one of the most painful exhibitions of human weakness" (310). Holmes realizes that much of his wider audience neither respects him nor loves him; he is a victim of the wondrous worldwide nervous system created by the new media of his time, which has been used against him by hordes of forthputting people. His response is to write a scathing set of form letters to various sorts of requests, unrelieved by generosity and any pretense to gratitude.

God and Self

Religion, the last of his persistent concerns that Holmes takes up in *Over the Teacups*, is both a personal and a cultural issue for him. If there is any core principle that Holmes stood for throughout his imaginative-prose works, it is freedom of conscience in determining one's stance toward existence. No individual or group had the warrant to interfere with how a person made their peace with life, if they succeeded in doing so. When the Mistress, the only representative of traditional Calvinism at the table, asks the Dictator how old people consider religious questions, he refuses to answer.

Holmes does not expose his personal beliefs in his writings; they are his own serious business. Yet he writes at length about religion as a cultural institution; it is the meaning that society gives to itself and to individual life, and the basis of morality. Considered culturally, the religious beliefs into which people are indoctrinated play a great part in shaping social relations and have profound effects on personality and psychological well-being.

Holmes lived to see the Calvinism that he fought in his youth and early middle age lose its grip on New England culture. Along with the forthputting new society had come the more promising humanization of faith that he had advocated all his adult life. Early in *Over the Teacups,* he writes: "Every age has to shape the Divine image it worships over again,—the present age and our own country are busily engaged in the task at this time" (40). Holmes looks forward to the rise of a "kindly, humanized belief" (40). He is pleased that in "the more intelligent circles of American society one may question anything and everything if he will only do it civilly" (251). The liberalization of religious culture is the one change that he experienced in his lifetime that Holmes can affirm unequivocally, and he had been an important contributor to it.

When Holmes addresses religion late in *Over the Teacups,* he restates, clarifies, and expands on his lifelong defense of the Broad Church based on Jesus-centered humanism. His remarks do not form an integral part of the narrative, but are presented in compact form as a reply to questions that correspondents have asked him about anti-Semitism, a lay sermon presented by the Dictator, and his final after-thoughts. In the process of working through his final judgments on religion, Holmes closes the loop linking his theory of the self and religious culture.

Holmes uses his remarks on the Jewish question to restate his ecumenical position on religion in the most precise and radical terms. Noting that he grew up walking "in the narrow path of Puritan exclusiveness," Holmes admits that he inherited the idea that the Jews "were a race lying under a curse for their obstinacy in refusing the gospel" (194). He had been taught that Calvinism was the only true religion, surrounded by a "multitude of detestable, literally damnable impositions, believed in by uncounted millions, who were doomed to perdition for so believing" (194). Holmes has now come so far from his origins that he argues that the Jews had their own good reasons for refusing Jesus's claims: "The Jews are with us as a perpetual lesson to teach us modesty and civility. The religion we profess is not self-evident. It did not convince the people to whom it was sent. We have no claim to take it for granted that we are all right, and they are all wrong" (197).

Praising his friend James Freeman Clark for having written a book on the ten great religions, Holmes advances his ecumenical principle: "If the creeds of mankind try to understand each other before attempting mutual extermination, they will be sure to find a meaning in beliefs which are different from their own" (196). He is not concerned with formulating a universal creed, but with proposing an "etiquette regulating the relation of different religions to each other," based on mutual comprehension, respect, and appreciation—"the true human spirit" (195–96). When considered as a cultural institution, religion only serves its proper social function when it is inspired by an ethic of sympathetic benevolence; any creed that gets in the way of ethical practice should be discarded. Holmes supposes that the Jewish and Christian communities will only establish "intimate relations" when they have been sufficiently "rationalized and humanized" to render their differences "comparatively unimportant" (199). He finds hopeful signs of humanization on "the extreme left of what is called liberal Christianity and representatives of modern Judaism" (199).

Having established his ethical-religious humanism as an overarching principle, Holmes moves in his next reflection to the issues of Christian theology that had occupied him throughout his adult life and had dominated his first two novels, *Elsie Venner* and *The Guardian Angel*. Holmes's lay sermon is another reply to correspondence, this time to a request from a clergyman to contribute to a collection of essays, which Holmes refused. The topic is the afterlife, and Holmes says that "[n]o other interest compares for one moment with that belonging to it" (246). He is ready to tackle the Mistress's query, but he will do it within a cultural discourse.

The Dictator reports that the sermon grows out of frequent discussions with Number Five, and that they agree on all important points, both having undergone the "tremendous trial of one's nature" involved in growing out of an inherited "narrow creed" (247). Holmes's stumbling block in Calvinism had always been the doctrine of original sin, which he believed debilitated the personality, depriving it of confidence in its own potential for goodness and throwing it into anxiety, distrust of others, and chronic anhedonia. In addressing the afterlife, he quickly criticizes the doctrine of eternal damnation and traces it to the idea of original sin. For Holmes, justice between God and self is the issue: "What shall we say to the doctrine of the fall of man as the ground of inflicting endless misery on the human race? A man to be *punished* for what he could not help! He was expected to be called to account for Adam's sin" (252). No reasoning can, for Holmes, reconcile the "supposition of a world of sleepless and endless torment with the declaration that God is love" (253). The only God that Holmes cares to worship is the God of love.

Holmes is confident that the process of rationalizing and humanizing faith will overcome the notion of hell, which is simply an appropriation of the myth of Tartarus into Christianity. In particular, the evolutionary hypothesis of modern biology and sociology "changes the whole relations of man to the creative power. It substitutes infinite hope in the place of infinite despair for the vast majority of mankind" (255). Holmes does not claim to know what kind of afterlife is implied by the evolutionary hypothesis, if any; the worst to be expected is "rest," and perhaps there will be a better home than the one on earth (256). He has not answered the Mistress's question and has left the issue of the afterlife undecidable, whatever his personal beliefs might have been. The Dictator reports that he and Number Five are regular churchgoers; they attend services because a good sermon by a humanized minister "stirs up [their] spiritual nature," regardless of creed (258).

Although Holmes's reflections on religion are his most confident and optimistic in *Over the Teacups*, he does not let his ecumenical Christian humanism go unchallenged as a promising cultural formula. After the Dictator has delivered his sermon, Number Seven— the squinting brain—suggests that organized religion would disappear if the clergy did not have fear of transcendental punishment at their disposal: "Not only are the fears of mankind the whip to scourge and the bridle to restrain [men], but they are the basis of an almost incalculable material interest" (258). The religion of love does not count with fear and its manipulation by greed. Having decentered his cultural ideal through the oblique vision of his alter-ego, Holmes can only say: "Remember that Number Seven is called a 'crank' by many persons, and take his remarks for just what they are worth, and no more" (259). Holmes does not indicate what those remarks are worth.

In his last words on religion, Holmes moves to the question of final judgment, joining theology and psychology. He shifts the meaning of judgment from determination of fitness for heaven or hell to the plane of theodicy—each individual deserves an explanation from God of who they are and why they have led the life they did. The final judgment should be a justification of the ways of God to his creature, as much as an evaluation of the latter. The individual should have as able an advocate as possible, because no one knows who they really are: "He himself is unconscious of the agencies which made him what he is. Self-determining he may be, if you will, but who determines the self which is the proximate source of the determination?" (312). Each human being is "entitled to know the meaning of his existence, and if there was anything wrong in his adjustment to the moral and spiritual conditions of the world around him to have full allowance made for it" (313).

In *The Autocrat*, Holmes introduced his theory of the multiple self—the idea that the individual has of who he is, the ideas that others have of the individual, and who the individual really is, which is only known by God. Holmes's final thought is a generous demand for justice, a moment at which doubt and irresolution shed resentment and become affirmative.

We do not know who we are.

Annotated Bibliography

Oliver Wendell Holmes's Imaginative-Prose Works

Holmes, Oliver Wendell. *The Autocrat of the Breakfast-Table* (1858). Vol. 1 of *The Works of Oliver Wendell Holmes*. Boston: Houghton Mifflin, 1892.

———. *The Professor at the Breakfast-Table* (1859). Vol. 2 of *The Works of Oliver Wendell Holmes*. Boston: Houghton Mifflin, 1892.

———. *The Poet at the Breakfast-Table* (1872). Vol. 3 of *The Works of Oliver Wendell Holmes*. Boston: Houghton Mifflin, 1892.

———. *Over the Teacups* (1890). Vol. 4 of *The Works of Oliver Wendell Holmes*. Boston: Houghton Mifflin, 1892.

———. *Elsie Venner* (1861). Vol. 5 of *The Works of Oliver Wendell Holmes*. Boston: Houghton Mifflin, 1892.

———. *The Guardian Angel* (1867). Vol. 6 of *The Works of Oliver Wendell Holmes*. Boston: Houghton Mifflin, 1892.

———. *A Mortal Antipathy* (1885). Vol. 7 of *The Works of Oliver Wendell Holmes*. Boston: Houghton Mifflin, 1892.

Select Bibliography of Secondary Literature

The following bibliography lists the sources that were found to be most valuable for understanding Holmes's imaginative-prose works. Annotations are given of the most important of those sources.

Modern Biographies of Holmes

Hoyt, David. *The Improper Bostonian: Dr. Oliver Wendell Holmes.* New York: William Morrow, 1979.
A popular biography of Holmes that covers the same topics as Tilton's more serious work.

Small, Miriam Rossiter. *Oliver Wendell Holmes.* New York: Twayne, 1962.
A literary biography reviewing Holmes's entire output, following established lines of interpretation.

Tilton, Eleanor. *Amiable Aristocrat: A Biography of Dr. Oliver Wendell Holmes.* New York: Henry Schuman, 1947.
A serious, reliable, and informative biography that follows the main-line characterization of Holmes as a dilettante.

Commentary on Holmes's Table-Talk Books

With the exception of Peter Gibian's major study, criticism of Holmes's table-talk books is mainly confined to writers at the turn of the twentieth century.

Crothers, Samuel McChord. *Oliver Wendell Holmes: The Autocrat and His Fellow Boarders.* Boston: Houghton Mifflin, 1909.
Discusses Holmes's relation to the personae that he deployed in his table-talk books, the form of those works, and his moral critique of Puritan moralism.

Gibian, Peter. *Oliver Wendell Holmes and the Culture of Conversation.* Cambridge, England: Cambridge University Press, 2000.
Argues that in his table-talk books, Holmes defined a model of democratic discussion with similarities to Richard Rorty's contemporary writings.

Howells, William Dean. "Oliver Wendell Holmes." http://www.blackmask.com/books26c/whowh.htm. Downloaded 3/28/03.
Defines the form of Holmes's table-talk books as the "dramatized essay."

Jerrold, Walter. *Oliver Wendell Holmes.* London: Swan Sonnenschein, 1893.
Argues that Holmes's table-talk books reveal a model of "conversational freedom."

Lang, Andrew. "Oliver Wendell Holmes." http://www.mastertexts
.com/adventures;among;books/chapter00004.htm.
Downloaded 3/28/03.
Defines Holmes as the "unassuming philosopher."

Elsie Venner Criticism

Holmes's first novel, *Elsie Venner,* has attracted more recent critical
attention than any of his other imaginative-prose works.

Dalke, Anne. "Economics, or the Bosom Serpent: Oliver Wendell
Holmes' *Elsie Venner: A Romance of Destiny.*" *American Tran-
scendental Quarterly* (March 1988): 57–68.
Interprets *Elsie Venner* as a criticism of fortune-hunting in
mid-nineteenth-century American capitalist society and culture.
Gallagher, Kathleen. "The Art of Snake Handling: Lamia, Elsie Ven-
ner, and 'Rappaccini's Daughter.'" *Studies in American Fic-
tion* (1975): 51–64.
Garner, Stanton. "*Elsie Venner:* Holmes's Deadly 'Book of Life.'"
Huntington Library Quarterly (1974): 283–98.
Establishes the main line of *Elsie Venner* criticism, posing the
question of why the (anti-)heroine of the title was sacrificed
by Holmes rather than being allowed to be rescued.
Hamblen, Abigail. "The Bad Seed: A Modern Elsie Venner." *Western
Humanities Review* (1963): 361–63.
Hallissy, Margaret. "Poisonous Creature: Holmes's *Elsie Venner.*"
Studies in the Novel (Winter 1985): 406–19.
Continues the line of criticism initiated by Garner, arguing
that Elsie was sacrificed by Holmes because she was too
powerful a sexual figure to be rescued by repressed New
England Brahmins.
Petry, Alice H. "The Ophidian Image in Holmes and Dickinson."
American Literature (December 1982): 598–601.
Traister, Bryce. "Sentimental Medicine: Oliver Wendell Holmes and
the Construction of Masculinity." *Studies in American Fiction*
(Autumn 1999): 205–27.
Interprets *Elsie Venner* as a study in the constitution of the
masculinist role of physician.

Holmes's Depth Psychology

Holmes is widely regarded as a forerunner of depth psychology. The literature on his psychological thought explores his relation to Freudian psychoanalysis and the neurological science of his times.

Boewe, Charles. "Reflex Action in the Novels of Oliver Wendell Holmes." *American Literature* (November 1954): 303–19. Corrects the thesis that Holmes anticipates Freud's psychoanalysis by showing that Holmes's depth psychology and acknowledgment of the unconscious are extensions of the reflex-arc neurology of his times.

Oberndorf, Clarence. *The Psychiatric Novels of Oliver Wendell Holmes.* New York: Columbia University Press, 1944. Shows the anticipations of Freudian symbolism and themes in Holmes's three novels.

Wentersdorf, Karl. "The Underground Workshop of Oliver Wendell Holmes." *American Literature* (March 1963): 1–12. Draws out Holmes's theory of poetic creativity by emphasizing the role of the unconscious in his literary theory.

Holmes's Social and Cultural Criticism

Most commentary on Holmes's social and cultural criticism appeared between the two world wars and adopted a Jeffersonian and liberal-reformist perspective that cast Holmes as a romantic conservative who was unwilling or unable to acknowledge the changes attendant upon the emergence of industrial capitalism.

Clark, Harry Hayden. "Dr. Holmes: A Re-Interpretation." *New England Quarterly* (March 1939): 19–34. Places Holmes as social critic between a progressive critique of Calvinism and a nostalgic defense of preindustrial Federalist society and culture. Finds Holmes to be an anticipator of reformatory criminology and penology.

Hayakawa, S. I., and Howard Mumford Jones. "Introduction." In *Oliver Wendell Holmes: Representative Selections, with Introduction, Bibliography, and Notes.* New York: American Book Company, 1939.

Helps define the main line of Holmes criticism that interprets him as a political and social reactionary and a literary dilettante, albeit an intelligent and insightful one.

Gougeon, Len. "Holmes's Emerson and the Conservative Critique of Realism." *South Atlantic Review* (January 1994): 107–25. Places Holmes in literary history as a romantic idealist who was eclipsed by the literary realism of the generation that succeeded him. Establishes a parallel in literary criticism to the main line of interpretation that positions Holmes as a nostalgic Federalist of the "Genteel Tradition."

Parrington, Vernon L. *The Romantic Revolution in America.* 1927. New York: Harcourt, Brace, 1954.

Establishes the interpretation of Holmes as a romantic conservative politically and a progressive liberal religiously.

Other Studies

Faderman, Lillian. "Female Same-Sex Relationships in Novels by Longfellow, Holmes, and James." *New England Quarterly* (September 1978): 309–32.

Corrects the thesis that the relation between the two female protagonists in Holmes's *A Mortal Antipathy* is a sublimated lesbian relation by showing that nonsexual same-sex intimacies among young women were common in nineteenth-century America.

Matson, J. Stanley. "Oliver Wendell Holmes and 'The Deacon's Masterpiece': A Logical Story?" *New England Quarterly* (March 1968): 104–14.

Corrects that line of criticism that interprets Holmes's poem "The Deacon's Masterpiece" as a criticism of Calvinism, arguing that it is a broader attack upon driving systematic logic to extremities.

Thrailkill, Jane F. "Killing Them Softly: Childbed Fever and the Novel." *American Literature* (December 1999): 679–707.

Shows pro-feminist implications of Holmes's positivistic approach to medical science as opposed to individualized approaches; e.g., his statistical argument that childbed fever was spread by the unhygienic practices of doctors.

Index

Adams, S., 52
Aeneid, 84
Afterlife, 192–93
"Anatomist's Hymn," 38
Aristocracy, 59–60, 133, 153–54
Artificial person, 25
Astronomer, 121, 123–25, 135–41
Autocrat, 24–46, 50–51, 117, 121, 170, 176
Autocrat of the Breakfast Table, 8, 9, 10, 11, 13, 16, 24–46, 55, 72, 73, 120, 121, 149, 171, 194, 195

Bacon, F., 7
Bhagavad-Gita, 105
Boewe, C., 94–95, 98, 112, 163, 198
Bradshaw, Murray, 15, 92–93, 94, 99, 101–4, 110, 113–14
Brain-women, 61, 154–55, 161
Broad Church, 18, 20, 63–66, 167, 191
Browne, T., 7–8, 16, 32, 36, 96

Carlyle, T., 8, 9, 132
Cather, W., 81
"Chambered Nautilus," 11, 32–33
Clark, H. H., 119, 198
Clark, J. F., 192
Common faith, 65
Comparative theology, 128–29
Conversational dogmatist, 8, 132, 150

Corinne: Or Italy, 147
Crothers, S. M., 25, 26, 27

Dalke, A., 80, 83, 105, 197
Darwinism, 127, 134
Death, 34–38, 40, 169, 172
Depth psychology, 13, 94–99, 109, 180
DeStael, G., 147
Determinism, 12, 22, 31, 69–73, 79, 90, 91, 119
Dewey, J., 19, 65, 129
Dexter, T., 189
Dictator, 170, 172–73, 174, 176, 180–81, 183, 187, 188, 190, 192–93
Dr. Butts, 10, 147–48, 153, 155, 156–57, 159, 161, 162, 163–66
Dr. Kittredge, 70–73, 78, 85–86, 88
Documentary novel, 143
Dramatized essay, 2, 26, 48–49, 120

Elsie Venner, 16, 49, 67–89, 90, 91, 92, 93, 98, 101, 105, 163, 192, 195
Emerson, R. W., 5, 23, 33, 143–44, 149, 181
Equality, 186–88

Faderman, L., 155–56
Fairweather, Rev., 73–74, 76–79
Feminism, 156–59, 161–62
Final judgment, 194

Forthputting, 187–90
Freedom, 22, 31, 56, 69–73, 76–77, 79,
    90, 102, 104, 109, 134; existential,
    36; institutional, 17, 54; of con-
    science, 18, 20, 21, 190; of opinion,
    53–55, 63, 191; spiritual, 17–18, 54,
    56, 58
Freudianism, 94–95, 198

Gallagher, K., 80, 197
Garner, S., 80–81, 83, 93, 197
Gibian, P., 5, 47–48, 56, 64, 196
Gougeon, L., 144–45, 199
Gridley, Byles, 92, 93, 94, 96–97,
    98–108, 110, 112, 113, 114, 122
Guardian Angel, 15–16, 90–115, 122,
    163, 176, 192, 195

Habit, 36
Hallissy, M., 80, 82, 83, 197
Hamblen, A., 80, 197
Hawthorne, N., 5
Hayakawa, S. I., 6, 119, 198
Hazard, Myrtle, 15, 93–115, 176
Heart-women, 61, 154–55, 161
Heidegger, M., 36
Honeywood, Rev., 70–76, 77, 90
Howells, W. D., 2, 26, 144, 149, 196
Hoyt, D., 6, 196
Hull, M., 95
Humanism, 19, 20, 158; religious, 19,
    22, 73–74, 75, 191–94; scientific, 19,
    125–30, 131–35
Hurlbut, Fordyce, 94, 101, 104, 107,
    112

"I Like You and I Love You," 182
Imagination, 38–42, 173, 175, 179
Imaginative prose, 2–4, 145
Intellect, 28; algebraical, 28–29; arith-
    metical, 28–29
Interviewer, 148, 150–53, 164
Iris, 49–50, 57–58, 59, 61–63

James, W., 22, 51, 175
James, H., 155
Jerrold, W., 6, 26, 196
Jesus, 63, 192
Jewish question, 191–92
Job, 140

Jones, H. M., 6, 119, 198
Johnson, S., 8, 9, 132, 149

Kant, I., 9, 28, 44, 125
Keller, H., 181
Kirkwood, Maurice, 146–48, 152–53,
    157–59, 161, 162, 163, 164, 166
Knights of Labor, 187–88

Lady, 124–25, 130–31, 137, 139
Lang, A., 50, 197
Langdon, Bernard, 80–81, 82–88
Language, 14, 19, 51–53, 129; spoken,
    29
"Last Blossom," 37
Leibniz, G. W. F., 127
Liberty, 17–21, 154, 190
Life Functions, 36; animal, 36, 40;
    organic, 36–40
Lindsay, Clement, 93, 94, 107, 108,
    111, 114
Little Boston, 49–50, 51–53, 55, 56–58,
    62–63, 73, 120, 177
Little Gentleman. *See* Little Boston
"Living Temple," 38
Longfellow, H. W., 155
Lowell, J. R., 5

Master of Arts, 8, 9, 19, 99, 117,
    121–35, 136, 139, 140, 177
Matson, J. S., 199
Medicated novel, 2, 67–68, 91–92
Metaphysical skepticism, 8–12, 19
Middle age, 24, 174, 182
Model of all virtues, 59–61
Montaigne, 7
Mortal Antipathy, 9, 10, 88, 142–67,
    180, 185, 195
Motley, J. L., 59

Nietzsche, F., 79, 133, 139, 140, 175
Number Five, 173, 180–85, 186,
    192–93
Number Seven, 176–79, 180, 181,
    193–94

Oberndorf, C., 94, 198
Old Age, 37–38, 158–50, 168–70,
    171–75
Ortega, J., 36, 118

Over the Teacups, 10, 13, 18, 20, 168–94, 195

Parrington, V. L., 118–19, 135, 199
Peirce, C. S., 129
Pepys, S., 7, 8, 132
Petrarch, 183
Petry, A. H., 80, 197
Physicians, 72, 128, 162–67
Physiological romance, 2, 67–68, 91–92
Plato, 26, 28, 125
Poe, E. A., 173
Poet, 38, 39, 116–17, 121–25, 126–27, 130, 131–35, 136, 137, 138, 139, 170, 176
Poet at the Breakfast Table, 8, 9, 19, 24, 116–41, 145, 149, 150, 177, 185, 187, 195
Poetry, 38–42, 44, 123
Portfolio, 2, 3, 142–43
Postmodernism, 4
Professor, 34–38, 39, 44, 47–66, 71, 75, 76–77, 79, 87, 90, 121, 170, 176, 180, 181, 183
Professor at the Breakfast Table, 11, 13, 14, 17, 18, 42–66, 73, 116, 120, 121, 126, 154, 177, 195

Reflex psychology, 95, 112
Relativism, 11–12, 30, 71–72
Religion, 18, 190–94; civil, 19, 65
Rescue romance, 42–46, 79–80, 88, 92, 120, 135–36, 145, 179–85
Responsibility, 68, 77, 90, 91, 95, 112
Reverence, 130–31, 134, 178
Richesse oblige, 106, 154, 162
Rorty, R., 47, 65
Royce, J., 130

Santayana, G., 65
Sartre, J. P., 36
Saturnians, 186
Scarabee, 117, 121–25, 126–27, 131–32, 135, 138
Schoolmistress, 43–46
Science, 117
Self, 150; multiplicity of, 13, 14–15, 31, 96–97, 112, 175–76, 177, 194
Self-determination, 12–16, 18, 20–21,

22, 31, 36, 69, 90, 93, 96, 98, 114, 173
Serene resolve, 114–15
Small, M. R., 6, 196
Socrates, 28
Specialization, 117–18, 122, 127, 137–38
"Spring Has Come," 41–42
Squinting Brain, 176
Stoker, Rev. Bellamy, 94, 102–3, 104, 107, 113
Swift, J., 163
Sympathetic benevolence, 16, 192

"Terrible Clock," 173–74
Thoreau, H. D., 23
Thrailkill, J. F., 199
Thought, 50–51
Tilton, E., 6, 24, 25, 27, 49, 54, 55, 90, 196
Time, 173–74, 178–79
Tower, Euthymia, 147–48, 152, 153, 155, 156–59, 160–62, 164, 166
Traister, B., 80, 83, 197
Truth, 27–34, 71
Tutor, 182–84

Unconscious experience, 13–14, 95, 96
Underground workshop, 95–96

Venner, Elsie, 68–89, 98
Vergil, 84
Vincent, Lurida, 147–48, 150–51, 152, 155–62, 164, 165, 166, 167, 180

Wentersdorf, K., 198
Whitman, W., 189
"Wind Clouds and Star-Drifts," 138–40
Wit, 30–31
"Woodnotes I," 181

Young Girl, 124–25, 135–38, 140–41
Young Man from Maryland, 57, 63–64, 116, 121

Zen Buddhism, 115
Zola, E., 144, 163